BIRMINGHAM TOURISM & HOSPITALITY MARKETING

CASE STUDIES IN
TOURISM &
HOSPITALITY
MARKETING

ROB HARRIS, LEO JAGO, BRIAN KING

PEARSON

Hospitality
Press

Pearson Education Australia
Unit 4, Level 2
14 Aquatic Drive
Frenchs Forest NSW 2086

www.pearsoned.com.au

Publisher: David Cunningham
Senior Project Editor: Carolyn Robson
Cover and internal design by Nada Backovic
Cover photograph: Laurie Strachan
Typeset by Midland Typesetters, Maryborough, Vic.

Printed in Malaysia

1 2 3 4 5 09 08 07 06 05

National Library of Australia
Cataloguing-in-Publication Data

Harris, Rob, 1957– .
Case studies in tourism and hospitality marketing.

    Bibliography.
    ISBN 1 86250 502 0.

    1. Tourism – Australia – Marketing. 2. Hospitality industry – Australia – Marketing.
    3. Tourism – Australia – Marketing – Case studies. 4. Hospitality industry – Australia –
    Marketing – Case studies. I. Jago, Leo. II. King, Brian, 1957– . III. Title.

338.479194

An imprint of Pearson Education Australia
(a division of Pearson Australia Group Pty Ltd)

CONTENTS

This book is dedicated to Ryan and Ben Harris,
Laura and David Jago, and Mimi King, in recognition
of the patience they exhibited as their fathers took
'time out' on occasions to undertake the writing of this book.

PREFACE

This book resulted from a casual conversation among the authors regarding the lack of Australian-based case studies in tourism and hospitality marketing. This gap, we believed, prevented teachers/lecturers (including ourselves) from providing a genuinely local context and grounding for the various research-based theories and practices that abound in international marketing literature. This book is our attempt to redress this situation.

Our criteria for selecting the cases that appear here was essentially one of identifying organisations that had a strategic approach to the application of the marketing process, and also were willing to allow us to report in a measure of detail on how this process operated in their specific context. We sought to ensure that the net we cast was wide enough to allow the complexities, nuances and challenges associated with the strategic marketing process within a variety of settings to be adequately embraced. One outcome of this decision has been the basing of some case studies on a period in the organisation's not too distant past where our research indicated that a more interesting or complex marketing situation existed.

Another area of concern for us as regards case study selection was the opportunity they present for students to compare and contrast marketing practices, not only between widely different tourism and hospitality organisations but also between ones that were similar in nature. Additionally, we were keen to expose students to the extent to which marketing research was being employed in real world situations. The intent being to allow them to form opinions on the degree to which literature-based research practices/techniques were in evidence in such situations, as well as how research outcomes were being used to guide marketing decisions.

Two contextual chapters have been included at the commencement of this book. The first seeks to provide an overview of the strategic marketing planning process used as the framework for examining each of the case studies, with an emphasis on the extent to which such strategic planning is underpinned by research activity. This chapter also briefly examines the characteristics of tourism and hospitality services that present specific challenges for marketers.

The second chapter looks at the role case studies play in assisting students to master the principles and practices of tourism and hospitality marketing, and suggests an approach to analysing the case studies that appear here. Again, we are attempting to emphasise the important link between research and practice and to show students that research skills, and the process of conducting research, are important underpinnings to an understanding of what is sometimes described as 'the real world'.

In order to focus student attention on what we consider the key marketing aspects of each case study, we have provided a number of questions at the end of each case. These questions require students to draw upon their previous marketing studies, and to refer to appropriate research sources such as academic journals, web sites and annual reports, in order to produce adequate responses. As a starting point for such research, a Bibliography has been included as part of this book. Additionally, while each case study is dealt with as a separate entity, the opportunity exists for lecturers to have students compare and contrast marketing practices among similar or dissimilar cases, and to set specific questions based upon such comparisons.

Finally, we hope that lecturers and teachers involved in the field of tourism and hospitality marketing will indeed find this book a useful text, or adjunct text, in their efforts to explore marketing theories/concepts and strategies within a localised Australian context.

Rob Harris, Leo Jago and Brian King
August 2004

ACKNOWLEDGEMENTS

The authors would like to acknowledge the contribution of the following people to the development of this series of tourism and hospitality marketing case studies. Without the detailed insights they provided as to the marketing practices of the various organisations that feature in this book, its completion would not have been possible.

Kristi Chambers
John Clunes
Geoffrey Conaghan
Kerri Edwards
Steve Eiszele
Adeline Goh
Sue Greenhalgh
Catherine Gutierrez

Jon Hutchison
Georgette Karagiozis
Jason Knack
Erin Lightfoot
Melanie McVey
Neelam Maharaj
Geoff Manchester
Richard Noon

John Perry
David Riley
Carina Slavik
Tom Smith
Norbert Uhlig
Paul Wiseman

PART 1: INTRODUCTION

1. MARKETING TOURISM AND HOSPITALITY SERVICES: AN OVERVIEW

INTRODUCTION

The purpose of this chapter is to assist students in their efforts at interpreting and critically assessing the tourism and hospitality case studies that have been included here. The chapter begins by examining the unique characteristics of tourism and hospitality services and the challenges these pose from a marketing perspective. It then moves on to overview the application of the strategic marketing planning process within a tourism and hospitality context. This process, which is used as the framework for examining each of the case studies, involves a number of key steps:

- analysing the marketing environment in which an organisation operates and the current 'strategic fit' between the organisation and this environment;
- establishing marketing objectives;
- setting a marketing budget;
- determining target markets;
- selecting an appropriate marketing strategy or strategies;
- developing a marketing mix to support the organisation's chosen marketing strategy or strategies; and
- implementing, monitoring, controlling and evaluating marketing actions.

While each of these steps is briefly discussed in this chapter, it is assumed that students will have a more detailed understanding of each of these areas from their previous marketing studies.

CHARACTERISTICS OF TOURISM AND HOSPITALITY SERVICES AND THEIR MARKETING IMPLICATIONS

According to Middleton and Clarke (2001), a number of features distinguish tourism and hospitality services from a marketing perspective. It is important that students of tourism and hospitality marketing have an understanding of these features as they influence the applicability of general marketing theories to the area, as well as directly influencing a range of marketing decisions. These characteristics are set out below.

Perishability

Tourism and hospitality services cannot be stored and used at a later date if they are not sold at the time they are made available. If a commercial aircraft, for example, flies with 50 of its seats unsold, revenue from these seats is lost forever. Contrast this situation with that of most goods, where if they are not sold one day they can still be offered for sale the next. From a marketing stand-point this situation creates the need to manage demand effectively through such means as pricing and promotion. Many of the case studies included in this book provide examples of how these tools, combined with a detailed under-standing of target markets, have been used for this purpose.

Tourism and hospitality services marketers also deal with this problem via the use of reservation systems. These systems allow them to 'store' demand for partic-ular time periods, thus allowing supply to be adjusted in line with demand in order to minimise wasted capacity. It is also noteworthy that some tourism and hospitality organisations specialise in the provision of reservation services (see *Travel Ys International* case study, page 209), or use such services as an integral part of their service offering (see *Flag Choice Hotels* case study, page 67).

Seasonality

Seasonality afflicts most tourism and hospitality organisations, and results in significant fluctuations in demand over time (i.e. day, week and month). During low demand periods, tourism and hospitality services marketers often find them-selves using price and promotion to drive interest in their services, as well as perhaps altering the nature of their service(s) (e.g. a ski resort offering horse riding and mountain bike treks during the summer months). In periods of peak demand, on the other hand, marketers are in a position to maximise profits by, for example, reducing or eliminating discounts and other incentives.

Tourism organisations sometimes attempt to enhance the appeal of seasons that would not normally be associated with high demand. In promoting Melbourne, Tourism Victoria (see page 104) describes its winter campaign as *Melbourne's Great Indoors*. By way of contrast, all other seasons are referred to directly (i.e. spring, autumn and summer). Tourism Victoria's intent in doing this is to minimise any negative associations with the poorer climatic conditions of winter.

High fixed costs

A number of tourism and hospitality organisations suffer from high fixed costs due to the substantial investment that must be made in buildings, equipment and labour before the point can be reached where they can make their services available for sale. This being the case, the actual cost of servicing individual customers is often relatively low. Given this situation, tourism and hospitality services marketers often find themselves concerned with stimulating additional or marginal sales as they constitute almost a straight revenue gain for little additional cost. The *Ocean Spirit Cruises Cairns* case study (page 83) provides an example of the use of both discounting and raised commission levels as means of simulating such marginal sales.

Intangibility

As tourism/hospitality services cannot be 'test driven' before being used, the issue of convincing potential customers of the capacity of such services to meet their needs can be a significant marketing challenge. Tourism and hospitality services marketers have responded to this challenge in a variety of ways, including: the use of printed colour/video brochures/CD-ROMs that seek to clearly (and in a motivational way) depict the types of places/experiences customers will have; the use of testimonials in promotional activities from people who have used the service; the conduct of slide/video evenings; and the employment of service guarantees designed to reduce the risk of using a service, particularly for the first time. Examples of these practices can be found in many of the case studies included here. Intrepid Tours and Trafalgar Tours, for instance, both make extensive use of high cost and glossy brochures as a way of bringing to life the experiences offered through their tours. In common with a range of adventure and small group tour operators, Intrepid also makes use of slide nights where experienced guides can provide some reassurance to potential clients as well as generate a sense of excitement about the product. An example of the use of service guarantees can be found in the *Flag Choice Hotels* case study (page 67).

Inseparability

The provision of most tourism and hospitality services requires interaction between a staff member(s) of the organisation providing the service and a customer. This being the case, staff can be said to be an inseparable aspect of the service offering. How they dress, talk and generally interact with customers will therefore likely influence customer perceptions of overall service quality. Given this situation, tourism and hospitality services marketers should seek a level of involvement in human resource issues such as the training, motivation and selection of staff, which are areas not traditionally seen as being of concern to them. This close interface between the marketing and the human resource/service function is particularly evident in the *Sydney Monorail* case study (page 120).

Interdependence between tourism and hospitality services, and tourist destinations where they are provided

Most tourists will use several tourism and/or hospitality services (e.g. accommodation, restaurants, local tours, and a visit to one or more local attractions). Some tourists will create such service 'packages' themselves while others will purchase pre-packaged services. In either situation, a tourist's experience at a destination has the potential to be positively or negatively affected by any of the number of services they use. Given this, and the importance of word of mouth in building demand, marketers of tourism and hospitality services need to take an interest in ensuring that certain minimum standards are maintained by all businesses dealing with tourists in the place(s) where they operate. Such an interest may find expression through participation in tourism/hospitality industry associations, and may lead, for example, to voluntary accreditation schemes. Additionally, tourism and hospitality services marketers need also to be concerned about broader issues such as environmental protection, tourist safety and the quality of interactions between tourists and local residents, as these matters also have the potential to influence demand for their services. The *Melbourne Airport* case study (page 177) provides clear evidence of this link between destination demand and demand for an individual organisation's services.

MARKETING PROCESS FOR TOURISM AND HOSPITALITY ORGANISATIONS

The strategic marketing planning process used by tourism and hospitality organisations is not significantly different from that used in other industrial contexts. Many writers (e.g. Weaver & Lawton 2002; Kotler, Bowen & Makens 2002; Middleton & Clarke 2001) have described this process within a tourism and hospitality context, identifying, while doing so, a number of sequential steps through which a marketer should move when developing a marketing plan. In essence, these steps are: research and analysis; objective setting; budgeting; determining target markets; strategy selection; marketing program development; and implementation, monitoring, controlling and evaluating marketing strategies and practices. An overview of these steps follows.

Research and analysis

This initial step in the strategic marketing planning process seeks answers to a variety of questions, which once obtained, provide a context for the marketing decisions that follow. Central amongst these questions are the following:

* What issues/trends exist in the external business environment that may influence matters such as service design, pricing, distribution and overall demand?

- What sales volume and revenue trends have been in evidence over recent years?
- What is the organisation's current customer profile, and to what extent is this the same/different from that of major competitors?
- How successful or otherwise has the current marketing strategy and associated actions been?
- What is the current market position of the organisation and/or its services compared with its competition?
- What developments/changes have occurred within current and potential markets that represent opportunities or threats?

In order to answer these questions, tourism and hospitality organisations need to draw upon a variety of sources. These sources include their own internal records, the outcomes of research they have conducted or commissioned, and industry specific statistics and reports. Sources of the latter include organisations such as Tourism Research Australia (previously the Bureau of Tourism Research), an arm of the newly created Tourism Australia, the Australian Bureau of Statistics, and State Tourism Commissions.

Once this information has been collected, it is then analysed, with the outcome commonly being a summary of key strengths and weaknesses, which are specific to the business itself, and opportunities and threats, which exist in the outside business environment. This summary document is referred to as a SWOT analysis.

Objective setting, establishing a marketing budget, and target market selection

Armed with the information gathered in the previous stage, decisions can be made as regards what objectives are reasonable to set in areas such as overall revenue/profit/sales/market share. Such objectives may be broken down further to a specific service or target market. Additionally, this information will act to inform decisions as regards what markets the business should direct its marketing activities at. Such target markets may be defined by reference to one or more distinguishing characteristics.

1. Location (e.g. local residents, day visitors from outside an area, domestic tourists, international tourists).
2. Demographic profile (e.g. age, sex).
3. Life cycle stage (e.g. newly married, empty nester, retired).
4. Frequency of use. Customers who make regular use of a tourism/hospitality service have the capacity to significantly impact on a businesses bottom line. This being the case, many tourism and hospitality organisations have

developed loyalty programs in order to capture and hold their existing customers.

5   Needs and benefits sought (e.g. novelty, escape, relaxation, interactions with people of a similar age group, luxury, exposure to different cultures, learning).

6   Purpose of travel (e.g. business, holiday, visiting friends and relatives, participating in a particular activity, such as attending a conference).

7   Lifestyle. Some tourism and hospitality businesses make use of or commission studies into personal identities, attitudes and values that group consumers into segments whose purchasing behaviour is then predicted (e.g. Morgan Value Segments).

8   Price (e.g. budget, luxury).

The marketing objectives ultimately set by a tourism/hospitality organisation will be influenced by its capacity to financially support the activities necessary to produce the outcomes that are sought. Such activities, for example, may involve new service development, or modifications to existing services, an expansion of distribution networks, and a range of promotional activities. Many tourism and hospitality businesses approach the task of setting a marketing budget by allocating a percentage of estimated sales revenue to marketing, while some simply use their judgement/experience to set a figure that they consider affordable (Kotler et al. 2002). Another way of approaching this task, that is increasing in evidence, is to use the objective and task method (Middleton & Clarke 2001). This approach involves identifying and costing what actions need to be undertaken in order to achieve the marketing objectives that have been set. In employing this approach it is necessary to: gather facts on matters such as advertising rates, commission costs based on projected sales through intermediaries, and new service development costs etc; and apply a measure of judgement and experience regarding exactly where money should be spent and how much. If, after engaging in this process, a total budget figure is reached that falls outside the affordable range, it may be necessary to reassess the marketing objectives that were originally set, or to consider directing more business resources to the marketing task.

Strategy selection

Once a marketing budget has been established and target markets selected, the next step is to identify what strategies are most likely to achieve the objectives that have been set. Essentially, a tourism/hospitality services marketer seeking to increase sales/revenue/market share has four major strategic options (Middleton & Clarke 2001):

1   Market penetration—capitalising upon an organisation's existing understanding of its markets, and its market position/brand image, by employing

aggressive marketing campaigns to increase demand from its existing markets;

2 Service development—adding new services to an organisation's current service range (e.g. a tour operator adding several new tours to its existing range of tour packages) and marketing these to its current target markets;

3 Market development—expansion of the range of markets an organisation currently serves with its existing services (e.g. a hotel that had previously only targeted business tourists might make the decision to target leisure tourists, particularly at weekends);

4 Diversification—addition of new services in order to serve new markets (e.g. a tour operator may decide to open a hotel in order, in part, to capitalise on the demand its tours are creating for accommodation services).

An integral part of pursuing whichever strategy, or strategies, that are selected is the issue of positioning. The tourism/hospitality services marketer will need to decide exactly what market position they will be seeking vis-a-vis their competitors. An integral part of this decision for many organisations is the 'brand' image they wish to project to their market and their intermediaries in order for them to be seen as different from their competitors. Branding may be based on a variety of attributes, including quality, reliability, expertise/knowledge, use of up-to-date/state of the art equipment (Holloway & Robinson 1995). The benefits of successful branding are many, including reducing perceived consumer risk by signalling the level of quality and performance that can be expected from a particular tourism/hospitality service.

Some tourism and hospitality organisations seek to position themselves as 'niche' operators, serving a very defined target group, that because of its relatively small size and specialist nature has been overlooked or ignored by larger firms. In this book, the efforts of the Hotel Sofitel Melbourne in seeking to position itself as 'Hotel for the Arts' provides an example of such a strategy.

Another key consideration in selecting amongst the broad strategic options noted previously is what stage in the product life cycle (i.e. introduction, growth, maturity, decline) individual services provided by a tourism/hospitality organisation are (Kotler et al. 2002). If an airline, for example, was the only one to be granted a license for a new route with high demand potential, it may be able to charge a high price until additional licenses are granted or demand begins to decline. Contrast this situation with an established route where multiple airlines operate. Under such a scenario, the previously noted strategy would likely not be sustainable due to the high levels of competition present. Instead, the 'mature' nature of the route would mean competition would take place via such means as product differentiation.

Marketing program formulation

In order to progress whatever strategies have been selected, an integrated marketing program needs to be formulated employing those key elements that determine demand for a business's services. Various listings of such elements can be identified (see, for example, Lovelock, Patterson & Walker 2001; Morrison 2001; Weaver & Lawton 2002). For the purposes of this chapter, however, the mix will be viewed as comprising four components (i.e. service, price, promotion and distribution).

Service

The foundation upon which tourism/hospitality services are created is an understanding of the needs of those markets the organisation has decided to target. This understanding should have been developed during the research stage of the strategic marketing planning process. Additionally, a regime of ongoing research needs to be in place to assess how successful or otherwise the organisation is in responding to consumer needs, and to monitor changes in these over time.

When designing tourism/hospitality services it is useful to think in terms of three levels: core, tangible and augmented (McColl, Callaghan & Palmer 1998). The core aspect of a service is the key benefit(s) that the service seeks to provide. It is these benefits that are emphasised when advertising a tourism/hospitality service. In the case of an under 35s tour of New Zealand, for example, such benefits might relate to fun, adventure, convenience over alternative travel options, and escape from routine. The tangible aspects of a tourism/hospitality service are the actual service 'ingredients' that have been developed in order to deliver the benefit(s) that are being promised. In other words, it is the advertised offering to consumers. The challenge at this level is to create services that are differentiated from those of competitors. In the case of the previously noted tour service, such ingredients might include: tour duration, type of transport and accommodation used, number of meals provided, presence of a driver/escort etc. The augmented aspect of a service refers to forms of added value that are built into the formal service offering in order to further differentiate it from those of competitors. Drawing again on the New Zealand tour example, such aspects of this service might extend to service satisfaction guarantees, discounts for future tours, and giveaways such as travel bags and guidebooks.

Price

The price at which a tourism/hospitality service is sold will be determined by a variety of factors. Central amongst these will be: the position that the organisation/service is seeking in the market (e.g. budget versus luxury end of the market); the marketing objectives that have been set regarding profit/revenue/sales/market share; the predicted responses to price by target markets; the legal and regulatory requirements (e.g. the need to collect government charges); and the cost of producing the service. Additional to these factors are a raft of other considerations that potentially further complicate the pricing decision for marketers of tourism and hospitality services, including:

* exchange rate fluctuations;
* the need to build into the final price commissions for intermediaries such as travel agents, inbound tour operators and tour wholesalers;
* seasonal fluctuations in demand that need to be managed through changes in price;
* high levels of price elasticity associated with the demand for leisure-based tourism services;
* high fixed costs of operation that can act to necessitate short-term discounting in order to stimulate demand for unsold (and perishable) services;
* propensity for competitors to engage in short-term tactical price changes whenever supply exceeds demand;
* use of price by some market segments as a measure of quality given the intangible nature of tourism/hospitality services; and
* long lead times (sometimes 12 to 18 months) associated with pricing decisions and actual service sales in areas such as tour packaging.

One pricing technique that is increasingly being used to try to ensure profit/revenue targets are met, given the complexities of pricing tourism and hospitality services, is that of yield management. This technique involves trying to maximise the revenue received from a given supply of a service (Dickman 1999). A hotel, for example, using this approach would first seek to estimate future demand (and the timing of this demand) for its services amongst its various target markets (e.g. business, holiday, conferences/meetings). Having done this, it would use these estimates to make decisions about how many room nights to make available at what prices and at what times with a view to maximising its revenue. Such decisions will, however, be the subject of constant revisions/adjustments in the light of real world conditions.

Promotion

Once a tourism/hospitality service has been created and priced, the next challenge faced by marketers is to persuade target markets to purchase it. If it is a new service, the challenge may first be one of creating awareness, then informing the market of the service's benefits and characteristics and finally persuading them to buy. If the service has been on the market for some time, the focus may be on drawing attention to improvements, or new features that have been added, as a prelude to seeking a sale.

The tools that can be used to move target markets to the purchase decision are many. They include:

* media and internet advertising
* creation and maintenance of an internet site
* brochures
* appointment of sales agents (i.e. travel agents)
* point of sale displays
* purchasing promotions space at consumer holiday and travel exhibitions/shows
* direct mail/email
* videos
* sales promotions involving short-term discounts
* temporary service augmentations (e.g. inclusion of added extras at no extra cost)
* public relations.

While communicating with end consumers is important, it must also be remembered that intermediaries such as tour wholesalers, travel agents and inbound tour operators also need to be communicated with. It may be, in the case of tour wholesalers and inbound tour operators, that personal representations will need to be made in order to try to gain agreement from them to include a particular tourism/hospitality service within one or more of their tour packages. In the case of travel agents, depending on the nature of the service, some form of formal agreement may need to be entered into before the service can be sold. Such is the case with airlines and car rental companies, for example. Such agreements sometimes extend to higher than normal commission levels, familiarisation trips and promotional assistance. Commonly, producers of tourism/hospitality services will advertise in media such as the tourism/hospitality industry trade press with the express purpose of informing retailers about such matters as service changes/new service developments and short term special offers etc. in order to aid them in the selling process, and to keep their service top of mind. Additionally some organisations employ sales representatives (either on a full time or contract basis) in order to service their retailers and/or encourage sales of their services through them.

Whatever promotional tools are selected in order to communicate with consumers and intermediaries, it is necessary to combine them in a coordinated fashion (a campaign) with a view to achieving established marketing objectives (Dickman 1999). Central to the campaign process are detailed promotional schedules stating what activities are to be undertaken, when they are to be undertaken, who within the organisation is responsible for overseeing them, and the costs associated with each promotional activity.

Distribution

The producers of tourism/hospitality services are often located at some distance from the markets that they are attempting to serve. This being the case, they need to 'reach out' to their markets via the use of intermediaries who can perform promotional/selling/representative functions on their behalf. Given the importance of these businesses to the success of many/most suppliers of tourism/hospitality services, it is worthwhile here overviewing who these firms are and the functions they perform (see Table 1.1).

Table 1.1: Major tourism intermediary firms/ organisations and their functions	
Inbound tour operators	Inbound tour operators (ITOs) put together packages of services (often called ground or land content) for use in a destination area by overseas tourists. These packages might include accommodation, airport transfers, entertainment and meals. The service packages developed by ITOs are not sold directly to overseas tourists. Instead, they are purchased by tour wholesalers, travel agents and incentive houses located in the tourist's home country. These businesses often incorporate the packages developed by ITOs into their own service offerings which are then sold directly, or via travel agents, to consumers or, in the case of incentive houses, to companies.
Tour wholesalers	Tour wholesalers package services from other sectors of the tourism and hospitality industry in the same way as ITOs. Tour wholesalers will often use ITO-developed packages within their own service offerings. Unlike ITOs, however, these businesses are located in a tourist's home region and the packages they develop are for use outside this area, such as in another state or overseas. Tour wholesalers sell their service packages to tourists either directly and/or via retail travel agents.
Incentive travel houses	An incentive travel house is a type of tour wholesaler. These businesses package tourism and hospitality industry services for corporations wishing to use such services as rewards designed to motivate their employees or the employees of companies with which they are associated.
Retail travel agencies	Retail travel agencies (RTAs) act to reserve, collect payments for, and complete documentation associated with the sale of various tourism/hospitality service providers' services. As it is through the sale of these services that they derive their income (commissions), they actively promote the services of the suppliers they represent to their clients and potential clients. This is achieved through the travel-consulting process, and also by other means such as advertising. Some

RTAs now operate solely through the internet, while many others have an online aspect to the services they provide.

Global distribution system (GDS) firms	Essentially, global distribution system firms provide the technology that links suppliers of tourism/hospitality services (particularly airlines) with retail travel agents in many countries around the world. This linking process is achieved by placing computer terminals within travel agencies that are connected to the GDS, commonly via leased telephone data lines. These lines allow electronic access to a large central database into which data can be entered so that reservations can be made, and information obtained. As part of this process, these systems provide gateways into the reservation systems of airlines, hotels, vehicle rental companies and other suppliers of tourism/hospitality services.
General sales agents (GSAs)	Many suppliers of tourism/hospitality services do not have offices in the particular countries or regions from which their customers are drawn. For this reason they appoint representatives in these locations to make reservations; provide information to consumers, or tourism/hospitality businesses; and to undertake promotional activities. Such businesses are known as general sales agents (GSAs).
Hotel representative firms	Many hotels will contract specialist firms to make reservations for them. These firms are known as hotel representative companies. These businesses may be national or international in the scope of their operations.
National/state tourism authorities and local and regional tourism associations	These organisations perform a number of functions, which might include booking tourism/hospitality services, partnering with suppliers of tourism/hospitality services to assist them to promote their services in specific distant geographic markets, and conducting events at which buyers and sellers of tourism/hospitality services are brought together.
Internet-based booking services	Accessed via the internet, some of these businesses specialise in a particular type of tourism/hospitality service (e.g. bed and breakfasts), while others concern themselves with a range of such services, but only within a particular region or area.
Convention and visitors bureaux	Generally city- or town-based, these organisations focus on attracting (through various promotional activities) large groups travelling for meeting or convention purposes. Membership of these bodies facilitates contact with the organisers of these events, who often need a variety of tourism/hospitality services such as accommodation, transport and tours.

Source: After Howard and Harris, 2001.

It should be noted that while many suppliers of tourism/hospitality services make use of intermediaries, these same businesses might also sell their services directly to consumers. It is also the case that some suppliers will not make use of intermediaries at all, preferring to distribute and promote their services to their chosen markets directly.

While market access is often a major function of a tourism/hospitality service supplier's distribution system, it is also the case that the system facilitates the sale of services in advance. From a marketing viewpoint the more advance sales that can be made the better as demand becomes easier to predict. Common approaches to stimulating advance sales include discounts and added value offers (e.g. two nights for the price of one) for bookings made for a particular time period.

The use of distribution channels does, of course, come at a cost. Such costs may include: commissions/fees/charges, maintenance of a sales force, service training for intermediaries, advertising, brochure distribution, general communication costs and familiarisation trips. Tourism and hospitality services marketers need to be aware of these costs, and how the various distribution 'channel' options they use, or potentially could use, compare. Such knowledge can lead to decisions to expand or reduce the number of channels on the basis of their cost effectiveness, or indeed to move towards more direct means of distribution (i.e. disintermediation).

Implementation, monitoring, controlling and evaluating

Once a marketing program has been determined, staff, many of whom would have participated in its development, need to be advised of its objectives, and their responsibilities as regards its implementation. Additionally, systems need to be developed and put into place to monitor progress, evaluate outcomes and ensure that implementation of the program proceeds in a planned fashion. Such systems should allow organisations, amongst other things, to: respond quickly when sales targets are not being met; make refinements to promotional campaigns; adjust overall marketing objectives in the light of changed circumstances; and generally learn what is effective and what is not as regards their marketing efforts.

As regards the monitoring process, various measures may be used, including:

* bookings against planned service capacity;
* customer satisfaction as measured by such means as complaints and surveys;
* awareness of consumers/intermediaries of advertising messages;
* level of sales response by consumers to advertising, special offers, price changes;

* level of sales generated through intermediaries as a result of changes in the level of marketing support etc.; and
* number of web site 'hits' and internet bookings made.

Information gained in these ways can be fed into regular (monthly/ quarterly) meetings of marketing staff, and used to adjust/refine marketing activities through appropriate tactical changes to planned actions. This process is commonly referred to as marketing control. Additionally this information can then be used as the basis for an overall evaluation of the outcomes of the strategic marketing planning process. Such a summative evaluation often takes place on an annual basis. Various contextualised approaches to monitoring, controlling and evaluating are in evidence in the various case studies in this book.

SUMMARY

Tourism and hospitality services present many unique challenges that marketers need to respond to: perishability; seasonality; high fixed cost; inseparability; intangibility; and interdependence between tourism and hospitality services and the tourist destinations where they are provided. This chapter has sought to overview these challenges and the approaches tourism and hospitality services marketers can employ in responding to them. It has also sought to describe, and provide insights into, the strategic marketing planning process that has been used as the framework for examining the cases included in this book. It is via the application of this process that organisations seek to establish a strategic 'fit' between themselves and the business environment in which they operate.

REFERENCES

Dickman, S. 1999, *Tourism and Hospitality Marketing*, Oxford University Press, Melbourne.

Holloway, C. & Robinson, C. 1995, *Marketing for Tourism*, Longman, Harlow, United Kingdom.

Howard, J. & Harris, R. 2001, *The Australian Travel Agency*, McGraw-Hill, Sydney.

Kotler, P., Bowen, J. & Makens, J. 2002, *Marketing for Tourism and Hospitality*, 3rd edn, Prentice Hall, New Jersey.

Lovelock C.H., Patterson P.G. & Walker R.H. 2001, *Services Marketing: An Asia-Pacific Perspective*, 2nd edn, Pearson Education, Sydney.

McColl, R., Callaghan, B. & Palmer, A. 1998, *Services Marketing: A Managerial Perspective*, McGraw-Hill, Sydney.

Middleton, V. & Clarke, J. 2001, *Marketing in Travel and Tourism*, 3rd edn, Butterworth-Heinneman, Oxford.

Morrison, A. 2001, *Hospitality and Travel Marketing*, 3rd edn, Delmar, Albany.

Weaver, D. & Lawton, L. 2002, *Tourism Management*, 2nd edn, John Wiley & Sons, Milton, Queensland, Australia.

2. LEARNING THROUGH CASE STUDIES

INTRODUCTION

This chapter examines the role that case studies play in assisting students to master the principles and practices of tourism and hospitality marketing. It begins by providing an overview of the origins of the case study approach and the various types of case studies students might encounter before completing their courses. The specific type of case study approach used in this book is then discussed before the advantages and potential pitfalls posed by this learning method are identified. The final part of this chapter suggests a method that students might find useful in analysing case studies of the type that appear in this book.

ORIGINS

According to Yin (1994) a case study is:

> . . . an empirical inquiry that investigates a contemporary phenomenon within its real life context; when the boundaries between the phenomenon and context are not clearly evident; and in which multiple sources of evidence are used (1994 p. 23).

The case study approach can be viewed as part of an intellectual tradition dating back to the ancient Greek philosopher Aristotle, who advocated an inductive approach to the pursuit and application of knowledge. Induction starts with particular cases or instances before proceeding to the formulation of generalisations. Since an individual will never have the time or opportunity to experience sufficient instances of a particular phenomenon to be able to arrive at a general principle, this approach emphasises the need to use intuition to overcome 'the gap' (Steane 1998 p. 63). Case studies, therefore, can assist students to improve their understanding by providing insights and information to facilitate such intuitive jumps.

The use of case studies in the contemporary era emerged during the late nineteenth century at Harvard University Law School. This led to the use of the expression the Harvard Business School 'method'. Harvard case studies examine examples of actual corporations within a particular business sector, providing insights into real dilemmas confronted by business organisations. This approach is particularly useful for students whose experience in the business environment may be negligible or non-existent. When operating within such environments, business managers are regularly confronted with challenges that have no single solution. Well-written case studies can highlight the complexity that surrounds such problems and how they may be addressed. Whilst case studies rarely contain all the information that is needed to explain a problem fully, this is also the situation that regularly confronts managers. In many cases the nature of the key or central problem is unclear. In instances where the relevant information appears to be available, it may be conflicting. Case studies aim to replicate such business scenarios and to challenge students into suggesting solutions to problems when they have access to only partial and inadequate information. Some students are more familiar with the textbook approach, where there are clear right and wrong answers, and find this approach uncomfortable. There is merit in encountering and confronting such frustration in a college or university setting rather than waiting for a rude awakening in business where failure may have serious consequences.

Employers appreciate the opportunity to recruit marketing and tourism graduates who have had experience with relevant case studies. They find that growing technological and marketing sophistication has increased the downside risk in instances where managers make decisions on a trial and error basis. Managers who have previous experience in handling the types of problems confronted in case studies should be better placed to apply the lessons of previous comparable examples.

CASE STUDY TYPES

Jensen and Rodgers (2001) outlined six major types of case study.

The first type is **snapshot** case studies. These profile the challenges confronted by an organisation at a single point of time. Such case studies often entail a narrative of decisions and processes including a considerable amount of detail. They are generally written from the point of view of the detached observer. The second type of case study identified is **longitudinal**. These cover a series of events that have occurred over a period of time and are outlined in chronological order. The major focus of such studies is the effect of time on either the whole organisation or on its divisions or subdivisions.

Pre-post case studies typically focus on a particular campaign, program or decision, and how it has been implemented. Such studies provide valuable baseline data covering the period prior to the introduction of a particular initiative, and then monitor the implementation phase. Since campaigns are an essential component of marketing, the pre-post approach is helpful for understanding the marketing process.

Patchwork case studies involve a greater degree of complexity. They comprise a series of studies for which different methodologies have typically been developed. They examine an entity at various points of time. Patchwork studies are valuable because they provide a more comprehensive picture of the complex issues confronted by an organisation.

The final two approaches to case studies, namely **comparative** studies and **meta-analysis**, involve greater complexity and provide a stronger basis for theory building. These methods are particularly suited to students at advanced undergraduate or postgraduate level. Comparative studies integrate the findings of multiple case studies often on different organisations or different parts of organisations. The commonalities that they identify may provide insights into particular processes, programs, campaigns or decisions.

The most sophisticated type of case studies involve meta-analyses. Meta-analyses attempt to overcome the criticism levelled at the snapshot approach that, it is argued, makes a minimal contribution to the advancement of knowledge generally and theory building in particular. A meta-analysis begins with the formulation of a research question. The author then synthesises the results and findings of any previous case studies that have focused on particular issues or processes that address this question. Because the meta-analyst sets out the research question at the start, the range of evidence that needs to be gathered is clearly delineated and the extent to which it is reasonable to arrive at generalisations is quickly ascertained.

In providing a descriptive overview of the strategic marketing systems of a cross section of tourism and hospitality organisations, this book adopts a 'snapshot' approach. The approach provides insights into the development and implementation of marketing strategies within these organisations at a particular point in time. This point in time in most instances is in the recent past. In the context of some case studies, however, an earlier time was selected when research identified a richer, more diverse set of marketing practices/challenges to be in evidence. The period covered by each case study is noted at the end of each one.

Each case study was developed in close consultation with the organisation concerned, and involved the use of a common framework as the basis for analysis. This framework was based upon the key stages in the strategic marketing planning process. Firstly, it involved examining the 'front end' aspects of this process—the marketing environment, identification of markets and use of marketing research. Next, it required a review of marketing objectives, marketing strategies and the marketing mix designed to deliver on these strategies. Finally, it involved an analysis of approaches to the monitoring, controlling and evaluating of marketing performance. Each case study also features a discussion of the involvement of marketing staff in the strategic marketing planning process (e.g. who was involved, what was the duration of the process and when did it occur?).

CASE STUDY METHOD—ADVANTAGES AND PITFALLS

Nelson (1996) outlined some of the advantages of the case study approach as follows:

* to describe examples of experience in 'real situations';
* to give a topic 'life' or 'human interest';
* to stimulate and focus discussion, and exchange experiences and views;
* to develop insights into types of situations and events;
* to practise analytical and decision-making skills, and develop judgement in a safe environment.

The approach has advantages for individual students by providing them with skills of independent analysis. It is also valuable as a stimulus for problem-solving at group level with the lecturer or tutor playing the role of facilitator rather than 'sage on the stage'. This approach can lead to a very active learning style that engages the interest and active participation of the student, encouraging, as it does, discussion, controversy and debate. In the context of this book, students have the opportunity to 'experience' strategic marketing planning in action in a variety of tourism and hospitality contexts, including, in some instances, organisations providing very similar services. The case study approach also allows them to reflect upon this experience. Their knowledge of marketing theories/concepts can be used to explain, critique, or propose alternatives to the marketing related actions or decisions evident in a particular case. In a number of the case studies presented here, students are also required to propose future marketing actions.

While case studies are an excellent means of providing students with a broad exposure to a range of real world marketing approaches and problems, students, according to Peter and Donnelly (1989), are prone to a variety of potential pitfalls. These include:

* inadequate problem definition;
* excessive belief in the existence of a single correct answer;
* frustration with an apparent insufficiency of relevant information;
* a sense that the proposed solutions are too general and lack specifics;
* wishful thinking—an alternative case is envisaged to avoid facing the realities of the current case;
* tunnel vision (e.g. assuming that the problem is one of price when it is likely that other elements of the marketing mix are also relevant);

- a lack of realism—e.g. solutions that require huge investments may be impractical for small firms with limited resources at their disposal;
- excessive reliance on marketing research. Research is a strong focus for university students but is rarely sufficient in itself as a solution to business problems;
- paraphrasing the case study. The emphasis should be on analysis and not description; and
- excessive enthusiasm for finding a quick solution. It is important to think through the various alternatives in a methodical manner.

PREPARING A CASE STUDY

Many authors suggest that students should approach case studies by following a series of steps (Berman & Evans 1995). While each student will likely develop their own working style to analysing case studies, the following is proposed as set of guidelines that will produce sound, well-reasoned responses to the questions that are asked at the end of each case study in this book.

1 Read through the case with the aim of 'getting a feeling for' the organisation and its strategic marketing system and marketing practices.
2 Read through the case again with a view to making summary notes regarding how the organisation has approached the strategic marketing planning process.
3 Read through the questions at the end of the case and identify what aspects of the strategic marketing planning process they are concerned with and exactly what the question(s) are requiring, for example:

- critically evaluate an existing practice;
- suggest alternatives/modifications/additions to an existing practice;
- propose a future course of action; or
- recommend a response to a specific marketing challenge.

4 Identify which aspect(s) of the case the questions are specifically referring to and what is known from the case regarding the matters referred to in the questions.
5 Determine what marketing theories/concepts are relevant to each specific question, and if any additional information (e.g. annual reports) will be required in order to answer the question.
6 Develop a response to each question drawing upon appropriate theories/concepts/additional information sources.

7   Ensure responses take into account any resources (e.g human, financial) or other constraints that reasonably might impact upon them.

Often students will find themselves developing responses to a case study as part of a group. If this is so, it is advisable for them firstly to work through their initial answers alone. Once they have done this, they will then be ready to engage in productive discussion with their fellow group members over possible answers. Students should always keep in mind as they engage in this process that there is often not a single correct answer to any specific question, and that any proposed answer must be supported by reference to appropriate literature or best practice examples.

CONCLUDING NOTE

Case studies have a fairly long history in terms of their use as educational tools within business programs, and it is likely that students will encounter a range of case study types as they move through their courses. A **snapshot** approach has been used in this book with a view to providing the reader with insights into the strategic marketing planning process and its outcomes across a range of tourism and hospitality organisations. To gain maximum benefit from the case studies, students are encouraged to adopt a systematic approach towards their analysis, and to avoid the pitfalls associated with the use of cases that have been referred to earlier in this chapter.

The authors believe that when students finally have the opportunity to engage in managerial decision-making in a business environment, they will value the 'real world' insights provided by case studies, and the opportunity they afford them to 'ground' the marketing theories and concepts that they have learnt. Case studies also provide students with an opportunity to work together in groups when examining marketing problems and issues. This is what often occurs within organisations. In simulating this reality, students will experience the frustration, excitement and challenges that are often associated with such interactions, leaving them better prepared for their future 'real world' roles.

REFERENCES

Berman, B. & Evans, J. 1995, *Retail Management—Strategic Approach*, 6th edn, Prentice Hall, Inglewood Cliffs, New Jersey.

Jensen, J.L. & Rodgers, R. 2001, 'Cumulating the Intellectual Gold of Case Study Research', *Public Administration Review*, vol. 61, no. 2, pp. 235–46.

Nelson, E. 1996, 'Producing and Using Case Study Material for Research and Teaching: a Workshop for Partners in Know-How Transfer Projects', *Journal of European Industrial Training*, vol. 20, no. 8, pp. 22–30.

Peter, J.P. & Donnelly, J.H. 1989, *Marketing Management Knowledge and Skills*, Richard Irwin, Homewood, Illinois.

Steane, P. 1998, 'History and Pedagogy of the Case Study Approach', in *Cases in Strategic Management*, eds. M. Brown, P. Steane & J. Forster, MacMillan, Melbourne.

Yin, Y.K. 1994, *Case Study Research Design and Methods*, 2nd edn, Sage Publications, Thousand Oaks, California.

PART 2: CASE STUDIES

3. SYDNEY CONVENTION AND VISITORS BUREAU

INTRODUCTION

This case concerns the Sydney Convention and Visitors Bureau (SCVB), a destination marketing organisation charged with attracting conferences, exhibitions and incentive tours to Sydney and regional New South Wales. The case begins by briefly examining the marketing environment within which SCVB makes its marketing decisions, before going on to look at the types of market research it engages in and its marketing planning process. Given SCVB's destination marketing role, discussion of its marketing mix centres on its marketing communication activities and how these activities have allowed it to establish a membership element to its operations. The final section in this case study emphasises the importance the SCVB places upon objective setting, and the associated measurement process, in gauging its marketing success.

BACKGROUND

The SCVB is a non-profit destination marketing organisation funded by the New South Wales State Government, Sydney City Council, membership fees and self-generated revenue. Its primary function is to secure and promote meetings, incentive travel programs, conventions, exhibitions and special events for Sydney and regional New South Wales (the latter though the New South Wales Convention and Visitors Bureau—a division of the SCVB). In performing this role, the SCVB undertakes a range of promotional activities, as well as providing advisory and other services associated with corporate event planning and coordination for individuals, corporations, associations and government departments. The SCVB's success in performing these various roles is evident from Tables 3.1 and 3.2.

The SCVB is overseen by a board of directors, with day-to-day management being the responsibility of a managing director. The organisation employs approximately 30 staff, and is divided into a number of functional units: marketing communication; membership sales; sales; research and sales development; and the New South Wales Convention Bureau (see Figure 3.1 on page 26).

Table 3.1: SCVB bids won from 1997/98 to 2001/02

Financial Year	Bids Won	Delegates	Delegate Days	Value
1997/98	24	28 450	144 050	$111 564 470
1998/99	40	38 020	168 010	$116 847 490
1999/00	30	35 850	176 000	$121 045 345
2000/01	37	58 420	240 460	$149 435 979
2001/02	32	29 600	131 110	$143 225 858

Source: SCVB, 2001/02.

**Table 3.2: Percentage of bids won by SCVB
and their associated value 1997/98 to 2001/02**

Year	% of Bids Won	Value of Successful Bids
1997/98	52%	$122 877 270
1998/99	59%	$195 225 672
1999/00	49%	$193 536 286
2000/01	65%	$201 921 800
2001/02	63%	$179 730 863

Source: SCVB, 2001/02.

MARKETING ENVIRONMENT

The 2001/02 year saw dramatic changes in SCVB's business environment, largely flowing from the collaspe of Ansett airlines, the September 11 terrorist attacks and a declining global economy. These events were followed in 2002/03 with the Iraq war and an outbreak of the severe acute respiratory (SARS) syndrome. These events in turn resulted in a reduction in the number of meetings, particularly corporate meetings, taking place. Compounding these difficulties has been the marked rise in the level of competition SCVB now faces. In the early 1990s, for example, there were only two major convention and exhibition centres in Australia, but by 2003 there were six. This number will again rise in the near future with new centres planned for Perth and the Gold Coast. This increase in competition is reflected in the number of pre-selection bids that the SCVB is now finding itself involved in against other Australian destinations. Such bids involve multiple cities presenting to an international corporation/association in order to have a single Australian city go forward to challenge international destinations seeking the same business meetings. There were 13 such bids in 2001/02. This rise in competition has not been confined to the Australian context. An increasing number of destinations within the

Figure 3.1: SCVB organisational chart

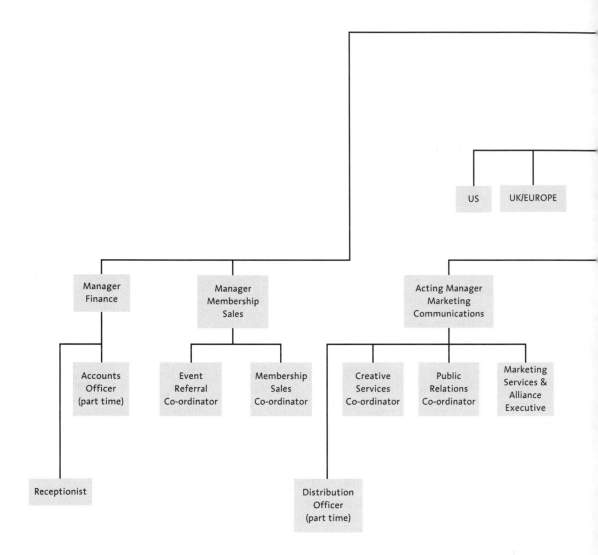

Source: SCVB, 2001/02.

region, such as Bangkok, Beijing, Seoul and Kuala Lumpur, and, further afield, London, Durban, Paris, Vienna, Madrid and Capetown, have invested in, or are upgrading, their meetings and exhibitions infrastructure.

Additionally, there are a number of general environmental factors that have, or have the potential to, influence the way the SCVB conducts its activities, and over which it maintains a watching brief, including:

* airline schedules and capacity into Sydney;
* relative prices of hosting meetings in Sydney versus major competing destinations;

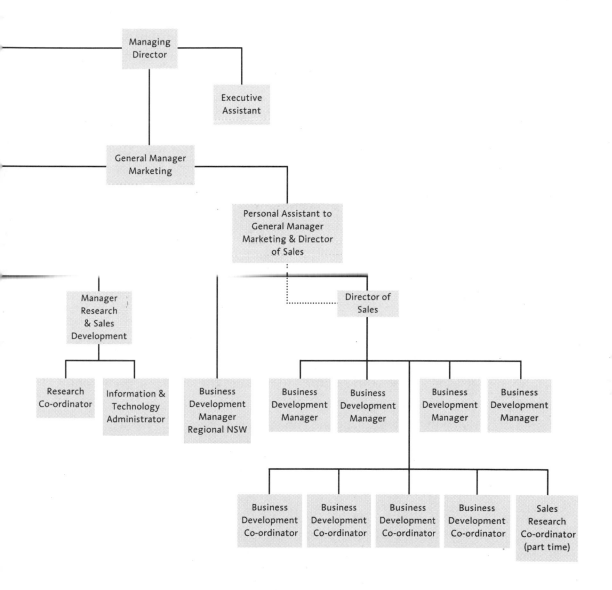

- quality, standard and capacity of business meetings infrastructure in Sydney/New South Wales;

- exchange rate differentials between Australia and major visitor source markets;

- the general world economic climate;

- market perceptions of safety and political stability in Australia; and

- the image and branding of Sydney and New South Wales as domestic and international tourist destinations (which is the responsibility of Tourism Australia, formerly the Australian Tourist Commission).

MARKET RESEARCH

Market research plays a vital role in SCVB's marketing practices. This is reflected in the existence of a research unit within the organisation that performs a variety of functions, including: identifying and qualifying leads for upcoming meetings; analysing statistical data on the meetings/convention/incentives market (from secondary sources); and commissioning market trend studies.

Key objectives for this unit of the SCVB as stated in its 2001/02 annual report included:

* increasing the number of lead opportunities for national and international meetings and events by researching new database sources;

* researching and producing an annual Sydney and Regional New South Wales Calendar of Meetings and Events providing details of planned events up to 10 years ahead that can be used by SCVB members in their sales and direct marketing efforts;

* undertaking qualitative and quantitative research of the meetings and exhibitions industry in Sydney and regional New South Wales to identify the economic value of the sector and measure the success of New South Wales as a meeting and convention destination; and

* continuing the development and enhancement of the SCVB's management information system to accommodate changing needs and new applications.

TARGET MARKETS

From Table 3.3 it can be seen that the SCVB directs the majority of its marketing efforts towards attracting international meetings/exhibitions/incentive tours. In seeking to attract these meetings/exhibitions the SCVB implements a multi-level marketing process targeted to individual organisations and their leaders. One important aspect of this process is the preparation of customised bid documents, with the intent of 'selling' the organisations/individuals behind the conduct of business events on the merits of Sydney/regional New South Wales as a location for their meeting/exhibition. Such organisations/individuals include national and international associations, national and international corporations, national and international exhibition organisers, and government meeting planners. In the context of its major overseas and domestic markets (North America, United Kingdom/Europe and Melbourne), the SCVB uses representative firms to assist it in the bidding process by:

* identifying potential business and bid opportunities;
* developing bid opportunities;

Table 3.3: SCVB performance indicators and results 2001/02

Performance Criteria	2001/02
Events won by Sydney (see Table 3.1)	32
Delegates	29 600
Total value	$143 225 858
International events	26
National events	6
Average size of meetings won	925 delegates
Number of events incorporating a trade exhibition	8

Source: SCVB, 2001/02.

- gathering market intelligence and undertaking competitive analysis;
- representing the SCVB at international tradeshows, roadshows and industry events;
- developing relationships with new and existing clients;
- distributing SCVB publications and marketing materials to key contacts;
- generating media interest in Sydney, and distributing media releases; and
- coordinating sales and promotional activities such as direct mail campaigns, and working in conjunction with industry partners in the local market.

It is noteworthy that different types of meetings will have different lead time requirements associated with them. It may be necessary, for example, to bid for an international association's annual conference four or five years out, while the bidding process for a purely domestic conference may occur 18 months to two years from its scheduled commencement date.

In terms of deciding what conferences and incentive programs etc. are to be pursued in its various geographic markets, the SCVB takes into account a range of factors. For example, there is little point in trying to attract meetings/ exhibitions/incentive groups at times of existing high demand for such services as accommodation. Instead, the SCVB identifies 'gaps' or low season periods where large groups can provide a real boost for the providers of business meeting services. Another significant factor in deciding what business to seek is the potential revenue that it will generate for Sydney/regional New South Wales both in direct and indirect terms as the multiplier effect takes hold. Associated with this consideration is the issue of the potential return on SCVB time and resources in undertaking a bid. The capacity of venues and hotels is also a determinant of business meetings sought. In this regard, the SCVB works with members of the business meetings industry and tourism agencies to high-light any limitations in this area to government.

In addition to the various business meetings-related markets the SCVB seeks to target, it also has an 'internal' market whose needs it must understand and service. This market comprises its more than 500 members who supply services and products to the business meetings industry, predominantly in the areas of:

● accommodation;

● tourist attractions;

● arts and entertainment;

● convention and exhibition services;

● restaurants;

● catering;

● shopping;

● transport and tours; and

● professional conference organising.

In order to meet the various needs of this group, five different types of membership packages have been developed: gold, silver, bronze, red and associate memberships. Each of these membership packages has its own benefits, and they range in price from approximately $19 000 per annum for gold membership through to $600 for associate membership (see further discussion under *Marketing Mix*).

MARKETING PLANNING

The SCVB works on the basis of a fiscal year (i.e. 1 July to 30 June). The marketing planning process commences in February each year at an annual marketing meeting where all staff discuss issues relating to the operation of SCVB and the achievement of its marketing goals, including the success or otherwise of the previous year's marketing efforts. Shortly after this meeting, all SCVB departments/units/divisions (i.e. overseas market development, research and sales development, marketing communication, membership, and the New South Wales Visitor and Convention Bureau) make a formal pitch for funds to support their current and planned activities for the following financial year. The merit of these claims is assessed by the general manager of marketing in the light of the organisation's overarching marketing strategy which is one of positioning Sydney as the business meeting destination of choice amongst its target audiences. Once this is completed, a new marketing plan and budget is developed for the coming year that contains marketing actions, along with their associated budgets. This draft plan is then submitted to the managing director for comment. Any changes to the plan resulting from this process are then made before a final version is submitted to the SCVB's board in June of each year for approval.

The SCVB's marketing plan is divided into two parts. The first provides a market overview of international and domestic markets, identifies marketing opportunities/problems to be addressed, and describes strategies for addressing these, along with the specific markets to which such strategies relate. The second section of the plan deals with specific projects, providing descriptions of such projects, and their objectives and performance measurement indicators. Separate budget sheets accompany each of these projects. In 2001/02, for example, one such project involved the development of a business development strategy for the Asian market which was identified as offering significant future growth potential.

A noteworthy aspect of the SCVB's marketing efforts is the strategic alliances it has developed with a number of organisations, including Tourism New South Wales, Tourism Australia and the Sydney Convention and Exhibition Centre (SCEC). The SCVB partners with these organisations in various promotional activities. For example, the SCVB builds a number of activities around Dreamtime, Australia's premier incentive travel event conducted by the ATC, and its overseas offices are jointly funded with the SCEC.

MARKETING MIX

In one sense the 'product' of the SCVB is Sydney and regional New South Wales and the attributes of these areas that lend themselves to being considered as business meeting locations. When viewed in this way, it can be observed that the SCVB has little direct control over what it has been established to 'sell'. Certainly, it can identify limitations in areas such as pricing, the capacity of venues, or the range of supporting services, and bring these to the attention of industry and government, but it cannot address such matters itself. Another way of looking at the 'product' of the SCVB is in terms of the marketing communication related services and activities it undertakes in order to progress its primary function. Viewed in this way the SCVB's 'output' can be said to be:

* sales calls, direct mail, telemarketing, and lobbying directed at those responsible for deciding on the location of an event;
* conduct of site inspections for those responsible for deciding on the location of an event;
* public relations efforts designed to position Sydney as a world class meeting/incentives/conference location;
* preparation of bid documents and their associated presentations;
* the development of strategies designed to allow the SCVB to compete against other Australian cities for the right to bid on events;
* undertaking and participating in promotional events such as road shows and Sydney on Sale;
* the production of marketing collateral to support the bidding process (e.g. flags, postcards, promotional videos and other give aways—see Figure 3.2);

- assisting in the development of promotional strategies to increase delegate attendance; and

- undertaking market research.

Figure 3.2: Sample marketing collateral

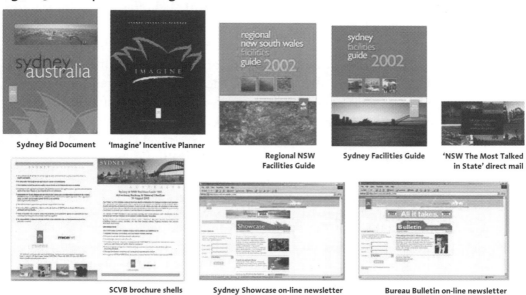

Sydney Bid Document   'Imagine' Incentive Planner

Regional NSW   Sydney Facilities Guide   'NSW The Most Talked
Facilities Guide   in State' direct mail

SCVB brochure shells   Sydney Showcase on-line newsletter   Bureau Bulletin on-line newsletter

Source: SCVB, 2001/02.

As bidding is the focus of much of the SCVB's activities, it is worth briefly overviewing here how this process takes place. A typical bid involves a number of stages from the initial follow up of a lead, until a final decision is made by the organising body, as outlined in Figure 3.3.

It is noteworthy that a majority of the SCVB's promotional tools and strategies are developed in-house as no advertising agency is expert in this specialist field. SCVB rely upon their own market intelligence and experience to advise external agencies on target markets and the best media to target each market. Advertising agencies, however, do play a significant role in the development of the creative component of promotional tools, and external firms are used for printing and design work for both domestic and international advertising.

From the perspective of many businesses involved in the conference/ exhibition area, the SCVB's marketing communication activities have the potential to create significant business opportunities. For example, the SCVB's web site was expanded early in 2002 to provide meeting planners with a range of easily accessible conference deals as part of the Bureau's *NSW: The Most Talked in State* promotional campaign, which attracted 1000 visitors to the site on the first day of the promotion. By June 2002 this promotion had attracted 6000 hits to the site and members were able to convert business to the value of $335 000 from these enquiries. Given this potential for expanded business

Figure 3.3: The business meeting bidding process

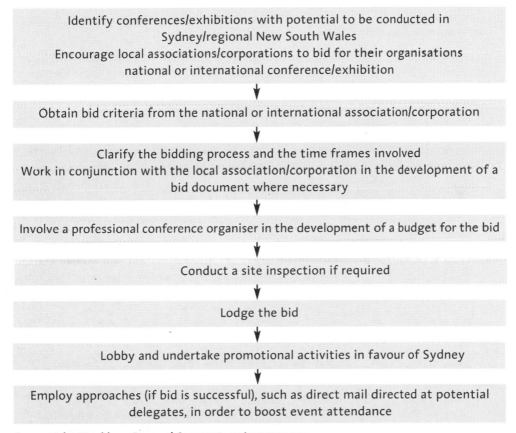

Identify conferences/exhibitions with potential to be conducted in Sydney/regional New South Wales
Encourage local associations/corporations to bid for their organisations national or international conference/exhibition

Obtain bid criteria from the national or international association/corporation

Clarify the bidding process and the time frames involved
Work in conjunction with the local association/corporation in the development of a bid document where necessary

Involve a professional conference organiser in the development of a budget for the bid

Conduct a site inspection if required

Lodge the bid

Lobby and undertake promotional activities in favour of Sydney

Employ approaches (if bid is successful), such as direct mail directed at potential delegates, in order to boost event attendance

Source: John Hutchison, Personal Comment, 15 January 2003.

opportunities, it is not surprising, therefore, that many businesses have sought to formally link with the SCVB through its membership program. The specific membership benefits provided by this program are outlined in Table 3.4.

SCVB seeks to attract new members through such means as public relations, advertising, sales calls, attendance at trade shows, member referrals and staff referrals. It also seeks to maintain its existing membership through ensuring it delivers on the various members benefits noted in Table 3.4.

It can be seen from Table 3.4 that participation in trade shows, and the conduct of roads shows and other events are a major aspect of SCVB's marketing communication efforts. In 2001/02, for example, the SCVB participated in nine domestic and international trade shows in an effort to raise the profile of Sydney/regional New South Wales in key target markets and generate quality business leads and bid opportunities. Additionally, the SCVB conducts its own road shows in major international and domestic markets, with members being invited to participate. In 2001/02, for example, a Sydney road show toured the North American market visiting Pheonix, Dallas, Boston, Salt Lake City, Minneapolis and St Louis. Within Australia, the SCVB conducted Sydney

Table 3.4: Sydney Convention and Visitors Bureau membership benefits

Convention and Incentive Sales Activities

Bid opportunities and participation	Meetings managers who are Gold or Silver members can join forces with the SCVB in bid document budget preparation for major meeting and convention business, particularly in the international arena.
Familiarisations and site inspections	The SCVB conducts regular familiarisations for national and international meeting and incentive planners and buyers, and visiting journalists. Members can showcase their products or services to these key contacts by becoming involved in familiarisation and site inspection programs, special events and business functions hosted by the SCVB.
International and interstate representation	The SCVB representatives in Melbourne, United Kingdom/ Europe and North America provide Sydney with a strong presence at trade shows and full sales representation across a broad range of sales and marketing activities.
Sydney and NSW on show	Selected membership levels have the opportunity to take part in roadshows to Canberra, Melbourne and Brisbane.
National and international trade shows	SCVB members have the opportunity to participate as a cooperative partner in national and international trade shows. It is essential that Sydney maintains a strong presence at these shows. By working in partnership, SCVB members can stretch their marketing dollar further and promote their product or service more effectively.

Marketing Communications Activities

Sydney Facilities Guide	This is the SCVB's main publication promoting Sydney and regional NSW. It is a comprehensive, full-colour guide to the city's meeting, incentive, convention and exhibition facilities and services. The SCVB distributes 12 000 copies nationally and internationally to a highly targeted database of corporate, association and government event planners and decision makers.
SCVB online newsletters	The *Bureau Bulletin* is a monthly newsletter emailed to SCVB members and VIPs which provides up-to-date reports on industry issues and information on SCVB's activities including the latest business won.
Sydney Showcase	*Sydney Showcase* is a monthly product and service update distributed domestically and internationally to over 8000 qualified business tourism contacts. All members have the opportunity to receive editorial coverage in this newsletter. All SCVB members can advertise in both newsletters.

| Imagine Sydney itinerary planner | The Imagine Sydney itinerary planner is the perfect itinerary promotional tool for all members who target the incentive market. This is a high quality, full-colour planner that profiles Sydney's capabilities as the world's premier incentive destination. It is distributed internationally and nationally to key incentive buyers. Members who offer products or services for the incentive market can take additional advertising in this publication. |
| Web site | The web site is an integral part of the SCVB's marketing and promotional strategy. All members are listed on the site, and advanced listings as well as tile and banner ads are available. The SCVB promotes the web site to key domestic and international meeting planner contacts and encourages them to request proposals online for their business events which are then distributed directly to SCVB members via the event referral service. |

Membership Activities

| Event referral service | The SCVB's event referral service is free to event planners searching for products and services. Through this service the SCVB is able to put members in touch with qualified business opportunities. Members receive the event profile based on their level of membership. |
| Membership functions | The SCVB prides itself on presenting regular opportunities for its members to network. These functions provide the perfect opportunity for members to meet with the other key players in the business tourism industry and form alliances that will see their businesses grow. The functions include networking lunches for all SCVB members, business networking breakfasts, and a series of lunches for Gold and Silver members. The SCVB invites buyers and corporate contacts to many of these functions, and key industry speakers are invited to deliver thought-provoking presentations relevant to the business tourism industry. |

Research and Sales Development Activities

| Educational forums | The SCVB places great importance on educating members on how to generate business opportunities and maximise their membership benefits. |
| Research and sales development activities | Calendar of Meetings and Events—a marketing tool members simply cannot do without, the SCVB's Calendar of Meetings and Events on CD-ROM lists the major events and meetings in Sydney, up to a decade in advance. The calendar includes details on the type of event, venue, date, number of attendees |

continued

Table 3.4: Sydney Convention and Visitors Bureau membership benefits (cont.)

	expected, and the organiser's contact details, providing you with the perfect opportunity to promote your business. The 2001 edition of the Calendar detailed 2065 confirmed meetings for Sydney and regional New South Wales up to the year 2012.
List rental opportunities	The SCVB maintains a comprehensive database of the national and international associations and corporate event planners that have the potential to bring business to Sydney. Blind list rental agreement is based on the premise that names are supplied to a third party mailing house. This refers to the fact that at no stage does the SCVB member receive a hard copy, a disk or labels of the actual names and addresses requested. Members can select the criteria for their target market and they will be provided with mailing labels direct to the mailing house.
Information/research	The SCVB is dedicated to keeping abreast of all the latest developments in the business tourism industry for the benefit of the Bureau and its members. As a member of SCVB you can access this research as well as the research SCVB conducts into the convention market.
Sydney on Sale	Sydney on Sale is the annual trade show presented by SCVB. This event provides members with the opportunity to exhibit and make contact with hundreds of qualified meeting, incentive travel convention and exhibition planners under one roof. The SCVB offers members special participation packages.

Source: SCVB, 2001/02.

and regional New South Wales road shows taking in Canberra, Melbourne and Brisbane. Qualified corporate meeting planners and buyers were targeted to meet with the SCVB members who participated in these events. The SCVB's most significant annual event is, however, Sydney on Sale. This event is designed to target: corporate event planners; association meeting and event organisers; marketing, public relations and advertising professionals; and government meeting and public event organisers. The primary goal of this event is to showcase the diverse range of professional business event products and services in Sydney, regional New South Wales, and, for the first time in 2002, other parts of Australia.

EVALUATION OF MARKETING PERFORMANCE

The SCVB establishes clear objectives for all areas of its marketing activities. These objectives act to direct its efforts and to provide benchmarks against which performance can be measured. In its 2001/02 annual report, for example, the following objectives were set for its marketing communications unit:

* to increase the profile and desirability of Sydney and regional New South Wales as a business tourism destination;
* to raise the profile of SCVB's members through cooperative marketing opportunities;
* to produce high quality marketing communications materials which promote Sydney, New South Wales and SCVB members;
* to provide support to the sales team's bidding activities; and
* to create and maintain a high quality web site, to meet the specific needs of key user groups.

In order to determine how it has performed against those objectives it has set, the SCVB gathers and analyses a range of appropriate information. For example, in Table 3.5 a range of criteria used to assess performance in the public relations area are given, along with quantitative measures of success (or otherwise).

Table 3.5: Public relations results 2000/01—2001/02			
Criteria	2001/02	2000/01	% change
Media coverage generated	$4 460 450	$5 086 119	–12% *
Media coverage generated by Sydney on Sale	$455 474	$902 426	–50% *
Media contacts on SCVB database	884	747	18%
Journalists hosted by SCVB	28	14	100%
Speeches given by SCVB management to key industry groups	42	56	–25%

*As Sydney on Sale was held in June 2002, most of the media coverage generated for this event will be published in the new financial year. This has impacted on the value of media coverage generated during 2001/02. In previous years, Sydney on Sale has been held earlier in the financial year and as such all media coverage was able to be recorded in the annual report.

Source: SCVB, 2001/02.

SUMMARY

The SCVB operates in a very dynamic environment exposing it to a variety of external factors capable of affecting its marketing practices and performance.

Nonetheless, the SCVB has been extremely successful in building the Sydney and regional New South Wales business meetings markets over a long period. The reasons for this success lie in its strategic approach to the marketing planning process with marketing decisions being based on research, input from staff and an analysis of the previous marketing efforts. It is noteworthy that the SCVB's marketing planning approach is, to a large extent, project based, acknowledging that different markets will present their own specific problems and opportunities. Objective setting and performance measurement, the key to monitoring, controlling and modifying future marketing efforts, are also strongly in evidence in the SCVB's marketing efforts. Additionally, the SCVB's success in developing strategic alliances with other destination marketing organisations and the Sydney Convention and Exhibition Centre, combined with its membership program, reflect its efforts to stretch its promotional expenditure as far as possible for maximum effect. Finally, it is noteworthy that the SCVB's 'product' can be viewed in two ways—the destination itself and the actual promotional activities that it uses its resources to undertake. When viewed as the former, the capacity of the SCVB to directly improve or modify its product is limited, which in turn can influence its actions in areas such as the type and size of business meetings it seeks to target. Aware of this, the SCVB works with the business meetings industry, tourism organisations and government to try to have any issues constraining its activities addressed. A recent example of this was the SCVB's efforts, in association with other organisations, to have the size of the Sydney Convention and Exhibition Centre expanded.

Primary period covered by case study: 2002/03

REFERENCE

Sydney Convention and Visitors Bureau Annual Report 2001/02.

QUESTIONS

1   Discuss the broad marketing functions performed by the SCVB. How important are these functions to the development of the business meetings industry in Sydney and regional New South Wales?

2   What marketing benefits do you believe those organisations that take up SCVB membership seek?

3   In what ways does this case study reflect 'best practice' from a marketing perspective? Can you suggest any changes to the SCVB's current strategic marketing approach?

4   Using the SCVB's annual report (see news and media section of the SCVB web site at <www.scvb.com.au>) as your source, briefly discuss how the SCVB has sought to quantify its performance in the research and sales, or marketing communications areas.

5 Briefly discuss how each of the general environmental factors listed in the *Marketing environment* section of the case study might potentially influence the SCVB's marketing actions.

6 What potential difficulties do you see, from a marketing perspective, in the SCVB's lack of direct control over the 'product' it is selling? In what ways has the SCVB sought to deal with this issue?

7 How significant is the SCVB's participation in, or conduct of, events in its overall promotional efforts? What strengths do you see in the use of events as promotional tools?

8 What value does the SCVB place upon evaluating its marketing efforts? Support your discussion by making reference to specific examples from the case study. Consider also using the SCVB annual report (see the SCVB web site at <www.scvb.com.au>) to identify further examples.

9 Construct a table listing the marketing communication activities undertaken by the SCVB. Try to classify these activities under a range of generic headings.

10 Briefly compare the stages involved in the SCVB's approach to marketing planning to that proposed by any major tourism/hospitality management marketing text. To what extent can the SCVB's approach be classified as similar to, or different from, that proposed in the text you have selected?

4. TRAFALGAR TOURS

INTRODUCTION

This case study explores the marketing planning process of Trafalgar Tours (TT), a multinational tour operator. In doing so it examines: the relationship between TT's head office and its country sales offices/general sales agents (with specific reference to its Australian office); the extent to which marketing research has guided its marketing decision-making; and the influence of an established market position on marketing mix decisions. Additionally, the case discusses how the internet is used by TT for strategic marketing processes, its approach to pricing and promotion, and the centrality of retail travel agents to its overall distribution strategy.

BACKGROUND

TT began operations in 1947 as Industrial Recreational Services (IRS), with the intent, according to its founder Bill Nunn, of 'organising group travel and entertainment for industry'. In 1949 IRS moved to Trafalgar Square in London—the landmark from which the company would take its name some 10 years later—and soon afterwards opened a travel agency called The Arcade Booking Office. The leisure side of the company's business steadily grew, and over the next 20 years a variety of group travel products were developed, including European coach tours and cruises.

In 1969 Trafalgar Tours was sold to a American-based tourism and hospitality group which is now known as the Travel Corporation. Under the new ownership the company expanded its operations significantly.

By the late 1990s Trafalgar had become a multinational business operating motorcoach tours of the United Kingdom, Europe and the United States with sales offices in nine countries, and general sales agents (GSAs) in a further nineteen. In 2002 the company employed approximately 800 people worldwide (60 in Australia) of whom 350 are tour directors. TT, it is worthwhile noting, is the largest escorted motorcoach tour operator for Australians travelling to Europe.

TT's holding company, Travel Corporation, has, over the past decade or more, pursued a strategy of horizontal integration, purchasing Contiki Tours (a specialist under-35s coach tour company), Creative Tours, New Horizons

Holidays, AAT Kings and Insight (once Trafalgar's main European competitor). Travel Corporation's last acquisition (in 2000) was Destination America, a major tour operator in the United States of America and Canada.

MARKETING PLANNING PROCESS

TT's marketing planning process is a relatively straightforward one. Each year in July/August the results of the previous year's marketing activities are reviewed and evaluated in terms of the marketing objectives that were set. These objectives relate to total sales revenue and passenger numbers, and are further broken down into specific country targets. As a result of this review, and in the light of current and projected market conditions for the next 12 months, new marketing objectives are established.

As part of the marketing planning process, TT's head office seeks information on market conditions from its overseas sales offices and general sales agents. This information along with data on the business environment in general serves as the foundation for decisions, particularly those relating to product (tour itineraries and frequency) and price. Promotion (with the exception of brochure design and development) and distribution matters are largely devolved to overseas offices and GSAs due to the importance of 'local' knowledge in these decisions.

EXTERNAL FACTORS IMPACTING UPON MARKETING DECISIONS

TT, like all well-managed tourism businesses, maintains a watching brief on a number of external factors that have the potential to impact upon its marketing activities. These include:

- exchange rates;
- fuel prices;
- infrastructure capacity constraints in popular tourist cities, particularly in Europe;
- airport capacity constraints;
- armed conflicts in destination, or surrounding, areas;
- prevailing economic climate in geographic markets;
- changes in the general level of disposable income within geographic markets;
- changes in available leisure time;
- health concerns with the potential to constrain, or influence the flow of, travel; and

- changes in the demographic market segments served within TT's various geographic markets.

Developments in these, and other areas, mean that TT's marketing process is very much a dynamic one that must be capable of responding to situations as they arise. For example, the outbreak of foot and mouth disease in the United Kingdom in 2000 had a significant impact on demand for tours of this region from the United States. This situation in turn meant TT had to work other markets harder, via such means as increased promotional efforts, in order to try to maintain overall demand levels. Compounding the potential volatility of TT's marketing environment is the relatively long lead times (12 to 18 months) involved in developing tour products and getting them to market. Such lead times can limit TT's capacity to respond to changed circumstances in areas such as product design or pricing.

MAJOR MARKETS

The consumer market for TT products is sometimes thought to comprise solely of the so-called 'blue rinse set', i.e. people over 65 years of age. This, however, is not the case as the majority of TT's passengers (50 per cent) are between 44 and 64 years of age, with approximately one-third of passengers being under 44. The majority of 44- to 64-year-olds are either 'empty-nesters' or on long service leave. As regards geographic market sources, North America (i.e. Canada and the United States of America) accounts for approximately 50 per cent of all customers, while Australia/New Zealand is responsible for 30 per cent of sales, and South Africa and the Far East (Hong Kong, Philippines, Korea, Thailand and Singapore) account for the remaining 20 per cent.

Price is used as a mechanism for further segmenting TT's market with most tour programs being offered at two levels, *First Class* and *Cost Saver* (see later discussion). Age is also used as a market segmentation tool with TT operating an extensive 21–35s tour program (*Breakaway Europe*).

MARKET RESEARCH

Market research plays a vital role in determining TT's marketing practices. The tour director at the completion of each tour conducts a questionnaire survey of tour participants. These questionnaires are analysed before a debriefing is conducted with the tour director so that matters raised in them can be discussed. Information gained from surveys is particularly useful in identifying aspects of tours that may need to be further improved, and to highlight areas of the service that are being performed at a high level. Additionally, focus groups are conducted from time to time with past customers for the purpose of identifying new product ideas and to gain insights into the nature of the Trafalgar tour experience.

As an example of how customer research has provided input into marketing decisions, TT cites its now defunct *Alpine Explorer* tour. This tour performed poorly in terms of sales in its first two seasons. The results of questionnaire surveys of passengers on this tour, however, indicated that they were very satisfied with it, with many considering that they had seen the 'best of Europe'. With this information in mind, rather than drop the tour from its brochure, Trafalgar decided to change its name to *Best of Europe*. It has since become one of TT's most successful tours in term of sales.

Travel agents in the various geographic markets are regularly surveyed by employing a 'shadow shopping' approach. This technique is used to determine the extent to which TT products are being recommended to agency clients and the level of product knowledge possessed by consultants. Sales data is also used to establish trends in booking patterns and to identify performing and non performing agencies.

Long-term trends within markets are monitored. One outcome of such monitoring has been the altering of the tour mix, particularly in Europe, in order to increase the number of regional- and country-specific tours. This has occurred in response to the growing number of repeat customers who wish to develop a greater understanding/appreciation of one, or a few, of the areas they had visited on more comprehensive tours. Additionally, market research has detected a desire for slower-paced touring and greater flexibility within each tour. In response, TT has adjusted some tours to allow for longer stops (two nights instead of one) and has built in more periods of free time on its tours.

OVERALL MARKETING STRATEGY

The overall marketing strategy of TT is essentially one of positioning itself as the best value escorted motorcoach tour operator (in terms of cost and quality) in the markets in which it operates. These markets include Europe, the United States of America and Canada, Australia and Asia.

Indicative of the involvement of local sales offices in implementing the head officer's marketing strategy is that of TT's Australian office. Typically, the marketing year for this office commences in October when new product for the following year is released. At this time a planned series of product seminars for retail travel consultants in both metropolitan and rural areas are conducted, and cooperative advertising campaigns, largely with retail travel agency chains, commence. Additionally sales representatives, of whom there are 11 in Australia, begin the process of communicating product changes to retail travel agents in their respective sales territories. These same representatives also provide information to management on market conditions via a weekly meeting. In addition to servicing retail travel agents, sales representatives work with retailers to conduct a series of consumer film seminars across Australia.

MARKETING MIX

TT's marketing mix is designed to link directly back to its overall positioning strategy, as can be seen from the following.

Product

TT offers a comprehensive range of escorted motorcoach touring programs in the United Kingdom, Europe and North America. The tours in Europe/United Kingdom offer two standards—first class and costsaver. For other destinations, first class tours are operated.

Additionally a 21–38s tour program is operated in Europe. Other than accommodation, the main ingredients of TT's tour packages are coach transport, the services of a tour director, local guide services, and meals. See Figure 4.1.

Figure 4.1: Trafalgar Tour products

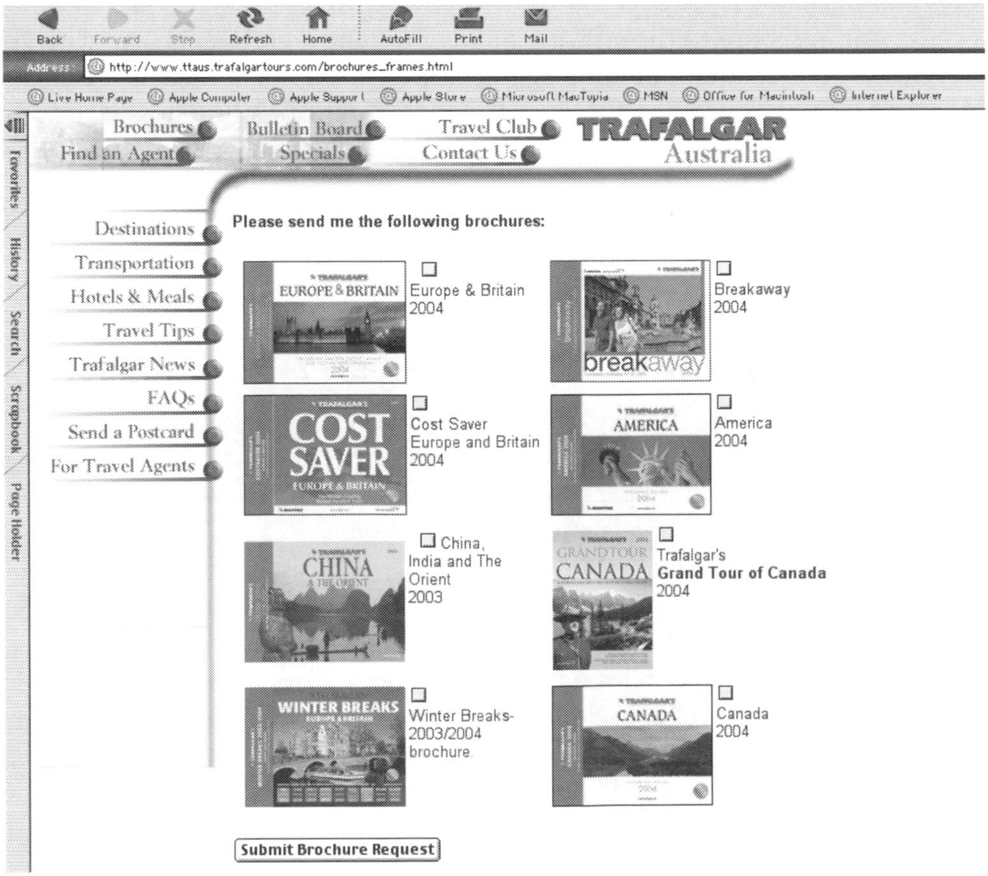

Source: <www.ttaus.trafalgartours.com>.

Trafalgar identifies the primary benefits sought by its customers as:

* opportunities for social interaction;
* removal of the worry and stress associated with making travel arrangements (all services are prearranged) or driving in unfamiliar countries;
* security and peace of mind;
* guaranteed product standards;
* flexibility (in terms of the amount of free time built into tours);
* convenient access to major tourist attractions; and
* information concerning historical and other attributes of places visited.

Service quality is central to TT's success, and it is an aspect of their product that features strongly in its brochures, as can be seen from the following excerpt from the *2002 Europe and Britain* brochure.

Quality control means a peace of mind holiday
There are many others who make your holiday special. Our professional licensed City Guides. Skilled professional drivers in whose safe and competent hands you'll travel. Dedicated staff who will welcome you on your arrival in Europe and help and advise you at your hotel. Also, reassuringly always present behind the scenes, our Quality Control team who are tirelessly committed to ensuring that every single detail of your holiday is as perfect as you could wish it to be.

To ensure they maintain a high standard of service, TT, amongst other things:

* employs tour directors with a minimum of five years' experience and monitors their performance on every tour;
* empowers front line staff to do whatever is necessary to meet customer needs;
* assesses all tour ingredients (e.g. hotels, restaurants) on a regular basis to ensure they meet designated standards. Quality control staff at TT's head office monitor such tour ingredients through client questionnaires completed at the end of each tour, and tour director reports. Quality control staff also spend time in the field and conduct on-site inspections of accommodation properties, and information from the bulletin board on the internet provides regular customer feedback on all areas of the operation; and
* utilises only late model, airconditioned coaches with reclining seats, on board washrooms and panoramic windows.

PRICING

The head office of TT sets all tour prices. In line with its positioning strategy of being the best value escorted motorcoach tour operator, prices are established with competitors firmly in mind, including those owned by the holding company of which TT is a part. In this regard, it should be noted, such companies are operated as independent profit-seeking businesses, and represent genuine competition for TT.

All prices for tours are based upon a break-even point, with tours being monitored on a regular basis to access where they stand in relation to this point. Should any tour 45 days (60 in peak season) from departure fail to reach its break-even number of passengers it might be cancelled, and travel agents and passengers are advised. Conversely, if excess demand is detected, additional departures may be scheduled. It is important to note that the break-even point is not the same year round and is calculated essentially on a tour-by-tour basis. For example, the break-even number of passengers for a winter tour departure may be 25, while this same figure for a summer departure of the same or similar tour might be in the vicinity of 37 passengers. This difference is largely due to seasonal variations in supplier charges.

Trafalgar accepts the need to develop strong partnerships with their suppliers, most particularly, their contracted hotels. For this reason, while the volume of business they generate gives them the capacity to bargain hard over room rates, they ensure they deliver promised demand in both off-peak and peak seasons. The track record that Trafalgar has developed with accommodation properties frequently has meant that they have been able to obtain lower rates than their competitors, with the bulk of these savings being passed on to their customers in the form of lower prices.

PROMOTIONAL STRATEGY
Promotional messages and tools

TT, while guided by its desired market position for its products, does not have a stated promotional strategy as such. It is nonetheless evident that it seeks to project an image of professionalism, efficiency and quality in its promotional activities. Evidence for this can be found, for example, in the imagery, design and copy of its brochures, as well as in the presentation of its staff and coaches.

It is noteworthy that TT has defined its competition as extending beyond other tour operators to alternative means of achieving a similar holiday outcome, specifically cruise ships and self-conducted rail or driving holidays. Indeed, it actively promotes its advantages over these alternatives, with its internet site noting:

When you travel with Trafalgar you WON'T have to worry about . . .
Frustrating parking problems!
The cost of gasoline!
Coping with foreign road signs!
Missing your train connection!
Getting lost in a foreign country!
Keeping track of your baggage!
Crippling continental road tolls!
Crazy European driving habits!
Finding hotel accommodation!
. . . Need we go on?

The design and layout of TT's main promotional tool, its brochure, is the responsibility of its head office. Additionally, the New York office is responsible for related developments, such as the production of videos. Other promotional activities, however, are essentially the responsibility of its overseas offices due to the need to adapt marketing communication efforts to local conditions. In Australia, for example, there is a heavy reliance upon cooperative promotional campaigns with major retail travel agency chains. These campaigns commonly involve the provision of promotional funds to agency chains as a lump sum. This money is then used, in combination with funds provided by the chain itself, to engage in advertising in various media, such as newspapers, television and radio.

In recent years, the internet has become a very important communication/ promotional tool in Trafalgar's marketing mix. The web site <www.trafalgartours. com.au> contains, amongst other things, general information on the company itself, details regarding its range of tours, information on booking conditions, an online brochure order form and a bulletin board. This last feature allows people who have been on a Trafalgar tour to tell others about their experience. It also provides an opportunity for those who are contemplating undertaking a tour to seek information both about the tour experience itself and on more general matters associated with travelling (e.g. should I take travellers cheques, cash or both?) or destination areas (e.g. what is the best place to buy leather jackets in Milan?). In recent times a group of past Trafalgar passengers using the bulletin board, banded together and formed their own online club, which they called 'Trafalgar Addicts'. This group has now grown large enough to allow it to approach Trafalgar concerning the conduct of tours specifically for its members. The 'ingredients' of such tours, that is the itineraries, inclusions, hotels, and even the drivers and tour managers, are worked out through online discussion between members.

The product design process evident in the context of the Trafalgar Addicts group reflects a significant departure from that which is employed for the company's other tours. Instead of the company itself acting to create a tour product and then attempting to sell it in the market place, customers themselves both create the product and undertake the selling task. This change in the product design and promotion process reflects how the personal empowerment allowed by the internet has the potential to change the traditional marketing practices of a company such as TT.

TT's overseas offices and GSAs undertake independent promotional campaigns directed at end consumers from time to time. TT's Australian office, for example, has in the past sponsored television programs, such as a direct telecast of Sydney's Channel 9's *Today* show from London. This same office has also provided product as prizes on television programs, undertaken radio and print advertising campaigns, facilitated inclusion of the company's product on travel-related television programs, and regularly participates in consumer travel shows.

Branding

The Trafalgar name features strongly in all print and media advertising, as well as in promotional material prepared for industrial markets, specifically travel agents. As Trafalgar sells over 250 000 packages per year, opportunities also exist to reinforce the Trafalgar brand and its market position to current customers, through such means as direct mail and via its internet site.

An example of the issues a powerful brand can create for a company such as TT is the internal debate the organisation had as to the difficulties its strong brand name, and associated image as a European motorcoach touring firm, might present as the company sought to expand its operations into the United States of America. Only after much debate amongst the company's management was it was decided that the brand name was more likely to convey an image of quality and value rather than that of a company with little knowledge of the United States as a touring destination. This being the case, it was decided to change the name of the tour operator it had purchased in the United States (Destination America) as the vehicle for its expansion there to that of TT.

Customer loyalty programs

Trafalgar operates a passenger loyalty program titled the 'Trafalgar Club'. Passengers are asked if they wish to join upon completion of their tour. Details are held in a central database that is used for regular product mailings. Past customers are also given a 5 per cent discount voucher for any future TT tour that they may wish to undertake. TT enjoys a high level of repeat business with approximately 58 per cent of clients having travelled with it before.

DISTRIBUTION

TT has pursued a strategy of distribution through retail travel agents, and is committed to this strategy for the foreseeable future. There are various reasons

TT has decided to act in this way. First, there is the complexity of the booking transaction itself. Tours are not often purchased in isolation. Often car hire, accommodation, cruises, air flights and other components are involved, requiring the seller to have expertise in a range of areas, as well as systems capable of completing transactions with a range of suppliers. Secondly, given the time that sometimes needs to be taken in order to 'sell' the product to customers, transaction times can be long, thus increasing the cost per booking. Lastly, the geographical spread of TT's customers would likely result in high toll-free telephone costs should it go down the direct booking path.

Most reservations by agents are currently made by phone. In the United States an online booking engine has been created for agents, and it is proposed to roll this out in Australia in the not too distant future. Additionally, TT is currently undertaking a complete review of its use of electronic distribution technology, and intends to launch a new web-based reservation system with agency access in 2005 for the 2006 season.

While Trafalgar maintains an internet site, it believes that its customer base requires the product knowledge and reassurance provided by retail travel agents, and as such this site does not provide a direct booking facility.

Trafalgar, in line with its distribution strategy, has entered into preferred product agreements with major agency chains. As part of these agreements a range of cooperative promotional activities, as noted previously, are engaged in. Additionally, Trafalgar maintains a sales force that acts to service travel agents by, amongst other things, arranging for brochure deliveries, dealing with client complaints and educating agents regarding product changes. Travel agents are also provided with familiarisations on TT to enhance their knowledge of, and enthusiasm for, the product.

SUMMARY

TT has positioned itself, over a number of years, as a provider of high quality coach tours in those geographic markets from which it draws its customers. Its centralised approach to product development, that draws on insights from its local offices and GSAs, combined with its own market research, has over time proven effective in meeting the needs of its target market groups. This centralised approach, however, has not extended to the areas of promotion and distribution, where 'local' knowledge has been deemed fundamental to success. Additionally, TT has not been tempted by the potential cost savings offered by the internet for direct bookings, instead maintaining a commitment to its trade intermediaries, believing this approach to accessing consumers is most appropriate given the nature of its product. This case also highlights the value of 'getting it right' in terms of product design and delivery, with 58 per cent of customers being repeat purchasers.

Primary period covered by case study: 2001/02

REFERENCE

<www.trafalgartours.com.au>

QUESTIONS

1   Describe the marketing planning process employed by TT. Do you consider the process you have described as formal or informal? Explain your answer.

2   What forms of market research does TT employ? Can you suggest any ways by which the current process of gathering market information could be improved?

3   Why has TT chosen to solely distribute its products through retail travel agents? Do you agree with its reasoning?

4   How does TT's marketing mix support its current market positioning?

5   If TT chose to control all marketing decisions centrally, what potential problems may result? Is it significant that TT's head office consults with, and provides automony in some areas to, local offices/GSAs?

6   What external factors have the potential to impact on TT's marketing planning efforts? Why can tour operators, such as TT, find it difficult to adapt quickly to changing environmental circumstances?

7   What form of market segmentation does TT use? Can you think of any other types of segmentation that might be able to be employed by a tour operator, such as TT?

8   Why has TT defined its competition so broadly? What advantages might there be in defining competition in this way?

9   To what extent is there evidence in the case study that TT is concerned about quality? Can you identify approaches it employs to ensure quality outcomes for its customers?

10   Why is TT concerned to develop strong partnerships with its suppliers? How might suppliers influence the overall perception of TT's products by its customers?

5. SYDNEY AQUARIUM

INTRODUCTION

The Sydney Aquarium faces a variety of marketing challenges as it seeks to maintain its position as one of Sydney's foremost tourist attractions. Central amongst these challenges is the need to stimulate repeat visitation from domestic visitors, adjust to changes in the business environment, further develop international visitation, and maximise yield per visitor. As this case study shows, these challenges are addressed via a structured marketing planning process that seeks to build an integrated marketing mix in order to achieve specific marketing objectives associated with admission and yield targets. Also in evidence in this case study is the significance of marketing intelligence derived from regular performance reviews and research to the marketing decision-making process.

BACKGROUND

In the original concept for Darling Harbour (a leisure and entertainment area on the edge of the Sydney CBD), it was envisaged that a government-funded aquarium would be built on the eastern side of the precinct at a site known as Pier 26. The cost of constructing Darling Harbour, however, was far higher than original estimates, causing the New South Wales Government to call for tenders for the construction and operation of a privately funded aquarium. The tender was won by Jonray Holdings Limited, who later contracted architects Philip Cox, Richardson, Taylor and Partners Pty Ltd to design the facility. They in turn designed the Aquarium in the shape of a large wave to complement both the underwater theme of the Aquarium itself and the maritime theme of Darling Harbour. Building of the complex commenced in May 1987, and it opened to the public on 13 July 1988. The cost of building and fit-out was $30 million.

Shortly after opening, the Sydney Aquarium was the subject of a leveraged buyout by an investor group comprising Byvest Management Buyout Group, EFG Securities Limited, and John Burgess. Interests associated with Ross Grant Management group subsequently invested in 1989. Elders IXL Limited, through Elders Finance and Investment Co. Limited (now known as ELFIC Limited), provided the majority of the debt financing for the group.

In June 1993, the Sydney Aquarium became a publicly listed company on the Stock Exchange. Some of the original investors retained their stake in the public company, while others considered it appropriate to realise their investment. Shares initially listed at $1.20. The annual report, available on the company's web site (<www.sydneyaquarium.com.au>) provides a current list of major shareholders in the company.

The Sydney Aquarium operates on a long-term lease from the Sydney Harbour Foreshore Authority which expires in 2037 with an option to extend for a further 50 years. It is a purpose-built facility that houses more than 11 000 invertebrates, fish, birds, reptiles and mammals, and comprises three large floating oceanariums as well as a general exhibit hall. In October 1998, a new $14 million Great Barrier Reef complex opened. Included in this complex is a 2.6 million litre tropical oceanarium, live coral cave, touch pool and coral atoll. As part of this development, the gift shop was doubled in size and the cafe was expanded so that it could accommodate 200 people in a mixture of internal and external seating. An external kiosk (takeaway food only) was opened mid-September 2000.

The Aquarium complex also includes a support building to the north of the main building within which there is a food preparation room for the animals, a water analysis room, quarantine room, staff room and some office space. The main staff offices are located in the Great Barrier Reef complex.

The Aquarium's revenues are derived mainly from visitor admission charges and sales from the gift and coffee shops.

The total number of full-time staff employed at the Aquarium is approximately 45, with a large number of casual staff being employed in various operational roles such as ticket sales and restaurant service.

BUSINESS GOALS, STRATEGIES AND MARKETS

Like any private company, Sydney Aquarium's primary goal is to maximise returns for its shareholders. It seeks to do this by positioning itself as one of Sydney's leading tourist attractions via the showcasing of Australia's unique aquatic life to both Australian and overseas visitors. In order to achieve this goal, Sydney Aquarium continually seeks to add 'new' experiences to both enhance the attractiveness of its offering and to encourage repeat visitation, particularly from Sydneysiders. Additionally, it has an ongoing program designed to enhance the quality of its existing exhibits.

Sydney Aquarium draws visitation from three key market segments—Sydneysiders, domestic tourists (intrastate and interstate) and international tourists. Set out in Table 5.1 is a breakdown of visitation from these markets over the past 14 years ending 30 June 2002. Prior to November 1994, it should be noted, the number of visitors within each market segment was based only on small daily sample surveys. Since November 1994, *all* visitors to the Aquarium have been surveyed for place of residence and this information coded into admission registers so that accurate demographic statistics can be obtained.

Table 5.1: Sydney Aquarium Limited visitor numbers 1989—2002 ('000s)

Year to 30 June	Sydneysiders	Domestic tourists	International tourists	Total
1989	n/a	n/a	n/a	1101
1990	379	222	206	807
1991	293	212	258	763
1992	207	176	321	704
1993	214	164	425	803
1994	213	195	517	925
1995	282	216	520	1018
1996	260	213	539	1012
1997	261	192	587	1040
1998	277	180	547	1004
1999	329	190	589	1108
2000	314	206	681	1201
2001	243	193	750	1186
2002	296	214	742	1252

Source: Sydney Aquarium, 2002.

From Table 5.1 it can be seen that visitor numbers in the year ended 30 June 2002 were the highest experienced by the Sydney Aquarium since it opened in 1988. A total of 1 252 000 people visited in 2001/02 compared with 1 186 000 in the previous year. This growth in visitor numbers is attributable to significant increases in the number of Sydneysiders (up 18 per cent) and domestic tourists (up 10 per cent). It can also be seen from Table 5.1 that the number of overseas visitors declined slightly (down 1.8 per cent) between 2001 and 2002. It is likely that the events of September 2001 and the collapse of Ansett airlines were significant factors in this decline, and it is possible that this decrease would have been significantly larger but for a relatively weak Australian dollar. A break-down of overseas visitor numbers (see Table 5.2) nonetheless shows that visitation from Asian countries other than Japan grew strongly. The economic difficulties Japan is currently experiencing, along with increased competition Australia has faced from destinations such as Hawaii, Italy and North America in this market, are likely to be responsible for this situation.

Also observable in Table 5.1 are the effects of the opening of the Great Barrier Reef exhibit in October 1998, with Sydneysider visitation growing by almost 20 per cent in the 1998/99 period over the previous year. Besides seeking to promote local visitation, the other aim of this new exhibit was to enhance the reputation of the Aquarium as a major international tourist attraction. Given that international visitation increased 7.6 per cent in 1998/99 and 15.6 per cent in 1999/2000, it could be said that this outcome was also achieved. Other interesting fluctuations in demand evident in Table 5.1 include the impact of the Asian currency crisis that was largely responsible for the decrease in overseas visitation in 1997/98.

In the context of international visitors, it is noteworthy that of the over 2.6 million international tourists who visited New South Wales in 1999 (Bureau of Tourism Research, 2000), approximately 26 per cent visited the Aquarium. Aquarium management believes, particularly in the light of the successful Sydney Olympic Games, that the long-term outlook for international tourism to Sydney is very positive and that international visitation to the Aquarium will continue to grow in both absolute and percentage terms.

International Market	000's	Growth over previous year
Europe	294	–2%
The Americas	92	–13%
Other Asia	210	+15%
Japan	93	–13%
Other overseas	61	+7%

Table 5.2: International visitation to Sydney Aquarium—2001/02

Source: Sydney Aquarium, 2002.

MARKETING ENVIRONMENT

Competitive

In February 1998, the Sydney Aquarium purchased its only other direct competitor, Oceanworld Manly. This smaller aquarium is situated on Manly Cove, approximately 11 kilometres from Sydney's CBD. At the time of purchase, visitation to Oceanworld was approximately one-fifth that of Sydney Aquarium's.

In a more general sense, the Aquarium competes with the full range of other Sydney commercial attractions, such as museums, art galleries, historic houses and various events, as well as natural attractions such as beaches and national parks. Some of these attractions, particularly museums and art galleries, are able to 'refresh' their product via regularly mounting new exhibits, making it easier for them to attract repeat visitors than is the case with the Aquarium. This weakness, however, is limited in its impact to the domestic market.

The schools market, which comprises some 15 per cent of the Aquarium's total Sydneysider market, is one of the most competitive. In this market the

Sydney Aquarium competes against a myriad alternative field trips available to schools. To attract and hold this market, the Aquarium has had to develop packages of interpretive materials such as educational kits that contain background information and student worksheets.

The Aquarium has also found that its relatively low entry prices, and associated commission rates, have prevented it from penetrating the international group travel market to any meaningful extent. This problem is one, however, that many attractions face (see further discussion under *Pricing*, page 62).

General business environment

Sydney Aquarium has identified a number of general external factors that have had, or have the potential to, impact upon either its visitor numbers and/or yield per visitor. These are:

* strong promotional campaigns offering cheaper and more attractive tourist destinations by other countries in international markets which are traditionally major visitor generators for Australia;
* economic recession in one or more major international markets;
* increased competition from other tourist destinations within Australia;
* any major disruptions to international and domestic arrivals in Sydney, such as industrial action or fuel crises;
* a strengthening of the Australian dollar relative to other countries, making Australia a more expensive holiday destination;
* major international conflicts;
* health-related travel warnings;
* shortage of hotel accommodation or increases in hotel tariffs; and
* changes that occur in government policy regarding taxes that affect international visitors, such as arrival and departure taxes and the GST.

MARKETING PLANNING PROCESS

Sydney Aquarium employs a formal annual marketing plan that is developed over a period of approximately two months. Although it is the marketing manager's responsibility to write and finalise the plan, input from the rest of the sales and marketing team is viewed as integral to the planning process. Key areas covered by the marketing plan include:

* objectives (usually expressed as visitation goals for each market segment and target admission revenue yields)
* analysis of key domestic markets
* analysis of key international markets

* analysis of budgets
* key strategies (general)
* key domestic strategies
* key international strategies
* analysis of front desk operations
* key strategies front desk
* marketing strategies—Oceanworld Manly.

In preparing the plan, significant consideration is also given to the success or otherwise of past marketing activities, along with the insights generated from market research activity. Once completed, the marketing plan is presented to the CEO for comment. Formal approval of the plan by the Aquarium's board of directors usually occurs at the June board meeting. Once approved, the plan operates for 12 months beginning 1 July. The sales and marketing budget is incorporated into the marketing plan. The gift shop and cafe also submit a business plan for approval that sets strategies for achieving specific revenue targets per visitor.

Marketing staff

The sales and marketing department comprises a marketing director, sales director, education officer, public relations/marketing co-ordinator, sales co-ordinator and marketing assistant. The marketing director and sales director report to the CEO, who is responsible to the board of directors for all the Aquarium's operations.

MARKETING MIX
Product

Sydney Aquarium comprises eight major display areas:

1   Murray/Darling River
2   Mangrove Habitat
3   Rivers of the Far North
4   Great Australian Bight
5   Sydney Harbour
6   Rocky Shores
7   Open Ocean
8   Great Barrier Reef

Additional to these product elements are a cafe and a gift shop.

The design of the Aquarium is such that it can comfortably be visited within a period of approximately 1.5 hours (indeed, this is the average visitation time). Given that many potential visitors have limited time, the Aquarium could be said to have a competitive advantage over other attractions requiring longer visitation periods, such as Taronga Park Zoo. Additionally, the Aquarium's long opening hours (9 am–10 pm) mean that it can easily be accommodated within a busy schedule involving multiple attractions. The all-weather nature of the Aquarium also means that it is not overly affected by weather events. Indeed visitor numbers tend to be higher on overcast and rainy days.

Sydney Aquarium can be viewed not only as an attraction in its own right but as part of a larger 'attraction', the Darling Harbour precinct. This area contains:

* over 4000 hotel rooms;
* Australia's biggest convention and exhibition complex;
* shopping, entertainment and restaurant complexes;
* the Australian National Maritime Museum;
* the Powerhouse Museum;
* Imax Theatre;
* Chinese Gardens;
* Star City (casino);
* a monorail/light rail linking various parts of Darling Harbour with Pyrmont and the central business district; and
* ferry and charter boat operations (at Aquarium Pier and King Street Wharf).

The combined effect of these various attractions has been to create Sydney's major tourist precinct that attracts some 16 million visitors per annum. Of particular note, given the importance of international visitors to the Aquarium, is that 65 per cent of total international visitors to Sydney visit the area.

Sydney Aquarium has a range of products that can broadly be grouped under two headings, Aquarium only and Aquarium packages (see Figure 5.1), the latter being aquarium entry combined with one or more services from other businesses. An annual pass (*Club Aqua*) has also been recently introduced that entitles holders to, amongst other things, unlimited entry to both the Sydney Aquarium and Oceanworld for a year from date of purchase, discounted merchandise and food, discounts at major attractions, and discounted parking.

In addition to Sydney Aquarium's various entry-based product offerings, it also derives income from several other sources. At its front desk various items are sold, including site guidebooks in English, German and Japanese (the three

Figure 5.1: Selected Aquarium product offerings

Aquarium Only

General admission	Purchased at Aquarium and involving full fee entry charge or discounts based on this amount for families, students and pensioners.
Pre-paid admission tickets	Discount tickets sold through social clubs etc. to their members.
Backpacker discount tickets	The backpacker market is offered discount entry (25%) through peak organisations such as Youth Hostels Australia, Nomads, VIP etc. There are also discount entry coupons in backpacker magazines.
Discount entry vouchers	Distributed in response to requests from local community based organisations e.g. Parents & Citizens Associations and charities.
Inbound operator exchange vouchers	Vouchers issued to inbound tour operators (ITOs) for distribution to their clients. These vouchers are exchanged for admission to the Aquarium. ITOs are later invoiced based on the number of vouchers exchanged.
Internet coupon	A 10% discount entry coupon can be printed from the Aquarium's web site.
Meal deal	Admission to the Aquarium plus a meal at the Shark Bite cafe.

Aquarium Packages

Aquarium cruise ticket	Admission to the Aquarium plus a Captain Cook Cruise (sold only through Captain Cook Cruises).
AquariumPass ticket	Admission to Aquarium plus Sydney Ferries trip (only sold through Sydney Ferries).
Darling Harbour superticket	Admission to Aquarium, cruise with Matilda Cruises, meal at the Shark Bite cafe, Monorail ride, Chinese Garden entry plus discount vouchers to other Darling Harbour attractions.
'Shark-Park' ticket.	Combined car parking/entry ticket. This has been developed in response to Sydneysider demand.
Sydney bonus deluxe ticket	Admission to Aquarium, a Captain Cook Cruise's coffee cruise and entry to AMP Sydney Tower/Sky Tour. (This package is a wholesale ticket only.)
Sydney for seniors	Aquarium entry, Captain Cook Cruise's cruise with educational commentary, monorail journey, and option of entry to the Powerhouse Museum or Maritime Museum.
SEE package (Sydney educational excursions)	Aquarium entry, Captain Cook Cruise's cruise with educational commentary, monorail journey, and option of entry to the Powerhouse Museum or Maritime Museum.

Source: Sydney Aquarium, 2002.

major languages used by visitors), film, disposable cameras, Sydney Aquarium souvenir videos, and Sydney Aquarium souvenir phone cards. Audiophones with pre-recorded site tours in six languages (English, Japanese, Cantonese, Mandarin, Korean and German) are also available for rent at the front desk. The gift shop has an extensive range of Sydney Aquarium branded merchandise as well as aquatic themed clothing and accessories, home wares, jewellery, toys, books and souvenirs. Food and beverage sales at the Aquarium's cafe also contribute significantly to the company's bottom line (see *Pricing* section).

In May 2002 Sydney Aquarium announced a new development to cost some $29 million on its site at Darling Harbour. This development will comprise a two-storey facility of approximately 7000 square metres to be known as Australia's Animal World. It will comprise a series of large open-air enclosures displaying a wide range of Australian native animals (e.g. kangaroos, wombats, koalas and emus), as well as an insect display, butterfly house, and aviary. Visitors will have the opportunity to view more than 10 separate exhibits as they walk through an air-conditioned, all-weather viewing corridor in a journey that will take approximately 1.5 hours. By extending its product mix in this way, the directors of Sydney Aquarium believe (based on extensive research) that they will be able to, amongst other things: greatly increase per visitor spend (as international visitors in particular are likely to visit both attractions); increase group bookings as it will be possible to pay higher commissions to tour wholesalers and inbound tour operators via the sale of combined Aquarium/Animal World tickets; and encourage greater visitation from educational groups.

Promotional activities

In a general sense Sydney Aquarium's promotional efforts are designed to maximise awareness and interest amongst its target markets within Australia and overseas. Most promotional effort, however, is directed at its international markets as they are believed to offer the greatest growth opportunities for the company. In terms of expenditure, including salaries of marketing staff, approximately 6 per cent of the Aquarium's total revenue is allocated to promotional activities. It is also noteworthy that all advertising collateral is produced in-house by a full-time graphic designer, with the exception of Japanese print advertising and creative for television commercials (TVCs), which is handled by agencies.

Domestic

Most domestic advertising takes place on television, is timed to coincide with school holidays, and is organised through an advertising agency. Prior to 1998/99, all such advertising was confined to Sydney. In 1999/2000, however, it was decided to expand such efforts to encompass two regional areas. The success of this expanded effort resulted in the decision to maintain such regional advertising activities. The main demographic targeted by television advertising is children 5 to 12 years and their parents. To complement and reinforce the impact of these television advertising efforts, a public relations program focusing upon new animals/exhibits, and special offers/promotions with other attractions (e.g. the launch of a marine-based family movie) is also undertaken. To gauge the success of this program—a media monitoring service is engaged to collect press clippings.

Interstate advertising is minimal and predominantly aimed at air travellers (e.g. airport advertising) and motorists (e.g. roadside billboards), the two most favoured modes of domestic transport for visitors to New South Wales.

To communicate with the schools market, direct mail advertising is used to target specific curriculum coordinators. Advertising in publications targeting teachers is another means used to access this market. To entice teachers to consider the Aquarium as a possible future excursion venue, free entry is granted to teachers only. Additionally, for the past three years, teachers using the Aquarium for this purpose have had access to educational kits either on interactive CD-ROM or from the internet (see <www.sydneyaquarium.com.au/AquaSchool/CLA030.asp>).

Other promotional practices used in connection with the domestic market have included, in the recent past, joint promotions with suppliers such as Coca Cola where discount entry coupons were placed in their Sydney Royal Easter Show bags, and the inclusion of free child tickets in Sydney hotel accommodation packages as a means of stimulating family visits.

International

In order to communicate with international visitors prior to departure a variety of promotional media are used. Sydney Aquarium is fortunate in that its status as a major Sydney attraction means that most tourist guidebook publishers (e.g. Lonely Planet, Eyewitness Guides, Frommers) include material on it in their Australian publications at no cost. Additionally, given the ever increasing use of the internet by overseas travellers as a trip planning tool, the Aquarium has invested significantly in updating its web site so that it better reflects the quality of the visit experience. The site now includes, for example, a virtual tour. Some in-flight airline publication advertising is also undertaken which is placed directly with the publisher.

Upon arrival in Australia international visitors are communicated with via several means. As, according to the International Visitor Survey (Bureau of Tourism Research, 1999), some 73 per cent of international visitors stay in a hotel/motel/resort, the placement of brochures in places such as CBD hotels and backpacker establishments is an important means of accessing this market. Additionally, such material is also placed in Tourist Information Centres in the Sydney area. The Aquarium advertises, and places editorial in, tourist guides commonly distributed through the same accommodation houses.

Those individuals whose job causes them to provide information to tourists (e.g. hotel concierges, tourist information centre staff, taxi drivers) are also encouraged to visit the Aquarium on organised familiarisation programs, as their word-of-mouth recommendations to clients and guests is regarded as the most cost-effective form of promotion.

To maximise overseas group visitation, it is necessary to ensure that decision-makers (e.g. wholesale product managers) are aware of the Sydney Aquarium. This is achieved via:

* overseas sales missions to key markets conducted either independently or through organisations such as Tourism New South Wales. Key markets visited at least once annually in this way are Japan, Korea, Taiwan, Singapore and Hong Kong. Such visits to Europe and the United States are not deemed cost-effective as much of the business from these markets is FIT-based;

* participation at Australian Tourism Exchange (ATE), a trade show organised by the Australian Tourist Commission for overseas wholesalers and conducted in either Sydney or Melbourne; and

* sales calls to local and interstate inbound companies. Major accounts are visited monthly, while smaller accounts are visited on a less frequent basis.

Tourism New South Wales, the Australian Tourist Commission (now Tourism Australia) and the Sydney Harbour Foreshore Authority (a New South Wales government agency that has authority over the Darling Harbour precinct) conduct various promotional programs in which attractions, hotels and tourist-based services can participate. As there are usually significant cost savings in participating in such cooperative programs, Sydney Aquarium selects those activities that complement its marketing plan. For example, all of the previously mentioned organisations operate visiting media programs that can generate significant overseas publicity for the Aquarium. Also, as noted previously, the Aquarium participates in cooperative overseas sales missions organised by such bodies on a regular basis.

Sydney Olympics

While the previous discussion reflects general promotional efforts, it must be remembered that such efforts need to be adapted to changing circumstances. The Sydney Olympics, for example, necessitated a revised approach to September school holiday promotional efforts that had in previous years largely been based around a television advertising campaign. Because of an expected change in visitation patterns (increased international visitation and decreased domestic visitation), and because of the 'premiums' being charged by Sydney television stations during the Olympic period, a decision was taken not to use television.

Instead, advertisements were placed in airline magazines, tourist publications, and Olympic guides published by the *Sydney Morning Herald* and *Telegraph* newspapers. Street advertising was also undertaken using mobile billboards on two trucks that were driven through CBD streets. Additionally, new roof signage designed to make the Aquarium more visible to Darling Harbour (an Olympic venue) visitors was installed. A free media desk was established within the Aquarium to encourage media visits and a new interactive CD-ROM and video featuring the Aquarium was developed and made available to journalists.

These promotional efforts were instrumental in boosting international visitation compared with the same period of the previous year which acted to more than compensate for the decline in domestic visitation (see Table 5.3 below).

Table 5.3: Sydney Aquarium visitation and trading for the periods Sunday 17 to Saturday 23 and Sunday 24 to Saturday 30 September 2000.

Visitation and Trading	First Week	Second Week	Total
Internationals 2000	15 699	16 926	32 625
Internationals 1999	10 503	10 612	21 115
% change	49.5%	59.5%	54.4%
Domestic 2000	9418	11 293	20 711
Domestic 1999	11 445[1]	15 330	26 775
% change	–17.7%	–26.3%	–22.6%
Total visitation 2000	25 117	28 219	53 336
Total visitation 1999	21 948	25 942	47 890
% change	14.4%	8.8%	11.3%
Revenue 2000			$1 175 500[2]
Revenue 1999			$819 500
$/visitor 2000			$22.04
$/visitor 1999			$17.11
% change			28.8%

1 This week was not school holidays in 1999.

2 Net revenue excluding GST.

Source: Sydney Aquarium, 2000.

Pricing

Admission prices are set by Sydney Aquarium's board of directors, with per visitor yield being the prime consideration (see Table 5.4). The FIT (fully independent travel) market is regarded as the high yield segment.

Table 5.4: Revenue per head growth (excluding GST) from 2000/01			
	2001/02 ($)	2000/01 ($)	2001/02–2000/01 Increase
Admission	13.04	12.74	0.30
Gift shop & cafe	5.43	6.00	(0.57)
Total	18.47	18.74	(0.27)

Source: Sydney Aquarium, 2002.

Domestic admission pricing

The majority of domestic visitors are part of a family group (56 per cent), approximately one-third are adults unaccompanied by children and the remaining 10 per cent are school children. The domestic market is more price-sensitive than the international market and therefore to attract these visitors a variety of discounts are employed. For example, family tickets offer substantial discounts (up to 30 per cent) on full adult and child entry prices, and concession rates (around 30 per cent) are offered to Australian pensioners and seniors. Group rates are also available and these apply to pre-booked adult, child/student and senior groups. Educational groups are offered discount entry with supervising adults being admitted free.

Social clubs (corporate, ethnic, senior, etc) have the option of pre-purchasing admission-only type tickets or joint product tickets at a discounted price, as well as receiving a commission for their sale. Additionally, the members of some organisations, such as NRMA and Australian Geographic, are afforded discount entry in return for that organisation's promotion of the Aquarium.

Annual access cards (*Club Aqua*) are also sold. These are particularly attractive to those people who regularly visit the Sydney Aquarium and/or Oceanworld. The cards are valid for one year and there is unlimited access to both venues along with other benefits. The cost of membership is about 1.9 times the normal full entry rates, and adult, full family and single family membership is available.

International admission pricing

Given the exchange rate between Australia and the Sydney Aquarium's major international markets, entry prices represent excellent value for money. It is therefore the case that inducements in the form of discount entry offers are not generally employed in the context of international markets. However, there are a couple of exceptions to this generalisation that require some explanation.

To attract the international group market, it is necessary to offer discount entry rates to inbound tour companies. Margins are important to these companies as they need to factor into their pricing a commission for themselves as well as the overseas wholesalers they represent. Additionally, in some cases, it is necessary to reward companies that provide a high level of support (i.e. in terms of volume of visitors) with a lower rate, or to offer inducements or rebates for achieving set targets. Also, in the case of some overseas markets, specifically Korea and China, and to a lesser extent Taiwan, which are particularly price sensitive, it is essential to offer a lower entry price than the normal discounted inbound rate to attract groups.

Even with the various commission levels and inducements provided to inbound tour operators and wholesalers, it is still difficult to attract tour groups as admission prices (and therefore commission levels) are relatively low in comparison with the usual holiday package inclusions of airfares, car rental, accommodation and other higher priced activities, such as dinner cruises. It is therefore the case that Sydney Aquarium is often only included in tours as an optional extra. To try to capture more of this business, inbound tour operators are provided with 10 per cent discount vouchers that they can distribute to their clients. If they are used, the operator receives a 10 per cent commission.

Sydney Aquarium also offers tour wholesalers and inbound operators packages which include entry into selected attractions as well as transport services at the same level of commission as provided by each individual attraction. Such packages offer greater administrative convenience, as they involve a single transaction with one supplier, rather than multiple transactions with a number of suppliers. The Sydney Aquarium offers two such products to tour operators and wholesalers, the Darling Harbour Superticket and the Sydney Bonus ticket.

MARKETING PERFORMANCE EVALUATION AND MARKET RESEARCH

Statistical sheets are produced for each day's trading. These show visitor demographics, and admission, cafe and gift shop revenues compared with budget and with the same day the previous year. Month-to-date and year-to-date comparisons with the previous year's trading figures are also produced. This analysis provides a concise summary of trading and visitation patterns. Sales and marketing reports are tabled at each monthly board meeting outlining all activities for the month and plans for forthcoming months, including a breakdown of marketing spend by market. On a quarterly basis the Aquarium is benchmarked against other attractions/cultural institutions in terms of visitation to identify any significant shifts in market share.

To assist it in assessing the effectiveness of its promotional efforts directed at the Sydney market, Sydney Aquarium uses the results of the Venue Monitor survey. This is a bi-annual telephone survey of the leisure time activities of

400 randomly selected Sydney adults. It measures recency of participation in a range of activities within and outside Sydney. It also measures the recency of visiting specific Sydney leisure and tourism venues and provides detailed information about these visits and intentions to visit in the future. The survey is conducted jointly by the Environmetrics Centre for Visitor Studies and Newspoll.

In order to assess customer perspectives on exhibits and overall visitor satisfaction levels, Sydney Aquarium employs exit surveys on a regular basis. This information is then used to further refine/improve aspects of its product, including service levels.

SUMMARY

Sydney Aquarium is today one of Sydney's premier tourist attractions. It has reached this position in large measure because of its understanding and application of the marketing process to its specific circumstances. It can be seen from the preceding discussion that Sydney Aquarium has a sound understanding of its markets and their needs, clear marketing objectives, an appreciation of the business environment in which it operates, a marketing mix designed to achieve its yield and visitation objectives, and an appreciation of the importance of both monitoring marketing performance and market research. It is also evident from this case study that Sydney Aquarium is aware of the specific marketing challenges attractions face regarding repeat visitation and the associated need to 'refresh' product regularly. The importance of yield as opposed to simply visitation numbers can also be seen from this case study. Indeed, Sydney Aquarium's decision to expand its product mix by developing Animal World would likely have been significantly influenced by yield considerations. Finally, the benefits of locating within a tourist precinct where attractions and other businesses can cooperate in order to create service packages, and where potential visitors are likely to be present in large numbers, is also evident in this case study.

Primary period covered by case study: 2000/02

REFERENCES

Bureau of Tourism Research, 1999, *International Visitors in Australia*, Canberra.

Bureau of Tourism Research, June 2000, *International Visitors to Australia*, Canberra.

Sydney Aquarium Annual Report 2001.

Sydney Aquarium Annual Report 2002.

Sydney Aquarium, 2000, *Interim Report*.

Sydney Aquarium, 2002, *Interim Report*.

QUESTIONS

1   Why is product 'refreshment' significant in the long-term success of attractions such as aquariums? What examples of this process are in evidence in this case study?

2   What is meant by the term 'yield' in the context of tourism businesses, such as Sydney Aquarium? Why is this concept significant, and why might it be seen as being of more importance than absolute visitor numbers by the management of Sydney Aquarium?

3   How vulnerable do you believe Sydney Aquarium is to changes in its external environment? What evidence (if any) is there of such vulnerability in the case study? Can you suggest ways by which Sydney Aquarium could reduce such vulnerability?

4   From the perspectives of product development and visitor demand, what benefits are in evidence in this case study flowing from the decision to locate Sydney Aquarium within a leisure/entertainment precinct?

5   Why is the approach to pricing used by Sydney Aquarium in the context of its international markets different from that used for its domestic markets?

6   Why is Sydney Aquarium's capacity to attract international tour groups constrained by its entry fee? How has Sydney Aquarium sought to deal with this issue? How might the opening of Animal World change this situation to some extent?

7   Compile a table comprising two columns in which the promotional activities presently being undertaken by Sydney Aquarium for its domestic (column 1) and international (column 2) markets are listed. Critically review this table and suggest other promotional actions that Sydney Aquarium might consider undertaking.

8   How has Sydney Aquarium sought to develop the schools market? (Note: Before answering this question you should consult the Aquarium's web site.)

9   How would you describe Sydney Aquarium's core, tangible and augmented product?

10   How does Sydney Aquarium monitor its marketing performance and what types of marketing research does it conduct? Can you suggest refinements/additional approaches to the ways it goes about these tasks?

6. FLAG CHOICE HOTELS

INTRODUCTION

This case study documents the transition of Flag Inns from an Australian-based marketing cooperative into part of a global franchise. An increasingly competitive market coupled with the need to have an internationally recognised brand name prompted this change. With this change comes a recognised and diversified global brand portfolio (enabling effective market segmentation), access to a comprehensive promotional strategy, global marketing and sales teams, improved distribution, and improved technological capability. The outcome of this change should be an enhanced capacity to recruit new accommodation properties in both Australia and New Zealand.

Whilst this structural change offers many benefits, there are also a number of potential downside risks associated with it, including the challenge of replacing a strong well-regarded brand name (Flag) with one (Choice) of which the Australian market has little, if any, knowledge.

BACKGROUND

The history of Flag International provides an illustration of the significant changes that have occurred in the Australian hotel industry in the past 40 years, and highlights the importance of branding in the twenty-first century.

Established in 1961, Flag International Limited was launched by a break-away group of 26 independent motel owners from the Motel Federation of Australia (MFA), Australia's only motel marketing cooperative at the time. This group was dissatisfied with the marketing and business opportunities provided to them by MFA, seeing it as focusing more on the needs of larger members to the exclusion of smaller businesses like their own.

In the early days, Flag Inns operated as a friendly non-profit, marketing cooperative. Members knew each other well and, every member, irrespective of the size of his or her business, had an equal say in how the group operated. The organisation's key role was as a referral group, driving business amongst member properties. It was not for many years that business from the corporate sector became an important focus of the group.

By 1988, Flag Inns had become the largest accommodation group in the

Southern Hemisphere whose members collectively accounted for 30 000 rooms (Dunstan 1991). Although the Flag brand was widely known throughout Australasia, the emergence of global hotel franchising chains with immense marketing and distribution capabilities led to Flag Inns looking at new ways of doing business in order to remain viable in the increasingly competitive global market.

Flag's board was concerned that the group was not in a position to capture future business growth opportunities. Its forecasts suggested that the majority of growth would come from offshore markets, and that whilst the Flag brand was well-established in Australasia it had little recognition overseas. As a result, the board developed three options to address this problem. They were for local members to put more resources into marketing the brand offshore, to float Flag Inns on the Australian Stock Exchange, and to become part of a global franchising chain. Members were asked to vote on these options and the majority of members opted to join forces with a global franchising chain.

The decision to join a global franchising chain led to Flag Inns corporatising and establishing in 1997, a 20-year master franchise agreement with Choice International Inc., the second largest hotel franchisor in the world. As part of the agreement, Choice Hotels International took a minor shareholding in Flag Inns (thus creating Flag Choice Hotels) with an option to purchase more of the company at a later date. Effectively a strategic alliance, the relationship between Flag Inns and Choice Hotels International gave Flag access to Choice's internationally recognised brands of Comfort Inn, Quality and Clarion, and provided its members with new, significant global marketing and reservation opportunities. As some members had concerns about moving to a franchise, members had the right to decide whether they would continue to operate under the Flag brand or join the franchise.

As at December 2002, Flag Choice Hotels was the largest franchise accommodation group in the Southern Hemisphere, with over 400 independently owned and operated hotels, inns, resorts and apartments, in the three to five star range. This amounted to a combined total of just under 23 000 rooms operating throughout Australia, New Zealand and the South Pacific. Sixty-five of those properties were franchised properties opened under the Choice brands, and 346 were franchised hotels operating under the Flag brand.

In July 2002, Choice Hotels International exercised its option to purchase more of the Flag Choice Hotels business, which resulted in Choice assuming majority shareholding of the Flag Choice Hotels group. The change of ownership resulted in a number of flow-on effects: Choice took over managerial and operational control of the group; and the Flag brand is being replaced over a two-year period by the three Choice brands of Comfort Inn, Quality and Clarion. As Flag already had a strict quality control system in place, Choice Hotels International guaranteed that every property in the Flag Choice Hotels group would be able to migrate to one of the three Choice brands. In addition,

Choice Hotels International promised that if a property required adjustments in order to fit into one of its brands, it would provide the operator with assistance to make these adjustments.

In January 2003, Choice Hotels International announced it had acquired the remaining 45 per cent interest in Melbourne-based Flag Choice Hotels from Flag International Limited, bringing its ownership of its Australian subsidiary to 100 per cent. To date, over three-quarters of Flag Choice Hotels members have elected to move to one of the three Choice brands.

MARKETING ENVIRONMENT

The prosperity of the hotel industry is particularly vulnerable to external factors. Such factors include technological developments, changing travel behaviour, major international events, and global economic and security matters. All of these factors have the potential to significantly impact on the growth and profitability of the hotel/motel industry as a whole, and on individual businesses in particular.

In Australia, the halcyon days of the motel industry in the 1970s and 1980s saw demand for accommodation outstrip supply in many areas. Travellers felt obliged to book in advance to secure accommodation and, through its nation-wide marketing cooperative and the launch of Australia's first motel directory, Flag Inns positioned itself well to take advantage of this opportunity. However, with the introduction of toll-free telephone numbers at individual properties, as well as the greater availability of accommodation in most regions, the number of inter-motel bookings between Flag's members began to fall, thus reducing the value of membership of a cooperative marketing group such as Flag Inns.

Since the early 1990s, the worldwide accommodation industry has seen a significant change in the management structure of hotels and motels, with most properties moving from being independent stand-alone operations to being members of a cooperative or chain affiliation. The number of affiliated hotels in Australia, for example, increased from 46 per cent of the market in 1990 to 60 per cent in 2001. Additionally, in Australia, there was an influx of American-based hotel groups in the late 1990s as such businesses saw an opportunity to establish internationally branded properties in a market where few such businesses operated. The Sydney Olympics provided a significant opportunity to bring such brands into the country via re-branding and franchising (Worcester 1999). This trend towards the internationalisation of the accommodation industry is one that will undoubtedly continue into the future.

Recently, transport, economic and security issues have played major roles in shaping the hotel industry worldwide. The increasing flexibility of air travel throughout the world, and in particular, cut-price airfares, has led to a rise in demand for accommodation by leisure travellers. However, this increase is biased towards capital cities, as cut-price fares generally do not impact on travel to regional areas. The downturn in the global economy experienced during 2001, coupled with the terrorist attacks of September 11, have also had a significant impact on the performance of the industry. With prospective guests reluctant or unable to travel, hotel performances have suffered, leading to reduced royalty payments to the franchisor. This has resulted in a reduction in hotel development, and new hotel numbers are expected to decline further in the foreseeable future as funding from the hotel development lending market has decreased significantly (Flag Choice Hotels 2001).

One of the major business aims of the Choice Hotels International group is to reduce the impact of competitor activities and factors in the external environment by strategic planning. Its brand portfolio is well-diversified, incorporating a wide array of brands that meet the needs of many types of guests, and this portfolio can be developed at various price points for new and existing hotels. Choice's brand strategy ensures that it has opportunities for creating growth in different markets, with various types of customers, during both industry contraction and growth phases. It ensures that at times of low industry growth and tight capital markets, it can rely on gaining conversions from non-branded hotels due to higher levels of awareness and the proven performance provided by its brands. Conversely, when industry conditions are favourable, a greater portion of growth is expected to come from new construction.

Dun and Bradstreet rate Choice Hotels International's direct major competitors as the Cendant Corporation (the largest global franchisor with over 6275 franchised hotels), Hilton Hotels (1935) and Intercontinental Hotels (3200). Other competitors include the Best Western Group (with 4000 hotels in 80 countries), Six Continents (2314), Marriott International, Inc. (1916), Accor (1219), Carlson Hospitality (554), and Starwood Hotels and Resorts (377). Locally, the Best Western Group is the strongest competitor for the Flag Choice Hotels group, offering almost 300 properties throughout Australia in the three and four star categories.

Conflict amongst hoteliers, irrespective of the type of hotel management arrangement, has significant potential to impact on business performance. This is particularly true where there are new and significant strategic alliances that affect a number of businesses. The transition of the Flag Inns group from a co-operative to the Choice Hotels International's franchise system has the potential to create tension amongst members. Already there seem to be three conflicting attitudes amongst the group's existing members regarding the change of structure. Some embrace the idea, believing it will give them a competitive advantage in the global market. Others reluctantly joined the franchise, believing that there are few alternatives, whilst others are completely opposed to the franchise system, believing that it will result in them losing control of their own property. Whilst the latter view is understandable, it may well soften as the franchise becomes operational and its performance can be assessed.

OVERALL MARKETING STRATEGY

Initially established as a marketing cooperative, marketing has always been central to Flag's business. In the early days, Flag Inns was a leader in developing marketing initiatives for motels in Australia (Dunstan 1991), and some of these initiatives included the first accommodation directory (1962), the development of the free eighth night customer loyalty program, the first referral system, the first on-premise laundry system, the first point system for standards, the first telex, and the first computer booking system.

The Flag Choice Hotel's alliance with Choice Hotels International will result in significantly increased marketing power and prowess for the organisation. Choice Hotels International is an experienced and successful global marketer, having introduced segmentation to the hotel industry through its Comfort Inn brand. The first hotel chain ever franchised, Comfort Inn is one of the fastest growing brands in the accommodation industry. In 1981, Choice Hotels International began its rapid worldwide expansion, and today it represents the full spectrum of accommodation products, from economy to upscale, and brings together 5000 operating, or under development, hotels in 46 countries under the brand names of Comfort®, Comfort Suites®, Quality®, Clarion®, Sleep Inn®, Rodeway Inn®, EconoLodge® and Mainstay Suites®.

Choice Hotels International has four core marketing strategies geared at maximising returns for franchisees and the organisation itself. They are:

1   Reach more consumers—this is achieved by committing a significant percentage of the marketing budget each year to reinforcing strong brand image and driving traffic to franchisees.

2   Deliver exceptional services—this is done by: designing the most effective tools (such as linkages to global distribution systems and Choicelink, Choice's computer reservation system); creating innovative services (such as Choice Privileges® loyalty reward program); providing resources to help franchisees create and manage successful hotels; and providing more field support than anyone else in the industry.

3   Build stronger brands—this is achieved by dynamic re-imaging programs and quality-standard enhancements such as: adding extra features like voicemail, data ports or meeting facilities to its brands aimed at the business market; and incorporating brighter lights, larger button phones and side handles in bathrooms for its brands aimed at the senior travellers. This focus on consumer needs has made Choice brands among the strongest in the industry.

4   Leverage size, scale and distribution—with over 5000 properties open and under development worldwide, Choice Hotels International has the scale to provide quality products and services at substantial discounts.

These strategies have successfully guided the business through both good and bad times. For example, despite the difficult business environment in 2001, following the downturn in the United States economy, and the September 11 terrorist attacks, Choice Hotels International experienced greater unit growth in 2001 than in 2000, and sold more franchises in December 2001 than in any other single month in the history of the company. This success is attributed to the company's operating model and the strength of its brands.

In line with the goal of becoming Australia's number one accommodation group, Flag's merger with Choice Hotels International in 1998 saw the focus of the marketing planning process become more globally encompassing. In accordance with the motto 'think global, act local', Flag's company name changed, as noted earlier, to Flag Choice Hotels as it moved to align itself with Choice Hotels International's global marketing strategies and adapt them for use within the Australian environment.

Franchising

The formation of strategic alliances, such as franchises, are driven by market uncertainty, the need for increased efficiency, the prospect of access to new markets, reduced costs, and the opportunity to develop joint product offerings and share expertise. In Australia, franchising in all sectors has grown consistently since the start of the 1970s, and demonstrated strong growth in the 1990s, expanding noticeably in the period from 1994 to 1998 (Frazer 2001).

Franchises provide hotels with opportunities for improved financial performance, as they usually offer a suite of business benefits, many of which would otherwise be unavailable to small- to medium-size businesses. These include resources for training and marketing, and reservations capabilities as well as other backup resources.

The alliance with Flag was Choice Hotels International's first master franchise agreement outside the United States. Master franchising arrangements are generally adopted to ease a business's transition into new markets (Mendelsohn 1991, in Frazer 2001) and are developed by mature franchisors, who typically seek to enter new markets once domestic markets have been established. Royalty and affiliation fees are the franchisors' principal sources of profits, with the main factors affecting returns being growth in the number of hotels, occupancies and room rates, the number and relative mix of hotels, and ability to manage costs. From Choice Hotels International's perspective, the alliance with Flag allowed it to benefit from Flag's dominant market share in Australia where it was the largest accommodation chain. This provided a platform for Flag Choice Hotels to expand into all segments within the Australian market.

From Flag Choice's perspective, the major objectives for moving to a franchise system were:

* to segment its product by linking it with a number of well known brands, with the aim of increasing the total number of rooms in any area and the overall number of properties and rooms; and
* to develop a consistency amongst products by segmenting them according to brands.

Other benefits included access to: Choice Hotels International's global marketing and sales team (including 23 call centres); hotel directory; state-of-the-art reservation system represented in the four major global distribution systems (providing access to 400 000 travel agents); internet distribution through WorldRes (with representation across more than 40 internet and intranet sites); and in-house public relations services. Additionally, Choice Hotels International offered building and financial assistance programs; start up training; opening support; and proprietary property management systems designed to assist in managing reservations, rates and inventory more efficiently and effectively. Flag Choice Hotels also benefited from Choice Hotels International's clearly defined brands and a capital injection of funds to improve and upgrade Flag Choice's infrastructure.

Flag International members sought a number of specific benefits from the merger including more business, better brand recognition, better marketing, product differentiation in the marketplace, and greater efficiency. In addition, as the levels of interest and investment amongst the group's members became more diverse, Flag's 'equal say for all members' policy was also considered to be holding the group back. Under this policy, even the very smallest Flag property had equal rights with the large capital city properties. The move to franchising was seen as a way of putting an end to this policy. Operationally, there were not many changes required of operators to transfer to one of the Choice Hotels International's brands other than new signage and changes to marketing materials.

MAJOR MARKETS

As a cooperative, and more recently as a franchisor, Flag Choice Hotels has always had two quite distinct customer groups for whom it must cater. They are:

1 the hotel patrons (current and prospective), to whom it must promote its members' properties; and
2 the hoteliers (members and prospective members) whose properties the company must promote and for whom it must provide marketing and operational benefits.

In relation to the former, the essence of Flag Choice's success is its appeal to a wide variety of consumers. The group focuses its marketing activities on two broad segments, the corporate market and the leisure market, and aims to achieve a balance of 50 per cent of its business from each. Currently, the corporate market accounts for approximately 60 per cent of Flag Choice's business in Australia. This tends to be high yield business, and it is crucial that the group provides properties that appeal to this market, particularly in capital cities.

For some of the group's members, the leisure market is particularly important. As a result, Flag Choice Hotels is now working hard to build this sector of the business, especially in the areas of domestic and international group travel. In order to achieve this goal, an alliance was recently formed with a tour operator, Australian Pacific Tours, which specialises in these leisure groups. Flag Choice Hotels is also developing new products for the leisure market focusing on key destinations such as the Australian outback, Tasmanian holidays, and special packages to Kangaroo Island. It is increasing its leisure-related marketing activities, targeting the interstate and intrastate markets. The group is also increasing its event marketing activities, and plans to be more active in packaging capital city accommodation in association with special events.

When marketing to hoteliers, the Flag Choice Hotels group seeks to recruit the best hotels within the accommodation markets that it targets. In doing so, it aims to provide superior marketing and operational support to those offered by its competitors believing that hoteliers choose franchisors based on perceived brand standing in the market, services provided and ultimate likely impact on the business's bottom line. In addition, it believes that hotel operators select a franchisor in part based on the franchisor's reputation among other franchisees, and the success of its existing franchisees.

SERVICE QUALITY

Service quality is taken seriously by Flag Choice Hotels, and the group aims to achieve a consistency of service across its properties (Travel Week 2000). At least once per year the group commissions a major marketing research study to test its current performance, and to assess potential new products. With the ongoing development of the group's web site, the amount and value of research relating to service quality is expected to be enhanced. Specifically, in the future, it will be possible to ask questions electronically and collect email addresses for specific follow-up questionnaires.

Recently, the group launched a customer-driven quality assurance program across all its brands. This was to ensure that every hotel within the group is consistently and effectively meeting the needs of its guests, and is accountable to guests for the standard of service delivered. The program guarantees guests 100 per cent satisfaction with their stay, or they will have their money returned by the individual property's management.

BRANDING

The task of making a brand image stand out amidst a crowded field of competitors is becoming more and more important, yet difficult to achieve in the increasingly competitive global hotel industry. The challenge for hotel companies is to make sure customers know who they are, what services and amenities they offer, and what values and prices to expect. The next step is growing that brand awareness and ultimately boosting loyalty through repeat visitation.

The emergence of international businesses in the Australian hotel industry has resulted in strategically important changes and has highlighted the importance of international brand recognition in the decision-making process of consumers. As the world's hotel market consolidates, and the industry's marketing and distribution power base moves to a few large companies, many operators of hotels not owned or managed by major accommodation companies have joined franchise chains as a means of remaining competitive.

Flag's first move towards achieving international brand recognition was in 1967, when it affiliated with a group of properties in New Zealand. In 1982, the group opened its first overseas marketing office in London, and a few years later it opened another marketing office in Los Angeles. Until the late 1990s, Flag's approach to branding was to have a single brand for all markets, with limited sub-branding opportunities for properties of architectural significance. However, this made it difficult to classify and differentiate between the wide range of styles and standards of properties in Flag's portfolio, and led to inconsistent standards across the Flag Inns brand. As a result, it was difficult for customers to confidently book accommodation at Flag properties, and it became necessary for the organisation to consider ways to introduce product segmentation and branding criteria to better meet the needs of its members and customers. The major outcome of such reflection was the decision to link with Choice Hotels International.

In recognition of the importance of branding, under the new company name of Flag Choice Hotels, they adopted three brands (Comfort, Quality and Clarion—see later discussion) from the Choice Hotels International group for the Australian market, ranging from the economy to luxury segments. These brands suit the needs of the local market, with each brand targeting a different segment and having a different brand personality and associated brand strategy. Aimed at identifying each of the Flag properties in ways that meet the needs of consumers, these changes, together with tightening of brand standards, seek to protect individual property investments, and give Flag customers a more satisfying experience. The recent changes in ownership of Flag Choice Hotels saw two-thirds of the existing Flag properties replace their brand name with one of the three Choice brands licensed in Australia by August 2002. The remainder of the Flag Choice properties will switch progressively to the Choice Hotels International brands over the next two years. The company will also seek to recruit more properties to join the Flag Choice Hotels group, particularly in the four-and-a-half to five star range.

The Comfort Inn brand is aimed at the middle market, and most feature restaurants, swimming pools and meeting rooms. Quality focuses primarily on the corporate traveller, offering licensed restaurants, professional business services and recreational facilities. Clarion is aimed at the lower upscale market to take advantage of upscale clients looking for value, and mid-range clients looking for extras. Besides the normal swimming, exercise and laundry facilities of Quality, these feature extra facilities for business travellers, such as a 24-hour Biznet centre, professional conference facilities, large work desk with data ports, two-line telephone and participation in a frequent flyer program.

To monitor the success of its brand strategies and brand modifications, Flag Choice Hotels commissions regular brand tracking studies.

CUSTOMER LOYALTY PROGRAMS

Customer satisfaction is considered to be one of the most important outcomes of all marketing activities at Flag Choice Hotels. It is only in this way that Flag Choice Hotels can increase its market share, and acquire repeat and referral business, all of which lead to increased profitability. According to Reichheld and Sasser (Bowen & Chen 2001), when a company retains just 5 per cent more of its customers, profits increase by 25 per cent. Loyal customers also aid in the promotion of a franchise or hotel brand through positive word-of-mouth communication, leading to opportunities for referral business. One significant means of establishing loyal customers is that of frequent stay programs. A popular franchise-driven feature that first became prevalent in the mid-1980s, these programs increase communications activity and provide another opportunity to build brand awareness. This activity is particularly useful in the early stages of launching a new brand if the new brand can be linked to established and well recognised brands, and can result in the strengthening of all brands.

Over the years, Flag has had a great deal of experience developing and implementing customer loyalty programs. The pioneer of the free eighth night scheme, in which travellers who spent seven nights in a Flag property received a free eighth night, much of Flag's leisure business was built on customer loyalty programs in the early years. Although Best Western's Travel Card proved to be difficult competition, and took back much of this business, Flag has continued to develop new schemes such as the highly successful Flag Corporate Card, which built and protected a substantial corporate business.

Recently, with the new alliance, Flag Choice Hotels has also developed partnerships with a number of the more generic, mainstream loyalty cards, including the Qantas Frequent Flyer, Thrifty Car Rental, American Express, Virgin Credit Card, Westpac Altitude and Qantas Visa programs. Under Flag Choice Hotels, such links have been maintained, and a major internal loyalty program Choice Privileges, has been developed, which targets and rewards frequent travellers for their loyalty.

PRICING

Pricing impacts on the business strategies of Flag Choice Hotels in two distinct ways. The first is the price that franchisees, and master franchisees, pay for the benefits of membership. The second is the need for each brand to represent recognisable price points.

To date, the pricing structure of Flag Choice Hotels has been a fixed fee structure, whereby members pay a royalty and marketing fee on a monthly basis regardless of the size or revenue of the property. A revised structure is, however, soon to be introduced whereby members will be required to pay a percentage of their gross rooms revenue, and the fees paid will depend upon the revenue earned per room at each property. The exact percentages of these components is often the topic of heated debate amongst franchisees, and suggestions to modify the group's pricing structure were always the most contentious issues at Flag Choice Hotels' annual general meetings.

Pricing also plays a major role in the group's branding strategy. Each brand represents various consistent attributes, such as a price point, and this facilitates differentiation and positioning in the market place.

PROMOTION

Choice Hotels International's promotional campaign is extensive, seeking to drive recognition of its brands in Australia and throughout the world. To date, the group's major marketing activities in Australia have focused on a combination of 'above the line' promotions, including TV advertising, print advertising, billboard signage and trade shows. The emphasis of these activities has been on increasing brand awareness of the group's major hotel brands.

Much of Flag's promotional budget in Australia is spent on advertising in media widely accessed by its target audiences. This includes magazine advertising such as in-flight and business magazines that are aimed at capturing business travellers, and advertisements in AAA Motoring publications, highway signage and advertisements on regional television and radio targeting leisure travellers. Flag Choice Hotels has also launched some destination-specific publications geared to the leisure traveller, such as a 12-page touring guide of New Zealand, containing maps, itinerary suggestions and a list of its 50 properties across the country.

With the international leisure traveller in mind, Flag Choice Hotels introduced the Flag *HotelPass* in Australia, New Zealand, Papua New Guinea, Singapore and Fiji. This is a pre-purchased accommodation voucher program that allows users to pre-book their accommodation or use open vouchers to travel as they please. Each property listed in the Flag *HotelPass* directory has a colour code and guests are entitled to use the Flag *HotelPass* open vouchers at properties with the corresponding colour codes. Colour codes range from:

* silver—luxury hotels centrally located in capital cities;
* red—deluxe hotels with excellent service and facilities;
* blue—first-class hotels in cities and resort locations;
* green—excellent properties with good facilities in cities and resort locations;
* pink—good quality, economical accommodation, mostly in regional locations; and
* yellow—most economical to good hotels and motels found in country towns (Flag Choice Hotels 2002).

Other major Flag Choice Hotels marketing activities include the annual Flag Choice Hotels Asia Pacific Accommodation Directory; an online conference and meeting guide; a 100 per cent satisfaction guarantee; the launch of the new loyalty program, Choice Privileges; and the Flag Choice Hotels Associations Program. The latter is aimed at registered associations and provides them with a variety of benefits for their members including a 10 per cent discount at Flag Choice Hotels and access to special deals and packages. Other promotional activities include giveaways and prizes.

Flag Choice Hotels is placing increasingly greater emphasis on new promotional activities. These include partnership marketing activities with organisations such as Amex and Qantas, direct mail and email. Internet marketing is also playing an important role in the group's overall promotional activities, with a full design and functionality revamp occurring during 2003.

A key component of the recent transfer of ownership was the tiered introduction of a multi-million dollar advertising campaign in Australia to promote the three Choice brands, and to explain the change of ownership and re-branding to the Australian public. The brand launch campaign will be introduced in three phases combining various media including television, radio, billboard and press advertising, complemented by a range of public relations activities.

DISTRIBUTION

The growing importance of technology in developing global reservations capabilities, and the large costs associated with the development and maintenance of such systems, was an important factor in Flag's decision to merge with Choice Hotels International.

Global distribution systems in the travel industry have had an enormous impact on the way in which businesses, such as Flag Choice Hotels and Choice Hotels International, operate. To ensure future business streams, it is virtually mandatory that organisations such as Flag Choice Hotels are linked into the major GDSs. As a stand-alone business, Flag Inns would have undoubtedly found the costs of being linked to these systems prohibitive prior to the merger.

In the future much more of Flag's distribution will be done via the internet, with the computer reservation system (CRS) being the Choice system 'Choicelink'. Choicelink is a real time, web browser-based system that can be used by any size property. It enables patrons to book directly via the internet and receive an immediate booking confirmation. Additionally, this system is very cost effective given that bookings made in this way rather than via a GDS are far less costly per transaction. Choicelink is also a useful communication engine, allowing individual properties to change their pricing immediately and to promote last minute specials.

SUMMARY

In becoming part of an international franchise, the Flag Choice Hotels group acquires well recognised global brands, obtains access to global marketing strategies and sales teams, as well as getting access to leading distribution and technology systems. It gives up some control over the Australian operation in return for these benefits.

Flag Choice Hotels intends to become the most profitable accommodation franchise in the Pacific (*The Age* July 2002), and the combination of Flag's local market knowledge and Choice Hotels International's franchise experience would seem to be one destined to succeed. A large proportion of the accommodation industry in Australia and New Zealand is still comprised of establishments that do not operate under a brand. As the Flag brand is arguably the most recognised brand in the accommodation industry in Australasia, this represents a significant opportunity for Flag's recruitment of new properties in the future.

Choice Hotels International plans to recruit new members in Australia, particularly in the four-and-a-half and five star categories, which are generally welcomed by other Flag Choice Hotels franchisees, so long as the increase in supply is based on the needs of the market. John Deeprose, owner of the Comfort Inn Macquarie Manor, is one franchisee in favour of recruitment in his area, as following the merger his will be the only branded property within Hobart's central business district. With only 18 rooms on offer, he believes that only by being able to provide a suitable supply of accommodation will the chain be able to win the business of large corporate clients.

The change of structure is not expected to significantly alter the nature of decision-making or the function of the Flag Choice Hotels board. Choice Hotels International has promised that the Flag Choice Hotels board, which is made up of Australian members, will remain unaffected. Concern about changes to the process of decision-making have existed for the past couple of years, and the issue was raised at last year's Flag Choice Hotels conference, where members voiced their concern that they would lose control of the brand and that all the power would be vested in the United States. To date, however, these concerns have proven to be unfounded.

There are two schools of thought amongst Flag Choice Hotels operators as to whether the move from one brand (Flag) to the three Choice brands will benefit owners and operators or be a liability. On the one hand, the Choice brands offer considerable marketing power and financial and human resources, and it would appear that most operators are positive about the impending changes. These operators are of the view that they could not continue operating in the way they were and, faced with the option of going alone and individually marketing themselves, or becoming part of an international franchise for a similar price, they would rather be aligned with an experienced global marketer such as Choice Hotels International.

On the other hand, significant concerns do exist amongst members as to the real costs of becoming part of a global franchise. These include: loss of power in the way they manage their properties; loss of uniqueness as their properties are expected to comply with brand guidelines; the possibility that a number of properties might leave the franchise thus weakening the overall position of the brand; and the potential for annual fees to rise significantly after the two-year handover period. Other concerns exist for re-branding existing properties, and it is felt that to make the Choice brands really work in Australia it may be necessary for new properties to be built which adhere to the Choice Hotels International brand and building guidelines.

Another concern amongst members is that of their properties losing their uniqueness due to the move to three brands each of which has strong brand requirements. The owners still operating under the Flag brand are very proud of their properties, and consider them to be somewhat unique, if not a little 'homely'. However, joining a franchise, with its standards and protocols, may result in a 'sameness' amongst properties and result in the property losing some of its appeal to guests. This situation is particularly the case with those properties (20) that were branded 'Flag Heritage' which will now find themselves grouped in with thousands of properties within a single brand.

It would seem that it was inevitable that the Flag board consider franchising as a serious option if it were to look after the best interests of its members and their businesses. Franchising has been a successful business model in many industries in Australia, and given Choice Hotels International's success as a franchisor globally, and its encouragement of local board level involvement, it seems to be a good match for Flag Choice Hotels.

The challenge for Flag Choice Hotels, and its members, is now to manage the transition to the three Choice brands in a consultative and fair process which enables each of the parties' objectives to best be achieved.

Primary period covered by case study: 2000/02

REFERENCES

Journals

Bowen, J. 1997, 'A market-driven approach to business development and service improvement in the hospitality industry', *International Journal of Contemporary Hospitality Management*, vol. 9, no. 7, pp. 334–4, MCB University Press.

Bowen, J. & Chen, S.L. 2001, 'The relationship between customer loyalty and customer satisfaction', *International Journal of Contemporary Hospitality Management*, vol. 13, no. 5, pp. 213–17, MCB University Press.

Choice Hotels International, 2001, *Form 10-K.*

Connell, J. 1992, 'Branding Hotel Portfolios', *International Journal of Contemporary Hospitality Management*, vol. 4, no. 1, pp. 26–32, MCB University Press.

Duluth, D. 2002, 'Choice Hotels International', *Hotel and Motel Management*, vol. 217, Issue 8, 6 May.

Dunstan, K. 1991, *Flag: The First 30 Years*, Flag International Limited, Melbourne.

Flag Choice Hotels, *2000 Annual Report.*

Flag Choice Hotels, *2001 Annual Report.*

Flag Choice Hotels, *2002 Annual Report.*

Frazer, L. 2001, 'Assessing Franchising Sector Maturity: Australian Evidence', *Australasian Marketing Journal*, vol. 8, no. 2.

Kandampully, J. & Suhartanto, D. 2000, 'Customer loyalty in the hotel industry: the role of customer satisfaction and image', *International Journal of Contemporary Hospitality Management*, vol. 12, no. 6, pp. 346–51, MCB University Press.

Mattson, B. 1999, 'Hotels Strive to Stand Out in the Midst of a Crowded Industry', *Primedia Intertec*, 1 September 1999.

The Age, 2002, 'US Group's Takeover Lowers Flag Brand', 12 July.

Worcester, B.A. 1999, 'It's a "G'day" to be a US based Hotel Operator in Australia', *Advanstar Communications, Inc.*, 20 September.

Internet

Business Wire. 1998, 'Choice Hotels International Enters Strategic Alliances With Australia's Largest Lodging Chain—Flag International', *Dow Jones Interactive*, 17 June, <http://ptg.djnr.com/ccroot/asp/publib/story.html>.

Flag Choice. 2002, 'International Visitors', 27 February, <http://www.flagchoice.com.au/html/international_visitors.php>.

Travel Trade Gazette UK & Ireland. 2000, 'Oz gets set for long term', *Dow Jones Interactive*, 9 November, <http://ptg.djnr.com/ccroot/asp/publib/story.html>.

Travel Week. 2000, 'Agents to gain access to self-drive itineraries', *Dow Jones Interactive*, 4 December, <http://ptg.djnr.com/ccroot/asp/publib/story.html>.

Travel Week. 2000, 'FCH to offer "100% Guarantee" ', *Dow Jones Interactive*, 16 August, <http://ptg.djnr.com/ccroot/asp/publib/story.html>.

Travel Week. 2001, 'Chance to win a car,' *Dow Jones Interactive*, 31 January, <http://ptg.djnr.com/ccroot/asp/publib/story.html>.

QUESTIONS

1   In joining with Choice Hotels International, the Flag brand is being split into three sub-brands catering for different markets. As a result of this, the consumer may not recognise the connection between the different brands, which will diminish the value of remaining as a single group. Discuss.

2   The vast distribution network of Flag Choice Hotels results in some areas receiving higher levels of international business compared with their smaller regional counterparts. Discuss the strategies that the organisation could take to ensure that the benefits of linking with an international brand flow to all properties, not just those in areas patronised by international visitors.

3   Discuss the strategies that Flag Choice Hotels can adopt to maximise the carry-forward into the new Choice brands of the favourable consumer sentiment that exists towards the Flag brand name.

4   Discuss the approaches that can be adopted to ensure that the marketing efforts of Flag Choice Hotels does reflect the Australian market and is not seen as simply an 'add on' to an overseas campaign.

5   Given that the accommodation market tends to be seen as either corporate or leisure, should both markets be catered for by each of the three Flag Choice Hotels brands or should the different brands focus on one or the other key segments?

6   Consistency in the standard of product offering is an important feature in most product markets. Given that there is substantial variation in the physical structure of motels, does the fact that Flag Choice Hotel properties are operated by individual owners under a franchise system rather than company owned make the delivery of a consistent product difficult in the very least? What steps can Flag Choice Hotels take to ensure a consistent level of product delivery at properties within the group?

7   In the Australian accommodation market, identify the key competitors to Flag Choice Hotels. Discuss the strengths and weaknesses of the Flag Choice Hotels group in relation to these other competitors.

8   Introducing multiple brands under the Flag Choice Hotels name allows the group to introduce more properties to a particular region under its different brand names. Is such an approach likely to lead to increased business within the group overall or simply result in the existing level of business being shared amongst a larger number of properties?

9   Customer loyalty programs have been in existence for many years, especially in the airline and hotel business sectors. Although these programs were generally set up to encourage patrons to purchase only a single brand, nowadays many consumers are members of a range of competing loyalty programs. This appears to be increasingly the situation in the accommodation market. What can Flag Choice Hotels do to encourage true loyalty amongst its patrons?

10   Discuss the reasons why franchising has become such a popular form of business operating structure in the accommodation sector.

7. OCEAN SPIRIT CRUISES CAIRNS

INTRODUCTION

Ocean Spirit Cruises Cairns is part of the Melbourne-based Macro Corporation. As a tour operator in a competitive market, it faces a number of marketing challenges, including establishing and maintaining a brand identity, understanding its markets, ensuring service quality, developing and maintaining relationships with intermediaries, and managing demand. These challenges in turn have given rise to a range of marketing responses which are examined in this case study. These responses collectively reflect the complexities of marketing small- to medium-size tourism businesses in Australia.

BACKGROUND

Macro Corporation is listed on the Australian Stock Exchange and is headquartered in Melbourne. This company has three major operating divisions, namely Ocean Spirit Cruises Cairns, Ocean Spirit Cruises Sydney, and Ocean Spirit Dive (Cairns). As reported in Macro Corporation's 2000 annual report, revenue was approximately $10 million ($9 942 347) in 1999 (Macro Corporation Limited 2001).

Ocean Spirit Cruises (OSC) Cairns, the subject of this case study, operates two sail catamarans from its Far North Queensland base to two islands—Upolu Cay and Michaelmas Cay—located within the Great Barrier Reef Marine Park, a World Heritage listed area. Operating as OCS does in this marine reserve brings with it certain legal obligations associated with environmental management, as well as the potential to leverage off the strong image this area has for promotional purposes.

MARKETING PLANNING

Within the OSC operation, there are two general managers who are responsible for the effective operations of the Cairns and Sydney ventures respectively. The general manager in Cairns at the time of writing was Steve Eiszele. A Sydney-based director of marketing is responsible for the marketing of the Sydney and Cairns products. The first marketing plan for OSC was prepared in 1996 and provided a general guide to future directions rather than precise targets or objectives. Over subsequent years, the organisation underwent a number of changes of personnel and restructures, including the relocation of Macro from Sydney to Melbourne. The company operated without an ongoing marketing plan until mid-2000 when the director of marketing presented a draft plan to the company's board. This plan covered both the Cairns and Sydney operations and aimed to achieve maximum economies of scale and synergies between the two divisions. The plan covered a one-year time frame and emphasised measurable targets in each market by geography and purpose of visit. Performance was assessed against annual financial targets measured in terms of both revenue and profit. It is the responsibility of the senior management team generally, and the Sydney and Cairns general managers in particular, to ensure that these targets were met. Monthly updates were provided by the Cairns general manager to keep Macro briefed about short-term market and performance fluctuations.

MARKETING PHILOSOPHY

Eiszele regards OSC as a marketing-driven organisation with products designed and regularly adapted to satisfy consumer preferences. The physical properties of the two sail catamarans, which constitute the OSC fleet, have a major influence on market positioning. Although there are several Cairns-based cruise operations, few operate sail-based vessels, with most using larger capacity motorised vessels. Whereas the vessels operated by Ocean Spirit Cruises have a capacity of 150 and 100 respectively, other operators, such as Quicksilver and Great Adventures, feature vessels with the capacity to carry 400 (or more) passengers. In part, the considerable distance between Cairns and the Great Barrier Reef, and an associated belief that many potential passengers would be reluctant to spend extended periods travelling, particularly in rough conditions, has led to the use of these larger vessels. Additionally, large vessels may be perceived as being faster and safer than smaller ones by some segments of the market.

While larger vessels may have some distinct advantages for some markets, the smaller scale of the Ocean Spirit boats provides a more personalised experience, allowing OSC to charge higher prices than many of its competitors, particularly those targeting the backpacker market. In positioning its vessels in what is a very competitive market, OSC has sought to stress this point, as well as emphasising its many years of operation. The latter is significant in terms of differentiating the company, as competitors are constantly entering and leaving the market with vessels of different configurations and levels of luxury. Additionally, emphasis is placed in marketing communications on OSC's enthusiastic staff, the quality and elegance of its vessels, and the 'we take care of every detail' aspect of customer service. The relatively low staff to passenger ratio of 1:10 makes the process of delivering on such promises a lot easier. Overall the 'small is beautiful' philosophy has worked well to date, though the fierceness of the competitive environment means that direct competition could arise at anytime.

BRANDING

It is Eiszele's view that the OSC brand is well established in Far North Queensland and that it is directly associated with high standards of service. The two vessels that operate in Cairns have a similar appearance and configuration, further facilitating the positioning of the brand. To date it has faced less direct challenge from competitors than other operators with diversity of product types.

The securing of market positioning is a feature of niche operators that are more able to differentiate their product offer and avoid a perception that they are 'me too' products. This dilemma was evident previously on Sydney Harbour where Macro operated a less technologically advanced vessel (inherited from previous management) under the banner 'Vagabond', and two sail catamarans under the 'Ocean Spirit' brand.

A key aspect of the Ocean Spirit brand in Cairns is the emphasis on merchandising. The main Ocean Spirit offices and booking centre operate as an office selling merchandise such as T-shirts, caps and videos. The merchandise on display is of high quality and, as such, is designed to reinforce the company's positioning efforts. It is intended that cruise customers, as well as those who purchase only merchandise, will associate this quality with the cruise product.

MARKET RESEARCH

OSC cites the relatively small scale of its operations and, associated with this, limited financial and staff resources, as reasons for undertaking little primary research. Most of the consumer research that is undertaken consists of on-board customer satisfaction studies. Distributors of OSC's products, specifically inbound tour operators, travel agents and overseas-based tour operators, are also asked for their feedback so that the director of marketing can assess which markets are most worthwhile targeting. As regards travel agents, it is noteworthy that surveys often accompany familiarisations that are conducted for this intermediary group.

Eiszele acknowledges that greater emphasis needs to be placed on consumer surveys as a matter of urgency given the importance of such information to product design and delivery systems. The provision of five star 'full-service' is currently viewed by management as a core component of the brand. Confirmation is needed, however, that consumers share this view. Another form of marketing research that is undertaken is 'shadowing', whereby researchers sample the products offered by competitors and make observations about product quality. This approach to research is rather basic, but provides useful baseline information about performance relative to competitors.

MAJOR MARKETS

Unlike Ocean Spirit Cruises on Sydney Harbour where the corporate market is important, the customers of OSC Cairns are almost exclusively tourists. Most of the clients of the two vessels (*Ocean Spirit One* and *Ocean Spirit Two*) are from overseas, particularly Europe, North America and Japan. As regards the Japanese market, it is noteworthy that OSC has a dedicated Japanese sales executive based in Cairns. Domestic clients comprise a smaller, but nonetheless significant market, and typically come from Melbourne or Sydney. Commonly passengers have either booked as part of a group tour or are fully independent travellers (FITs). Group-based travellers will typically have booked their cruise through an operator based in their home country. FITs will more commonly book on arrival in Cairns. Visitors who book overseas are valuable in that they are making a commitment in advance. Having pre-paid, they are also willing to travel to the Reef in less than perfect weather conditions, which is not the case with those who book locally. The latter will often postpone their trip when weather conditions are anything less than perfect. On the other hand, the distribution costs are high where a booking is made through a travel agent and/or tour operator/wholesaler. Maintaining a balance between bookings made locally and those purchased through an operator overseas is an important challenge for the marketing department in order to ensure an adequate yield is achieved. The pursuit of yield is a complex issue. High distribution costs may dilute the yield for certain market segments in terms of the purchase price, but the same clients may compensate by making on-vessel purchases.

One market dilemma being confronted presently is the strong backpacker orientation of Cairns as a destination. Many sophisticated domestic and international visitors are shifting their preference towards Port Douglas, located an hour to the north. Many backpackers are willing to purchase relatively costly tour products, but their product preferences are not always compatible with the inclusive tour market. For example, a cruise product that has proved very popular in Cairns with the backpacker market is *Passions of Paradise*. A noteworthy feature of this vessel is its loud rock music and the loud screams from participants as the vessel returns to dock. While OSC could develop similar cruise products, it has been reluctant to do so out of a concern that they would negatively impact upon its brand identity.

KEY COMPETITIVE STRENGTHS

Ocean Spirit Cruises is an established brand in the marketplace and enjoys a strong reputation with tour operators due to the quality of its services. This reassurance is particularly important within the member countries of the European Union, where consumer laws are strong and the tour operator may be liable for substantial compensation if the experience that was promised to the customer is not delivered. Additionally, according to Eiszele, OSC enjoys excellent relations with its other intermediaries, and this constitutes a kind of 'goodwill' for the business.

Working in tandem with Ocean Spirit Cruises is Ocean Spirit Dive, another subsidiary of Macro Corporation. Managed by Jason Knack, an experienced dive instructor, Ocean Spirit Dive offers the prospect of a special experience for those of the cruise clients who wish to add an extra dimension to their trip. (Knack has subsequently taken on the role of general manager of Ocean Spirit Cruises Cairns as well as the Dive operation.) Clients taking up this opportunity can also opt (at an additional cost) to have a video of their scuba diving adventure taken using digital technology. These videos provide customers with an opportunity to 'tangible-ise' their experience. This is particularly important for those who regard a trip to the Great Barrier Reef as a 'once in a lifetime' experience. Another feature of the OSC product of note is its use of fully-trained chefs on board its vessels. As it is the only operator to do this, it strongly emphasises this product feature in its promotional efforts. In 1997 the company won an award for the quality of its on-board catering.

A final competitive strength, according to Eiszele, is the fact that Ocean Spirit Cruises sails to coral cays (an insular bank of coral) that he describes as 'eco-destinations'. This approach contrasts with other operators that moor their vessels at pontoons located adjacent to reefs, typically in about 6 metres of water. Such settings are intimidating for customers who like the reassurance of dry land. The small-scale and fragility of the coral cays it uses, however, means that OSC has to be particularly concerned about briefing customers as to the dos and don'ts of interacting with such sensitive environments. External threats to these areas, such as the Crown of Thorns starfish, also require close monitoring if the company is to be able to maintain the quality of the visitor experience and hence its competitiveness.

SERVICE QUALITY

There is a close relationship between service quality and marketing. Though OSC is a a small operation, it employs a full-time staff member to handle human resources issues to ensure that training is undertaken thoroughly and that the company is complying with the various government occupational health and safety requirements. Sail catamarans are particularly challenging from an occupational health and safety standpoint since the working environment is cramped and involves close interaction with the guests. In addressing staff professional development, the company has attempted to provide opportunities for promotion and hence career development from within the organisation. This provides better career prospects for those who are employed with the company. Steve Eiszele, for example, was employed at an operational level prior to being promoted to General Manager.

Service quality is also reinforced through the company's approach to staff selection and training which emphasises the capacity of staff to offer personalised services. The manager responsible for human resources handles technical matters such as occupational health and safety considerations and requirements, recruitment, staff training and induction. Because the vessels are relatively small in dimension, and have limited opportunity to deploy the size of staff that would be needed to undertake each technical activity on an individual basis, there is a strong emphasis on multi-skilling. This being the case, as well as performing their customer service roles, staff participate in various activities associated with operating and maintaining the vessel.

CUSTOMER AND INTERMEDIARY LOYALTY PROGRAMS

Since the primary clientele of Ocean Spirit Cruises Cairns is from overseas and are infrequent visitors to Cairns, or even Australia, the prospect of repeat visitation is limited. The establishment of strong ongoing relationships with key suppliers of business is, however, an important dimension. One way of achieving this is the use of override commissions (i.e. commissions above those normally provided) once particular sales targets have been met. For this reason OSC monitors its sales to ensure that those who are most loyal are appropriately rewarded.

A number of incentives are also provided to build a profile amongst local residents. Local residents who book directly with the company are offered a 25 per cent discount off the normal price on Sundays, a day when load factors are typically low. Encouraging local purchases also leads to positive word-of-mouth communication within the community. This is significant because many international clients book after arrival in the area. This is important for maintaining the company's local (and ultimately international) reputation.

PRICING

There are four major products offered by OSC. These are:

1   day cruises on the vessel *Ocean Spirit One* to Michaelmas Cay ($150.00 per adult);
2   day cruises on *Ocean Spirit One* to Upolu Cay ($121.00 per adult);
3   a scuba diving package with *Ocean Spirit Dive* ($188.00 for an introductory dive plus cruise to Upolu Cay); and
4   a dinner cruise around Cairns ($70.00 per adult).

Pricing is influenced by the activities of major competitors such as Quicksilver and Great Adventures. The price for *Ocean Spirit One* is set deliberately at the upper end of the scale because of the perceived quality of the vessel including the aesthetic appeal of sail and the commitment to including a full range of services within the price charged. Since tickets are sold locally, and through overseas distributors, the selling price must allow for a considerable margin including commissions. In the case of tour operators which generate the highest volume of business, this may involve the setting aside of 35 per cent of the selling price. Local retailers of OSC products commonly receive less than this amount, often around 20 per cent of the selling price. Such commissions are unavoidable for any operator who is serious about attracting overseas visitors and/or is dependent on a network of distributors.

The pricing of cruises on *Ocean Spirit Two* to Upolu Cay has been the subject of an ongoing discussion within the company. The current selling price of $121.00 is only $29.00 less than *Ocean Spirit One*. This has prompted customers to inquire about the difference, if any, between the two products, particularly since the two destinations (coral cays adjacent to the Great Barrier Reef, and a range of impressive coral formations) are similar.

Load factors on *Ocean Spirit Two* are currently lower than those experienced on *Ocean Spirit One*. At the time of writing, the board of Macro and the management team at OSC had just devised a strategy to re-position *Ocean Spirit Two*. The options they considered included moving the product up- or down-market, focusing on a particular overseas target market, or reducing the overall price by making some of the service components into 'optional extras'. The upshot of these strategy discussions was the decision to increase load factors on *Ocean Spirit Two* by decreasing ticket prices to $89.

A compulsory 'Environment Management Charge' of $4.00 per passenger is an additional element in the pricing process. This charge is collected by operators on behalf of the government and exemplifies the 'user pays' approach to the use of natural resources such as the Great Barrier Reef for tourism or other purposes. Since such charges apply to all operators they do not directly affect competition in the market. They do, however, add to the price of cruise products relative to, for example, trips inland from Cairns where no such charges are applied.

A final issue for consideration in the pricing strategy is the inclusion of a dive option for tourists. Since Ocean Spirit Cruises is positioned as a day tour product rather than as a specialist dive operation, it is largely dependent on the chance that those who have selected and purchased the day tour product will be interested in a dive experience. Ocean Spirit Dive is dependent on a steady flow of cruise customers to achieve viability. Pricing needs to be competitive. Most of those who opt to dive when at the destination are inexperienced or first-time divers.

As previously mentioned, one innovation of OSC is the opportunity for participants to purchase a video highlighting their diving efforts. For overseas visitors in particular, a visit to the Great Barrier Reef is a once in a lifetime experience. Jason Knack, General Manager of Ocean Spirit Dive, believes that this fact makes customers responsive to the offer of a personal video-making service. It also constitutes a value-added element that enhances revenue.

Ocean Spirit Cruises does not operate a formal yield management system. Since the pricing structure is relatively uncomplicated, the main issue of concern is to keep the costs of distribution under control and to make sure that the distributors of the product are sufficiently motivated to sell the product.

PROMOTIONAL STRATEGY

Overseas tour operators generate approximately 40 per cent of the turnover of Ocean Spirit Cruises Cairns. These operators plan their schedules 18 months to two years in advance. In such an environment, the cultivation of long-term relationships and the determination of appropriate rates are critical to ensuring the necessary volume of business. There is little opportunity for discounting given the long lead times. There is, however, the opportunity to do this in the context of local suppliers such as Destination Cairns Marketing (DCM). Indeed, supplementary commissions are introduced during periods of low demand to such firms to provide a boost to sales. Discounts are also used from time to time to stimulate walk-on business. The dinner cruise product may, for example, be discounted from $70.00 to $60.00 and the offer displayed at sales outlets around Cairns. Discounts are also used at specific times of the year such as during school holidays ('kids go free' option), Fathers' Day and Mothers' Day.

The advertising component of OSC's promotional strategy is focused on print-based media, specifically newspapers, trade publications and brochures, and to a lesser extent, radio advertising and billboards (notably at Cairns Airport). Because a large proportion of business is booked within Cairns itself, the displaying of high quality brochure collateral at the various local tour retail outlets is critical. Ensuring that such brochures are available in sufficient quantities and displayed prominently is a key role for the local sales executive. This staff member is responsible for enhancing the profile of the operation in Cairns and Far North Queensland.

Another costly, but critical, component of promotional strategy is participation at key international tourism trade shows such as the International Tourism Borse (ITB) in Berlin. Participation in such shows is important for raising product awareness amongst overseas operators, but is only effective where thorough followup is undertaken with suppliers. Within Australia, participation in the Australian Tourism Exchange (ATE) is also important because international tour operators and travel agents are present, as well as inbound tourism operators. Australian product suppliers seeking to attract overseas visitors via overseas wholesalers and/or inbound tourism operators communicate the rates that they have determined for forthcoming periods, and enter into important contractual obligations at these events.

In early 2000, an override commission of 10 per cent was offered to outlets selling *Ocean Spirit Two*. To ensure that this did not lead to an ongoing expectation of high commission rates by distributors, the promotion was limited to a two-month period. According to Eiszele, the results were disappointing and the initiative was discontinued. This highlights the dilemma facing sales promotions. If the period of trial is short, the evidence of whether success was achieved may be inconclusive. However, the other option of continuing the offer over a longer period may be unacceptable because of the perceived danger of creating a precedent. How to handle such trials is a key challenge for marketing managers.

In 2000 OSC's promotion budget amounted to approximately $400 000 excluding salaries. The largest items of expenditure were brochures (15–20 per cent) and print media costs (20–25 per cent). Sales trips and trade shows were also significant budget items.

Ocean Spirit Cruises Cairns does not make large-scale use of external marketing-related consultancies because of the relatively small scale of its operation. Some assistance is sought with the production of brochures and video materials.

INTERNET

Ocean Spirit Cruises Cairns was a relatively early adopter of the internet (the web site was installed in 1995/96) as a means of communicating with potential customers. The OSC pages are linked to the Destination Cairns Marketing site. Whilst key competitors are also displayed prominently on this site, the link does provide an additional promotional medium and a strong association between the individual product and the destination region as a whole. At the time of writing, the main current initiative of OSC was the establishment of an online booking facility on its web site. It is intended that this will move their web presence from being primarily about information dissemination to an active channel for direct bookings. Additionally, revisions to their site will allow for customer feedback on their products as well as providing the opportunity for merchandise to be purchased online. Over the financial year 1999/2000 OSC's site received approximately 5000 'hits'. The web address is <www.oceanspirit.com.au>.

DISTRIBUTION CHANNELS, TECHNOLOGY AND SERVICE

As mentioned previously, overseas distribution is critical to providing OSC with its flow of customers, and with advance bookings from which it can project future demand levels. Not only does this mean linking with overseas intermediaries, but also with inbound tourism operators (most of whom are located in Sydney) and local retail travel agents. In addition to international visitors who are attracted via tour operators and travel agents, domestic travellers particularly from Melbourne and Sydney are targeted by OSC through having its products incorporated into the packages of major domestic tour wholesalers—Qantas Holidays and Sunlover Holidays (operated by the Queensland Government's Tourism Queensland). It is noteworthy that the domestic market is primarily leisure-based with corporate and conventions being of less importance. This is largely to do with the inability of OSC's vessels to handle large groups.

SUMMARY

Ocean Spirit Cruises Cairns is an interesting example of what appears on the surface to be a straightforward product configuration—two sail catamarans. In practice, however, the management of this small-scale business is anything but simple. The need to distribute the product in key international markets— Europe, Asia and North America—poses considerable challenges for a small organisation with limited resources to devote to marketing. The location of much of Australia's inbound tourism industry in Sydney, remote from Cairns, adds an additional layer of complexity, albeit compensated for by the presence of Ocean Spirit Cruises Sydney in that marketplace. There is also the challenge of maintaining a strong presence in the local market with a view to attracting impulse purchases by both local residents and tourists. Finally, this case raises the issue of how to respond to changes in a given market place (e.g. the development of the backpacker market) without compromising the integrity of a well established and respected brand.

Primary period covered in case study: 2000/01

REFERENCE

Macro Corporation Limited. 2001, *Annual Report 2000*, Melbourne.

QUESTIONS

1 How would you describe the 'product' offered to clients by Ocean Spirit Cruises Cairns?

2 What are the particular challenges confronting small enterprises such as OSC in attempting to adopt a strategic approach to marketing?

3 To what extent are smaller enterprises, such as OSC, especially vulnerable to external shocks affecting the business environment?

4 What types of promotional material would you expect to be most appropriate for products such as the sail catamaran experience offered by OSC?

5   Do you believe that potential exists for the two OSC vessels to be marketed as distinct visitor experiences?

6   a) What product attributes has OSC management emphasised in developing an overall brand?
    b) What other methods could be considered by OSC to strengthen its branding in Far North Queensland?

7   In what ways is the distribution function such a critical success factor for a business such as OSC?

8   a) Is OSC's price-setting process best characterised as complex or straight-forward? Why?
    b) What potential consequences should OSC management consider before determining the final price structure for their products?

9   Prepare the basic elements of a market research plan for OCS that could address its information needs concerning consumers and intermediaries.

10 Discuss the 'pros' and 'cons' of the various options considered by OSC management before proceeding to decrease ticket prices to $89 and thereby increase its load factors on Ocean Spirit Two. Do you believe that the right decision was made?

8. SOFITEL MELBOURNE

INTRODUCTION

The present case study provides insights into the marketing activity of a five star hotel located in a central business district. It also examines the issue of market positioning in some detail based on Hotel Sofitel Melbourne's campaign to be known as Melbourne's 'Hotel for the Arts'. This process involved a conscious strategy to distinguish Hotel Sofitel Melbourne from other equivalent accommodation properties by building a close association with the arts community, including both artists and customers of the arts—both visual and performing.

BACKGROUND

Accor is a French-based diversified tourism and leisure group whose operations extend to retail travel, car rental, service vouchers and accommodation. It has over 3000 hotels worldwide with a portfolio of properties in every category from budget to up-scale and resort hotels, causing it to claim that it is the world's largest hotel network. At the time of writing, it operated more hotels in Australia than any other company, with 13 properties in Melbourne alone.

In 1996 the Accor hotel group took over the management of the Regent Hotel, a five star hotel with 363 rooms located on the 35th to 50th levels of a high-rise tower in Melbourne, from the Four Seasons group. The hotel was located at the 'Paris End' of Melbourne's principal thoroughfare, Collins Street. Once in Accor's control, the hotel was re-branded a 'Sofitel' (the Hotel Sofitel Melbourne), Accor's luxury brand, and thus became one of a network of 110 Sofitel properties internationally.

Hotel Sofitel Melbourne has performed well financially for Accor, with average annual revenue in recent years of approximately $40 million per year, with the rooms division accounting for just over half of this amount and food and beverage for the remainder. In 1998, Hotel Sofitel Melbourne had a room occupancy rate of 76.4 per cent that was equal to the Grand Hyatt Hotel, its major direct competitor, and ahead of all other Melbourne hotels. The achieved average room rate of $188.85 was second only to the Grand Hyatt Hotel.

MARKETING PLANNING PROCESS

As is the case with many large hotel groups, Accor provides its member properties with a pro forma marketing plan that is then adapted to local circumstances. The scale of the plan varies according to the size of property with certain sections applicable only to larger hotels. According to Hotel Sofitel Melbourne's General Manager, Norbert Uhlig, the group aims to ensure that one of its properties operates as the 'market leader' in any given competitive setting, and his hotel had been chosen to achieve this position in the 'up-market' five star hotel category in Melbourne.

MARKETING PHILOSOPHY

According to Uhlig, the Accor philosophy emphasises the need for diversified hotel groups to appeal primarily to the 'middle market'. Whilst five star, up-scale properties are a critical part of the product mix, they account for only a small part of aggregate demand and are sensitive to economic downturns. Consistent with this philosophy, Accor general managers are not appointed to a five star hotel on the basis of their familiarity with the luxury end of the market (though this helps), but because they possess the skills and knowledge to operate accommodation as a business entity. There are, for example, 330 Novotel and 400 Mercure properties worldwide, but only 110 outlets bearing the Sofitel deluxe brand. Because there are relatively fewer Sofitel properties, and because the Sofitel brand occupies a distinct marketing positioning, managers of these properties have a higher degree of autonomy than their counterparts in other properties within the group. This is particularly the case with the Melbourne property, which is one of only two Sofitel properties in Australia (the other is the Sofitel Reef Casino Hotel in Cairns). A second property was recently added to the Sofitel portfolio in Melbourne through acquisition—the Grand Hotel. This property is, however, only managed under the Sofitel name and is not formally branded as a Sofitel hotel.

MARKETING POSITIONING AND BRANDING

Hotel Sofitel Melbourne has taken a relatively unusual and bold step in aligning and branding itself with a particular activity—the arts. The hotel's promotional material describes the property as the 'Hotel for the Arts'. This positioning was adopted because of the widely-held view (shared by Norbert Uhlig), that most five star hotel brands lack personality and have a tendency to blandness. According to Uhlig, the management of the hotel, prior to the Accor takeover, was heavily focused on the corporate market and paid little attention to leisure travellers. By adopting the positioning of embracing the arts, Uhlig determined that the property would be less 'exclusive' and more welcoming.

The 'Hotel for the Arts' positioning strategy has provided a focus for a range of marketing activities including sponsorships, promotions, merchandising, product presentation and public relations. The initiative is an interesting one partly because it is so unusual—relatively few five star hotels pursue such a clearly defined and communicated positioning. The choice of focus was opportunistic in that no other five star hotel in Melbourne had secured a positioning as a place of, and for, the arts. The location was also important to the initiative because of the reputation of Melbourne as a 'Home for the Arts' with a vibrant calendar of artistic events. When Accor took over the management of the property, the State Government of Victoria was in the process of emphasising the credentials of Melbourne as an 'events capital', with a range of supporting services, including hotels. This created an opportunity for tourism organisations to associate themselves with the government's push focusing on sporting and/or cultural events. Given that five star hotels are perceived as 'up-scale' or 'up-market', the potential connection between 'fine arts' and a 'fine hotel' offered considerable potential.

The Hotel Sofitel Melbourne, in pursuing its desired position, devised a strategy involving six main components, namely:

* a program of arts exhibitions;
* a program of performing arts sponsorships;
* communication activities including advertising, brochures and in-house promotions;
* the hosting of in-hotel events;
* public relations based on its arts activities and associations; and
* submission of the 'Hotel for the Arts' initiative for tourism and arts awards.

Additionally the slogan 'Hotel for the Arts' was adopted, under whose umbrella the hotel has sought to:

* cultivate corporate and social networks;
* enhance the profile of the hotel through a range of communication activities;
* link hotel promotion with city-wide arts promotions such as the Melbourne Food and Wine Festival and the Melbourne Fashion Festival;
* grow room and food/beverage revenue; and
* create a lively hotel ambience built around the arts.

Indicative of this last point is the use of four public areas of the hotel as gallery spaces. Local artists, who provide the artworks, are charged only 10 per cent commission for their works if they are sold. This commission level stands in marked contrast to that of commercial galleries that charge up to 40 per cent, and therefore assists the hotel in building goodwill amongst the arts community.

Like any coordinated effort at positioning, it is important for internal and external aspects of any associated promotional efforts to be fully integrated. As regards internal promotional efforts, a range of collateral material has been developed to support the 'Hotel for the Arts' concept, including:

* door cards
* restaurant cards
* an arts brochure
* in-lift advertising
* exhibition flyers through the concierge.

Supporting external communication efforts take a number of forms. The hotel produces a magazine *At the Sofitel*. This publication has a mailing list of 8000, an active association with the Hotel Sofitel web site and the 'Hotel for the Arts' concept, and advertising/sponsorships that emphasise this connection. The hotel has also become a major (or associate) sponsor of a cross-section of strategically selected activities, as opposed to a more exclusive approach of being a principal sponsor for one or two organisations. This is an interesting strategy given Melbourne's recent success in reducing seasonality of visitation by spreading events throughout the year (King & Jago 1999). Consistent with this approach, Hotel Sofitel Melbourne deliberately sought to create an arts profile for 12 months of the year, not simply when an opera or symphony season is scheduled.

Although 'opening up the hotel' was one aspect of the 'Hotel for the Arts' strategy, an exclusive hotel cannot move away entirely from concepts of exclusivity. In this regard Hotel Sofitel has created an Arts Club. To qualify, members must use Hotel Sofitel for corporate or leisure accommodation to gain access to a range of arts-related benefits such as invitations to the opening of arts-related events.

The 'Hotel for the Arts' initiative has been a major financial commitment, but has also generated revenue. It was 'never intended primarily as an income-generator' (Hotel Sofitel Melbourne 2000). In 1999, for example, revenue of at least $250,000 was derived from in-hotel performances, dinners, other events, additional accommodation booked by arts organisations, and commissions on art works.

The ultimate aim of the 'Hotel for the Arts' initiative is to provide Hotel Sofitel Melbourne with a clear positioning and a distinct identity amongst five star Melbourne hotels. Whilst it is difficult to provide a precise cost benefit measurement, there is no question that this initiative has helped Accor to convince the skeptics that the move from the Regent of Melbourne could be achieved smoothly and without sacrificing the identity and market position of the property.

It is noteworthy, as Uhlig has observed, that the Sofitel brand lacks a distinct identity internationally, something that Accor itself has acknowledged, resulting in a review of its branding strategy. Confident that Hotel Sofitel Melbourne has already resolved the issue of brand identity through its 'Hotel for the Arts' strategy, Uhlig has submitted a proposal to the group suggesting that other members of the group should position themselves as a 'Home for the Arts', adopting the Hotel Sofitel Melbourne ethos. At the time of writing, this proposal was still under consideration by Accor.

MARKETING RESEARCH

According to Uhlig, Accor produces a modest volume of consumer research for use by its member properties. The focus of such research is to facilitate the attainment of performance targets, especially the maintenance of service delivery standards. The Accor Asia-Pacific Headquarters in Sydney implements a process called 'Qualivision' on a quarterly basis. This involves contacting (by telephone) current clients of each of its properties and determining the level of service that they encountered, based on a rating scale. This approach to research is common amongst many larger hotel groups, where there is, of necessity, a strong emphasis on the achievement of specific business targets.

Despite the widely held view that room-based customer questionnaires are used excessively and are consequently of decreasing value, Uhlig is insistent that they are an invaluable tool for hotel general managers. The questionnaires used by Hotel Sofitel Melbourne are brief and allow considerable opportunity for general comment. This improves response rates and allows the general manager to identify any problem areas that are in need of attention. Uhlig notes that there is a strong correlation between dissatisfaction expressed by customers and patterns of staff departure.

MAJOR MARKETS

Common in the case of up-scale downtown hotels, the major target markets for Hotel Sofitel Melbourne are:

* corporate
* domestic leisure
* inbound leisure
* conferences.

The corporate market provides the dominant contribution to revenue. It accounts for about 40 per cent of room occupancy with domestic leisure responsible for a further 20 per cent, conference for 12 per cent and inbound leisure for 12 per cent. Geographically, Sydney is the key source market of both corporate and leisure travellers. The United States, Europe and Japan are the major international markets. Whilst New Zealanders have a reputation for attending Melbourne-based sporting and cultural performances in large numbers, Hotel Sofitel Melbourne is not a major beneficiary of this traffic. According to Uhlig, relatively few New Zealanders stay in five star properties when travelling to Melbourne.

Packaging is an important tool for the hotel, particularly as the connection with the arts offers an opportunity to develop 'value-added' product combinations and propositions. As a key component of its arts profile, Hotel Sofitel sponsors a wide range of arts events and consequently is able to secure complementary or heavily discounted tickets, which may then be incorporated into an inclusive price. The hotel makes widespread use of arts events packaging with accommodation or pre-dinner drinks. The preference for 'value adding' over discounting may be considered as a useful way of ensuring that the 'Hotel for the Arts' branding is not viewed as devaluing the perceived luxury of the property or the experience of staying there.

The potency of Hotel Sofitel's approach to packaging is exemplified by the recent response from viewers of Channel Nine's *Getaway* program. In this program a package was featured incorporating accommodation at the Sofitel and seats at the *Sound of Music* that was then playing at the Princess Theatre in Melbourne. According to Uhlig, over 400 telephone calls were received in the course of 90 minutes, and the number of packages made available could have been sold two or three times over.

KEY COMPETITIVE STRENGTHS

Uhlig regards the hotel's food and beverage operation as a key competitive strength and views the hotel as a culinary leader and as offering banquets of the highest quality, particularly in association with the conference and meetings markets. He cites the various awards won by the hotel's fine dining restaurant, Le Restaurant, as an indication that management pays particular attention to the food and beverage function within the property. The hotel also operates an in-house training school known as Academy Sofitel. The Academy enables the hotel to incorporate a strong training dimension into its pursuit of food and beverage service excellence. Academy Sofitel was established as Victoria's first training school within a five star hotel. The Academy collaborates with Victoria University to provide students with an opportunity to proceed to degree level study.

The physical dimensions of the property also provide a competitive advantage. Whilst the vistas from the guest rooms (not to mention the floor-to-ceiling windows in the public toilets!) are impressive, it is the openness of the lobby area that offers particular appeal by suggesting inclusivity and a sense of arrival and welcome. Uhlig claims that consulting reports have shown that Sofitel enjoys a higher satisfaction level than other five star hotels in Melbourne and perceives this as a competitive strength. The benchmark is for Hotel Sofitel Melbourne to achieve a minimum of 80 per cent of respondents in the 'exceeded expectations' category for the guest questionnaires. He states that the percentage of respondents indicating that their expectations have not been met is approximately 2 per cent.

Technology is also used as a means of differentiating Hotel Sofitel Melbourne's product offerings. The main current technological development is the installation of 'highest speed' internet access in the guestrooms. The other key innovations also concern internet-based access. Conference activities taking place in one part of the hotel will be able to be viewed in guest rooms through the internet using Cat Six Broadband technology. The hotel has also made provision for the installation of movies on demand accessed through the internet. Guests will be able to view such movies as they wish, with a facility for fast-forwarding and re-winding.

CUSTOMER LOYALTY PROGRAMS

According to Uhlig, research commissioned by Accor in Australia indicates that offering a 'frequent user' program would be a major operational expense and would be unlikely to have any significant impact on purchasing patterns. The Accor philosophy is to make maximum use of the database of some 80 000 previous guests and to undertake periodic and highly targeted promotions. Accor promotes a membership card called *Advantage Plus* that can be used throughout the Asia-Pacific region. It costs $195 and offers a free night's accommodation plus a range of dining privileges. There is a European-based Sofitel Club card, though this particular item is not sold in Australia.

In line with a practice that is common amongst five star hotels, Sofitel also contemplated the installation of an executive floor as an additional guest service. Again, research indicated that this initiative would not lead to an increase in revenue and the plans were aborted. These two initiatives are a reminder that relatively few of the various product developments that are subjected to a process of evaluation by organisations successfully overcome the viability test.

PRICING

According to Uhlig, pricing is highly sensitive to the actions of competitors and consumers in Melbourne. He states that the way of doing business is changing. Instead of paying travel agents a 10 per cent commission on sales, there is a growing tendency for corporate clients to prefer to deal directly with the hotel with a view to arriving at a net rate. After an initial call for tenders, the client will determine which travel business should be appointed to manage the operation. Under such an arrangement, the agent is typically paid a monthly management fee. To avoid excessive dependence on a small number of very large clients, Hotel Sofitel has been pursuing small- to medium-sized corporate accounts that might, on average, book 150 room nights over the course of a year. These groups are sometimes attracted to the prestige offered by a Collins Street address and are less price- and volume-driven than some large corporations.

Different markets display different approaches to contracting, and to the conduct of business. German and European clients seek absolute reliability because of the strict consumer laws that apply throughout the European Union, such as the *European Communities Directive* 90/314 concerning package travel, package holidays and package tours. Europeans are an important source of business for Hotel Sofitel Melbourne and it is difficult for other properties to lure this business away because of the strict demand by clients for proven reliability. Like German and other European guests, Japanese visitors emphasise the need for reliability. Other Asian markets have a stronger tendency for group-based travel, an activity that is largely price-driven. In view of the high cost of operating a five star property, it is rare to pursue these markets actively except in the case of fully independent travellers and corporate travellers. Uhlig states that the strictness of the European consumer laws are a portent of things to come, with consumer laws beginning to tighten in parts of Asia such as Taiwan.

A yield management system is operated group-wide, and properties are required to adhere to this approach. Uhlig emphasises that yield management systems are not a panacea for resolving supply and demand imbalances, especially when there is downward pressure on room rates due to external and uncontrollable factors. Achieving a high yield is desirable in theory, but lower yield business is worth pursuing during periods of weaker demand.

DISTRIBUTION AND NEW TECHNOLOGY

The hotel works closely with a wide range of distributors and tourism industry partners. Tourism Victoria has been an important partner in developing events that in turn generate additional bed nights for the accommodation sector, including Hotel Sofitel. Tour operators and travel agents are also important in generating leisure-based booking for the hotel. The hotel also seeks to build relationships with professional conference organisers (PCOs) who handle much of the conference and convention business in Melbourne. In this regard, Hotel Sofitel Melbourne's main relationships are with locally-based PCOs which are primarily concerned about issues of consistency and reliability rather than with price.

Uhlig is a strong believer in the value of well-established marketing techniques and states that an appropriately phrased letter from the general manager to previous guests is generally well received. Despite his support for the traditional approach, Uhlig is enthusiastic about the cost effectiveness of web-based distribution and particularly of the merit of 'hot links'. Hotel Sofitel Melbourne has very active links with the web sites of arts organisations in Melbourne. Other hot links have included the web sites of ninemsn (the holiday-based program *Getaway*) and the Australian Stock Exchange (ASX).

INTERNAL MARKETING

Uhlig acknowledges intra-organisational communication as a key, and ongoing, challenge for management. As a part of the staff induction process, he stresses the need for all employees to become involved in the marketing process and emphasises the importance of marketing to the success of the organisation. He stresses the central importance of relationships with clients as described by the former chief executive officer of SAS Airlines, Jan Carlzon (London Business School 1993). He regards the greatest communication risk as the imposition of ostensibly innovative marketing ideas on reluctant or poorly briefed operational staff. Ensuring that staff in all sections of the business are informed about marketing activities is critical, he believes, to creating a relaxed and focused working environment.

SUMMARY

In committing itself to the 'Hotel for the Arts' positioning, Hotel Sofitel Melbourne has shown how a corporate hotel can adopt an imaginative approach that links its identity to the key strengths of the destination (as an events capital). The association has facilitated the development of partnerships with government and with a range of arts organisations. Such partnerships are helpful to provide the property with community support at the highest level. This form of support is valuable in an era when corporations are moving their image from a focus on profit-taking to responsible corporate citizenship. Such responsibility is not purely the provision of philanthropy. Through skillful marketing, the development of a collaborative approach can yield commercial benefits. Other five star hotel properties, struggling to secure a clear identity in the marketplace, would be well advised to take note of the approach adopted by Hotel Sofitel Melbourne.

Primary period covered by case study: 2001/02

REFERENCES

Hotel Sofitel Melbourne. 2000, *A Discussion Paper—Hotel for the Arts*.

Hotel Sofitel Melbourne. 1999, *Submission for the Victorian Tourism Awards*.

King, B.E.M. & Jago L.K. 1999, *TTI City Reports*, No. 1 pp. 37–52, Melbourne.

London Business School. 1993, *SAS and Carlzon*, London.

<www.sofitelmelbourne.com.au>·

QUESTIONS

1   What marketing benefits has Hotel Sofitel pursued by positioning itself as Melbourne's 'Hotel for the Arts'?

2   How significant are Sofitel properties in Accor's overall product mix? What role do such properties perform for the Accor group?

3   Briefly discuss the relationship between the positioning of Hotel Sofitel Melbourne and that of the City of Melbourne.

4   What specific actions have been undertaken by Hotel Sofitel to position itself as Melbourne's 'Hotel for the Arts'? Please classify these actions under the broad headings of product, price, promotion and distribution.

5   What role does sponsorship play in Hotel Sofitel Melbourne's positioning efforts? Should sponsorship be viewed as an element of the hotel's promotional mix? If so, why?

6   What role does 'packaging' play in Hotel Sofitel Melbourne's efforts to stimulate demand for its services?

7   Briefly state and comment upon Hotel Sofitel Melbourne's web-based promotional efforts. Can you suggest any extensions/improvements to the current promotional mix?

8   It is indicated in the case study that 'different markets display different approaches to contracting'. To what extent does this influence the approach adopted by Hotel Sofitel Melbourne towards target marketing?

9   What types of market research are currently undertaken by Hotel Sofitel Melbourne? Do you believe that current market research efforts are adequate? Can you suggest other marketing research tools that could potentially be used to enhance the knowledge that hotel management has about its customer base?

10   What do you see as the benefits or problems of extending the 'Hotel for the Arts' strategy to other Sofitel properties as proposed by the General Manager of the Hotel Sofitel Melbourne?

9. TOURISM VICTORIA

INTRODUCTION

In the Australian environment, state and territory tourism commissions have played a key role in tourism development, particularly in marketing to domestic travellers. This case study examines one such body, Tourism Victoria, and seeks to explore its approach to overall marketing strategy development, marketing planning, market selection, branding and promotion. In examining these key aspects of its marketing the case study also seeks to: demonstrate the value of market research in shaping marketing decisions; highlight the importance of consensus building by tourist commissions as a precursor to marketing decision-making; and point to the difficulties faced by a body such as Tourism Victoria as it attempts to achieve its marketing objectives in the absence of direct control in areas such as product quality.

BACKGROUND

Tourism Victoria is the government organisation responsible for the marketing and development of tourism in the state of Victoria. It has counterpart tourism commissions in the other five states of Australia and in the two territories. The equivalent tourism organisation at the national level is the Australian Tourist Commission (which will be incorporated into the Federal Government's new body—Tourism Australia—in late 2004). Most of Australia's state tourism commissions originated through statute, and Tourism Victoria is no exception, having been established by the *Tourism Victoria Act 1992*. This Act abolished the previous organisation, the Victorian Tourism Commission, and sought to provide the new body with a measure of commercial freedom commonly associated with the private sector, while at the same time ensuring a level of accountability more often found in the public sector.

The chairman and board of Tourism Victoria are ministerial appointments and bring industry experience and knowledge to the overall direction of the organisation. Senior figures from prominent Victoria-based private sector organisations are members of the board. In the case of operational personnel, public service terms and conditions apply since Tourism Victoria operates as a government department. Consistent with the prevailing view that an appropriate balance must be struck between the public and private sector ethos respectively, the chief executive is jointly accountable to the board of Tourism Victoria and to the secretary of the relevant government department.

Restructuring of government tourism departments was commonplace across Australia during the 1980s and 1990s, and in the case of Tourism Victoria, included changes to the secretarial function. In 1992, Tourism Victoria was relocated into the Department of Arts, Sport and Tourism and subsequently (in 1996) into the Department of State Development. Since the election of a Labor Government in 1999, tourism has formed part of the Department of State and Regional Development, reflecting a trend across government towards a reduction in the number of departments.

According to David Riley, Deputy Chief Executive of Tourism Victoria, its location within a government mega-department provides Tourism Victoria with beneficial economies of scale. Activities such as personnel and finance are shared with other sections of the Department and thus are centralised, thereby minimising duplication. This avoids the need to develop stand-alone functions for a relatively small number of staff. This approach assists Tourism Victoria to focus on its key objectives. According to Riley, the tourism industry understands the merit of the government department approach and views Tourism Victoria as being strongly committed to the development of partnerships with industry operators. He believes that the potential criticisms of excessive bureaucracy tend to arise only if industry is dissatisfied with performance. This situation has not arisen because of Tourism Victoria's demonstrable and ongoing record of achievement.

MARKETING PLANNING PROCESS

The structure of Tourism Victoria operates within the ambit of government, but the organisation emulates the private sector by adhering to an annual business plan. As is the case with most destination tourism organisations in Australia, Tourism Victoria is predominantly marketing-driven, and any other activities, such as strategic planning, focus around the marketing core. The Tourism Victoria *Strategic Business Plan 1997–2001* sets out key directions and incorporates a range of performance indicators. The latter are becoming standard practice amongst state and national tourism organisations, though there is debate internationally about the appropriate level of detail that should be incorporated. Some critics have argued that targets are becoming too specific, thereby reducing the opportunity to be creative and hampering the capacity of tourism organisations to adapt to changing circumstances.

The preparation of Tourism Victoria's *Strategic Business Plan 1997–2001* involved two critical elements. First, high calibre expertise was drawn from outside Tourism Victoria including the formulation of special groups and the staging of 'brainstorming' sessions. Secondly, widespread consultation was undertaken throughout the regions of Victoria. Such liaison is a critical issue for state tourism commissions throughout Australia, particularly in view of the increasing acknowledgment by government of the needs and demands of rural constituents. Given the concentration of population in the respective capital cities, which makes it easy to communicate the interests of urban residents, it is doubly important that the concerns of the bush are given due consideration.

The marketing structure within Tourism Victoria is divided into domestic and international activity, in part a reflection of the different competitive environments that prevail in the two spheres. In the case of domestic marketing, the various tourism commissions compete vigorously for market share. Domestic tourism growth has been generally sluggish and expansion of tourism in particular states has often been achieved at the expense of visitation to other Australian destinations. International marketing involves a greater degree of cooperation with other states and, in particular, participation in the Partnership Australia (PA) agreement with the Australian Tourist Commission (ATC). Broadly speaking, under this agreement state and territory commissions take responsibility for determining those overseas markets which are most attractive to their particular geographic and product attributes. Since Victoria is the headquarters of many major corporations, there has been a strong emphasis on travel related to corporate activity including meetings and conventions. There is also a strong emphasis on markets that have direct flights to Melbourne. Tourism Victoria, for example, is less active in Korea and Japan than is Tourism New South Wales since there are no direct flights from Korea or Japan to Melbourne. Korean and Japanese travellers also generally prefer to take short trips. Melbourne does, however, enjoy frequent and direct flights from key gateways such as Singapore, Bangkok and Hong Kong, and this has prompted a stronger emphasis on the markets served by these airports.

Riley asserts that the strategic planning undertaken by Tourism Victoria is 'customer and research driven'. Tourism Victoria has aimed to provide industry leadership by interpreting and responding to the types of experience that will be sought by the consumers of the future. The Tourism Victoria *Strategic Business Plan 1997–2001*, subtitled *Building Partnerships*, was based on a combination of leadership and consultation over a 14-month period. The process involved review, consultation, research, strategy development and the setting of targets and methods of evaluation. The consultative approach included:

* input from more than 3000 people through workshops and presentations;
* 15 industry workshops which focused on international markets and specific market segments;
* some 330 letters to the industry inviting comment; and
* 23 business plan presentations across the state.

The approach adopted is depicted in diagrammatic form in Figure 9.1.

Figure 9.1: Tourism Victoria business plan approach

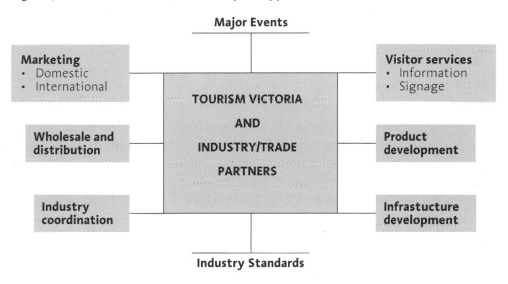

Source: Tourism Victoria, *Strategic Business Plan 1997–2001*.

EXTERNAL FACTORS AND MAJOR MARKETS

Tourism Victoria's *Strategic Business Plan 1997–2001* includes an assessment of the marketing environment, including the global scene, international markets, the domestic scene and a SWOT analysis (strengths, weaknesses, opportunities and threats). Assessment of external factors is a critical component of the strategic planning process. The Asian financial crisis is an obvious example of an external event with the potential to exert significant influence. The sudden drop in arrivals from key Asian source markets, such as Indonesia, Malaysia and Thailand, undermined many of the assumptions of the Plan, though Tourism Victoria was not unique in this respect, and other destination marketing organisations faced similar problems. In fact, Victoria suffered relatively less than several other states from the Asian financial crisis, being less dependent on South-East Asian sources. It benefited from having strong relationships with a number of Asian countries, such as China, that were less negatively affected by the financial crisis and continued to generate growth of traveller numbers, particularly in the education and visiting friends and relatives categories. Additionally, Tourism Victoria's traditional markets of the United Kingdom and Europe, New Zealand and North America were unaffected by this event.

The main domestic markets for Victoria are the cities of Sydney, Adelaide and, to a lesser extent, Brisbane. The three source markets display different characteristics. The Sydney market, by far the largest in terms of population, predominantly generates a substantial volume of short-break traffic using air travel. Adelaide, in contrast, is predominantly a 'self-drive' market. Brisbane's population is of similar size to Adelaide's but like Sydney it is characterised by short-break holidays based on air travel. Because of budgetary constraints, high cost promotional activity, such as television advertising, can only be justified in areas that generate large volumes of visitors. Sydney and Adelaide are critical in this regard, and high cost television advertising is largely confined to these cities. Television advertising is also undertaken periodically within Victoria with a view to encouraging intrastate travel.

Within these clearly identified geographical areas, Tourism Victoria targets particular segments. Like a number of other state and territory tourist commissions, Tourism Victoria bases its market measurement on the 'Value Segments' developed and copyrighted by the Roy Morgan research organisation. With a view to attracting those markets with the highest spending potential, Tourism Victoria specifically targets the 'Visible Achiever' and 'Socially Aware' segments. In recent times it has added the 'Traditional Family Life' group with a view to broadening the overall appeal of the destination. A campaign called *'You'll love every piece of Victoria'*, which commenced in 1993, focused on these specific segments. This campaign (initially at least) was significantly different from most of the promotional activity being undertaken by other tourist commissions at the time that tended to be concerned with general destination awareness raising. This highly targeted approach has been widely attributed as having improved Victoria's share of the domestic market.

In addition to targeting particular demographic groups, Tourism Victoria also targets special interest groups by identifying appropriate and appealing product types. Such products include nature- and heritage-based tourism, cultural tourism and special events tourism. The organisation also tries to disperse tourists throughout the state by targeting segments that may be interested in touring and in non-urban attractions such as wineries or national parks. This commitment to dispersal differentiates government-funded destination organisations from individual firms, which are usually reluctant to embrace such broad community-focused commitments.

To supplement its use of the Roy Morgan Values Segments, Tourism Victoria also uses a program called MOSAIC that provides tightly targeted information about consumers who live in particular localities. MOSAIC is based on information included in the national census. The information generated by MOSAIC is particularly useful as an underpinning for direct marketing campaigns.

MARKET RESEARCH

Bill Faulkner, a former Director of the Bureau of Tourism Research and, until his untimely death, a leading Australian tourism academic, characterised the marketing activity of the state tourism commissions during the 1980s and early

1990s recession as 'advertising fundamentalism' (Faulkner 1993). He asserted that there was insufficient commitment to strategic marketing supported by rigorous research. Since Faulkner made his comments, a number of the tourism commissions have devoted greater attention and resources to research. Riley's observation that Tourism Victoria is a 'research-driven organisation' is indicative of this change of philosophical emphasis.

In attempting to increase overall domestic tourism and to attract market share from other states and territories, Tourism Victoria has adopted a highly targeted research-based strategy. The Roy Morgan research organisation was commissioned to provide ongoing information about key market segments, and this information in turn forms the basis of a marketing information system (MIS). By tracking the purchasing behaviour of market segments against media and other consumption and behavioural characteristics, Tourism Victoria has been better able to target its marketing activity.

Tourism Victoria has also undertaken large-scale research projects such as the state-wide Regional Tourism Survey. Completed in 1995, this project involved surveying tourists at their chosen destinations, and aimed to provide Tourism Victoria with a better understanding of tourism activity in the regions. This survey, however, has not been repeated. In the post-1995 period, the Bureau of Tourism Research modified its research methodology, replacing the Domestic Tourism Monitor with the National Visitor Survey. This change introduced a more economic way of undertaking survey work by the Commonwealth Government and eliminated some of the urgency for individual states and territories to undertake their own dedicated surveys.

Tourism Victoria is a funding participant in the Commonwealth Government's Cooperative Research Centre for Sustainable Tourism (CRC Tourism). CRC Tourism is a partnership between government, industry and academia, and undertakes strategic research on issues of importance as determined by industry. Along with Tourism Victoria, the Victorian participants in the scheme are the City of Melbourne, Victoria University and La Trobe University. The focus of the Victorian component of the research to date has been events tourism. Different priorities are sometimes evident in the case of the various partners. Nevertheless, the Victorian component of the CRC Tourism is a positive sign of a commitment on the part of government and industry to strategically focused research and to a more holistic approach to tourism marketing.

Undertaking research on international markets is particularly costly. Tourism Victoria relies primarily on its participation in the Australia-wide International Visitor Survey that is coordinated by the Bureau of Tourism Research, and on the various ad hoc market segmentation studies undertaken by the Australian Tourist Commission (ATC). These activities are a significant element of the relationship between the ATC and its state and territory counterparts under the Partnership Australia scheme.

State tourism commissions generally recognise the value of marketing research as providing an element of objectivity to underpin strategic decisions. In the context of state government, objectivity is essential since such strategies that are substantiated with research can provide stakeholders with some reassurance about performance and accountability. A consistent rationale is required where additional marketing expenditures are being proposed for destinations that have been identified as offering the greatest development potential. This is not possible without timely and accurate research. Destination regions are not equal in terms of attractiveness to tourists or their ability to attract the mass market in a sustainable manner. Whilst good management and leadership at regional level may lead to some competitive advantage, state-based resources to assist with regional tourism marketing are limited. Research can assist tourism commissions such as Tourism Victoria to identify key attractions with a view to prioritising the allocation of resources. This, in turn, can form the basis for decisions about the resources that should be allocated to particular regions. A key research issue for Tourism Victoria is the identification of critical success factors for regional destinations as viewed by consumers.

OVERALL MARKETING STRATEGY

As set out in Tourism Victoria's *Strategic Business Plan 1997–2001*, its priorities are:

* maintenance and expansion of a commercially sustainable industry;
* provision of industry leadership and direction; and
* expansion of cooperative partnerships.

Under these overall headings, the key strategic issues for the period 1997/2001 were identified as being to:

* increase visitation to regional Victoria and encourage longer-stay holidays in the state generally;
* develop a comprehensive international strategy which is targeted and offers the highest overall return on investment;
* develop a consistent, international branding for Melbourne and Victoria;
* utilise developments in information technology to improve bookings and information provision;
* improve the delivery of visitor services;
* capitalise on the tourism opportunities generated by the Sydney Olympics and the centenary of Australian Federation in 2001;
* harness the power of the travel industry to expand the distribution of bookable Victorian product;

- develop new product which matches the needs and expectations of target markets, ensuring a more desirable and accessible product for visitors;
- foster development of tourism infrastructure;
- attract additional, direct international air services to Melbourne;
- capitalise on Victoria's natural assets while protecting the environment; and
- match increasingly tough competition in both domestic and international markets.

BRANDING STRATEGY

A number of tourism commissions in Australia, such as the Western Australian Tourism Commission and the Australian Tourist Commission, have embraced the concept of branding with enthusiasm and have devoted considerable resources to its development. According to Riley, Tourism Victoria has used the concept of 'accessible diversity', as epitomised by the *You'll love every piece of Victoria* campaign, as a key element in its branding efforts. Tourism Victoria has emphasised the importance of taking a long-term view and of maintaining brand consistency (see later discussion). Whilst the concept of branding features prominently behind the scenes via discussions with key partners, such as its advertising agency, Tourism Victoria has opted to be more low key in communicating a specific and literal branding. This approach appears to have worked well. Nevertheless, Victoria faces a challenge in that the logo of the ATC's Brand Australia is focused on the colours red (outback), yellow (sunshine) and blue (water). Riley argues that this depicts the centre of Australia, Sydney and Queensland but is different from the 'green' Australia of Victoria, South Australia and Tasmania (associated with natural attractions). The positioning of the 'green' relative to Brand Australia as a whole is a major challenge for the southern states and extends beyond Victoria's state-specific concerns.

Riley highlights the fact that Tourism Victoria's award-winning 'Jigsaw Campaign' *You'll love every piece of Victoria* has run over a seven-year period. Changes of emphasis were planned well in advance and in the context of a consistent message. The initial campaign involved a 'World Map' (to emphasise diversity and raise awareness) followed by the 'Melbourne Experience' (Melbourne as a gateway city), 'Touring Victoria' (with its emphasis on regional areas) and most recently a two-pronged approach of 'Melbourne Plus' (linking Melbourne with its adjacent regions) and a continuation of 'Touring Victoria'. Such continuity of promotional messages has been a key success factor. A number of other equivalent destination marketing organisations have made frequent changes to their promotional slogans and messages thereby missing out on the benefit of continuity and consumer recognition.

Another key element of continuity involves building connections between the various regional images or sub-brands. Some $2 million is allocated annually to cooperative marketing campaigns undertaken in conjunction with the regions of Victoria. The promotional materials that emerge as a result of these campaigns enjoy a high level of consistency, achieved through the development of good relationships. On the one hand, the individual characteristics of regions need to be acknowledged. On the other hand, funding inducements are needed to ensure the maintenance of consistency and professional standards of presentation in brochures and other collateral material. For most state tourism commissions the achievement of a consistent approach to branding is elusive because of the wide range of political pressures that must be accommodated. The need to give serious attention to regional agendas means that notable icons such as the Sydney Opera House and the Sydney Harbour Bridge in New South Wales, for example, may be down-played in favour of more generic imagery which is inclusive of regional themes and attractions. This is not necessarily a bad thing, but there are instances in which politics may push tourism imagery in a direction inconsistent with consumer preferences.

The balance between Melbourne and regional Victoria has been achieved through the 'Jigsaw' advertising campaign mentioned previously, with the regions of Victoria making up the various pieces. In reality, tourists love some parts of Victoria more than others, but the campaign has provided a voice for the tourism aspirations of all parts of the state and importantly has avoided the situation where any particular region feels excluded from direct exposure through television advertising. Since television advertising is the most prominent aspect of marketing for both customers and for the destinations themselves, this issue is taken very seriously in the regions. Under the continuing 'Jigsaw', Tourism Victoria, as noted earlier, has more recently moved to develop its 'Melbourne Plus' campaign. Again this involved an astute blend of political reality (regions must be seen to benefit as much as the capital) and commercial reality (many of the core market segments will stay in Victoria for a limited time and will not travel far beyond Melbourne).

The deft interplay of regional and urban tourism is important in Victoria because of the relationship between Melbourne and its hinterland. Victoria has always stressed its relative advantage of easy accessibility (a 1980s campaign was labelled *The Best is Within Your Reach*), but, unlike Sydney, Melbourne and Victoria lack attractions that enjoy icon status.

To a considerable extent the success of tourist commissions is determined by their ability to work through the relevant stakeholders, including governmental organisations at various levels, and to be commercially strategic and responsive (states are administrative conveniences and tourists are fundamentally not interested in political boundaries). Through the 1990s Tourism Victoria gained a reputation as having achieved its key objectives and for having found and maintained an appropriate balance between securing both private sector support and credibility within government circles.

KEY STRENGTHS

Riley believes that there are two aspects to the issue of competitive strengths, namely Tourism Victoria itself and the extensive range of Victorian tourism product. As regards the former, he sees Tourism Victoria as a significant asset in the state's efforts to position itself in the national and international market place. This is so, he believes, because the organisation is customer-driven, has a stable senior management team, has strong partnerships with the industry and the travel trade, and offers industry leadership. Riley also considers the strengths of the destination to be many, referring to the list provided in the Tourism Victoria *Strategic Business Plan 1997–2001*. In this document these strengths are stated as:

- the appeal of Melbourne as a city;
- the high level of commitment to tourism from the government of Victoria;
- the widely recognised and acknowledged jigsaw branding;
- diverse and quality products under the catchline *You'll love every piece of Victoria*;
- the high level of professionalism achieved because of the commitment by government to industry accreditation and quality assurance;
- wide-ranging boutique products which appeal to frequent travellers; and
- major events.

SERVICE QUALITY

Destination marketing organisations such as Tourism Victoria are constrained in their ability to influence service quality. Relatively few Tourism Victoria staff deal directly with tourists, their primary role being to work through the tourism industry to pursue their objectives. Nevertheless, Riley argues that Tourism Victoria is committed to building a high quality product, and that ensuring the availability of quality service in Victoria is critical.

The pursuit of service quality has an internal dimension (looking after your own staff and ensuring that they display the appropriate attitudes) and another that is achieved by exerting influence (introducing measures that will stimulate the provision of quality service). As regards the latter, Tourism Victoria has worked with the Tourism Accreditation Board of Victoria (TABV) to develop an industry accreditation scheme (see later discussion). This has been a key initiative of the industry development division of Tourism Victoria and is related to the overall marketing effort in that it will influence the quality of the product. In terms of internal quality control efforts, Riley points to the fact that a staff professional development and training strategy is in place, with all staff having a work plan that is linked to performance assessment. Staff are also required to undergo regular training and professional development.

As previously noted, Tourism Victoria cites professionalism as one of its seven key strengths. John Kennedy, previously Chairman of Tourism Victoria, announced that participation in cooperative marketing campaigns would only be open to organisations that have achieved an appropriate level of accreditation under the 'Better Business Programme' developed by the Tourism Accreditation Board of Victoria in conjunction with various industry organisations such as the Victorian Tourism Operators Association (VTOA). The accreditation requirement is being phased in over a three-year period. Victoria has been a leader in the field of operator accreditation and the move is now gaining momentum in other states and territories. Again a political element is unavoidable since certain operators may be uncomfortable about a process that is ostensibly voluntary but involves external judgements about which businesses provide a high quality product and those that do not.

CUSTOMER LOYALTY

Destination marketing organisations do not generally operate customer loyalty schemes, and Tourism Victoria is no exception. Gaining an understanding of what prompts visitors to return is, however, a key preoccupation for Tourism Victoria. Some international markets such as New Zealand consist predominantly of repeat business (over 90 per cent). Others are a mixture, with, for example, Singapore having slightly over 60 per cent repeat business factor and Japan (10 per cent). Assessments are also undertaken of the contribution made by visitor types to a destination. The level of repeat visitation is one factor in such assessments, along with volume, length of stay, expenditure, dispersal and seasonality.

To generate loyalty amongst its industry partners, Tourism Victoria offers discounted rates for participation in cooperative marketing activities to organisations that are members of their local tourism association. Participation in the tourism awards is also predicated on evidence of such membership. Since a key role for Tourism Victoria is to act as a catalyst, it is appropriate to provide an incentive to collaborate, particularly to industry partners.

PRICING

Destination marketing organisations rarely involve themselves in the determination of price, except where they operate their own tour wholesaling and retail function. Whilst this is the case with Tourism Tasmania's *Temptations* and Tourism Queensland's *Sunlover Holidays*, it is not the case with Tourism Victoria. The latter has chosen to rely on third parties to undertake the retailing and wholesaling functions. Tourism Victoria does, however, espouse a philosophy of 'value adding' rather than of discounting, and attempts to avoid competition based exclusively on discounting. An example of a campaign developed by

Tourism Victoria (in conjunction with the Australian Hotels Association–Victorian Branch) with a focus on 'value adding' is the *Melbourne's Great Indoors* campaign (see Figure 9.2). The campaign is aimed at encouraging travel to Melbourne during the off-peak winter months when hotel occupancy levels are traditionally low. The campaign offers consumers a $100 credit for use at participating hotels and retail outlets. This campaign was acknowledged by the industry when it received the National Tourism Industry Award for a marketing campaign in 2000. This approach is a way of minimising a proliferation of discount offers by suppliers, which may prove counter-productive for the destination as a whole. Like many destinations, Victoria wishes to position itself as a 'quality' product, and a climate of widespread discounting is inconsistent with such an approach.

Figure 9.2: Melbourne's Great Indoors

THE BEST OF MELBOURNE BOTH INDOORS AND OUT. WITH $100 CREDIT OFFER AT PARTICIPATING HOTELS AND DAIMARU.

www.visitvictoria.com/mgi

The World on a Plate

Dine at any of Melbourne's world class restaurants and you'll be pleased to discover outstanding cuisine, fine wines and a radiant atmosphere. Enjoy cosy intimacy for the perfect romantic evening, or gather with friends at a lively bistro for a night of tasty food, tempting wines and lots of laughs.

By day, the humble cafe is the heart and soul of Melbourne, a warm respite from winter. Through the door you will encounter a maelstrom of cappuccinos, lattes, muffins, mochas, and pastries. Kick your feet up and read a magazine, sip a latte with a blackberry muffin chaser or socialise with other cafe-loving souls. After all, this is the cool season.

Life After Hours

Whatever the occasion, whatever the style, Melburnians love putting on a show!

Winter is prime time for entertainment in Melbourne – catch a hit play or musical at one of Melbourne's classic gold-era theatres, or the more modern Victorian Arts Centre.

On any night, step into a Melbourne bar, order your first wine or cocktail, and take a look around. With a quality bar on nearly every street, lane and alleyway in town, the city delivers in a big way!

If your evening doesn't begin until midnight, Melbourne has a plethora of raging late-night clubs oozing with attitude.

Shop in Style

You name it, we've got it, and it's better here than anywhere else! The best of the world is on sale in Melbourne - there's an enormous pride in providing the finest fashions, the coolest accessories and the most unbelievable range of stores in the southern hemisphere.

A world of good buys awaits - a little exploring will be well-rewarded. You'll find everything you need and beyond right in the heart of the city, with major department stores and several mega-malls offering excellent service, competitive prices and a huge range of merchandise all under the one roof!

But don't stop there ... the markets and malls hide millions of great deals, and a jaunt out to some of Melbourne's villages like South Yarra and Richmond will yield a world of fashion, accessories and other desirables of every description!

Indulge yourself a little ... spoil yourself a lot!

continued

Figure 9.2: Melbourne's Great Indoors (cont.)

Melbourne Storm

In only two seasons, Melbourne Storm has become the biggest phenomenon in the National Rugby League. Combining the fierce on-field clashes with glamourous sideline entertainment, a Storm game is much more than just a sports event. Catch all the action as the defending premiers battle tough opposition from interstate during their charge to the finals series.
Address: Olympic Park, Swan Street, Richmond
Tel: Ticketek 132 849
Website: www.melbournestorm.com.au

Southgate Arts & Leisure Precinct

The river. The atmosphere. The passing parade. Southgate is leisure at its best. Whether its catching up with friends for a drink or a quick bite at one of Southgate's 20 restaurants, cafes or bars, or meandering amongst Southgate's 39 unique retailers, Southgate is the ultimate in dining, shopping and relaxing. Open daily.
Address: Southgate Arts & Leisure Precinct, Southbank
Tel: (03) 9699 4311
Website: www.southgate-melbourne.com.au

Melbourne Aquarium

Journey into subspace and be ready for anything as you step into Melbourne's amazing new aquarium. Dive into four levels of coral atolls, mangrove swamps, billabongs, and rock pools. Step through a transparent tunnel surrounded by fish and drop right off the deep end into the 2.2 million litre oceanarium. Splash into the simulator ride, the ultimate underwater experience. Open daily.
Address: Cnr Queenswharf Road & King Street, Melbourne
Tel: (03) 9923 5999
Website: www.melbourneaquarium.com.au

Daimaru

Daimaru is Australia's only international department store. With six levels of fashion, homewares, cosmetics, food, sporting goods and audio visual. The choice is yours from international brands that are unique to Daimaru and also the very best of Australian made. Open daily.
Address: 211 LaTrobe Street, Melbourne
Tel: (03) 9660 6666

Crown – A World of Entertainment

The world class Crown Entertainment Complex features a host of entertainment options, including Crown Casino, five-star Crown Towers hotel, some of the world's most prestigious luxury brand retailers, and a plethora of signature restaurants, bars, snack kiosks and cafes. Experiences range from international fine dining through to casual riverside cafes. Crown also offers nightclubs, cinemas, virtual reality interactive games and a huge range of activities. Open daily.
Address: 8 Whiteman Street, Southbank
Tel: (03) 9292 8888
Website: www.crownltd.com.au

The Sound of Music

After a record breaking season in Sydney, the beautiful new Broadway production of The Sound of Music is now playing at The Princess Theatre. The acclaimed cast includes today's hottest television star and multiple Gold Logie winner, Lisa McCune, film and stage star John Waters, television legend Bert Newton, international opera star Eilene Hannan, multi-award winning actress June Salter and Crazy For You star Anne Wood.
Date: From 21 March 2000
Address: The Princess Theatre
Tel: Ticketek 132 849
Website: www.ticketek.com.au

49th Melbourne International Film Festival

An annual showcase of the widest possible range of outstanding filmmaking from around the world, the 2000 Melbourne International Film Festival celebrates the finest achievements in film in all its forms. Over 18 days the Festival screens nearly 300 films presenting the latest developments in Australian and international film, plus a chance to meet the filmmakers.
Dates: 19 July – 6 August
Tel: (03) 9662 3722
Website: www.melbournefilmfestival.com.au

Source: Tourism Victoria, 2000.

PROMOTIONAL STRATEGY AND BUDGETS

Riley observes that organisations often associate promotion with advertising when in reality advertising is only a single element of the multi-faceted promotional mix. The emphasis at Tourism Victoria has been to place advertising in 'the correct context', namely as a single element within the overall promotional mix that is fully integrated with the other components. He says that in 1999 the 'visiting journalists program' involved an outlay of approximately $400 000 by Tourism Victoria, with the tourism industry contributing an estimated $300 000 in cash and kind. According to Riley, the program generated media exposure worth an estimated $300 million. This figure is based on a rule of thumb applied by Tourism Victoria, whereby a page of editorial comment is judged to be as valuable as three pages of above-the-line advertising. Readers and potential customers appear all too aware of the tendency of advertising to be biased in favour of the sponsor and regard editorial material or independent comment as more credible.

The selection of promotional medium depends on the intention of the campaign. Television, the most costly medium, is generally best suited to awareness raising. The exception is where Tourism Victoria provides the 'shell' of an advertisement and this then incorporates a message including a specific price offer from a particular supplier such as an airline. The challenge of converting awareness into actual purchase is generally undertaken in the daily press and in specified magazines. Riley observes that, overall, there has been a shift away from the use of mass media towards more targeted approaches.

Of its expenses of just over $45 million reported in the 1999 annual report, slightly in excess of $16 million was spent on advertising and promotion. A further $17 million was spent on grants, which included promotional activity such as the $1.9 million for the Regional Tourism Cooperative Marketing program and $1.85 million for the Melbourne Convention and Visitors Bureau.

Consumers have become increasingly demanding in their expectations of how destinations are promoted, including standards of presentation. Consistent with such pressures, Tourism Victoria has sub-contracted various activities to specialists viewed as capable of providing a high quality of service. For example, since 1993 Tourism Victoria has worked with the advertising agency Mojo Partners. This relationship has involved the provision of strategic advice by the agency as well as the more traditional roles assigned to advertising agencies such as the purchase of media space and provision of creative services. In the case of the production of printed and other materials, there is a short-list of seven graphic designers who may be engaged. This use of designers is a major shift of emphasis from the earlier period when Tourism Victoria operated its own production facility. As is the case in the private sector, a key challenge involves determining which services should be contracted out and which should be provided in-house. Balancing the provision of a service and minimising cost is a major challenge.

SERVICE STANDARDS AND APPLICATION OF TECHNOLOGY

Tourism Victoria has expressed its ambition to be the Australian leader in electronic distribution for the tourism sector with a view to bringing the industry online. In 1999, backed by state government funds of $7.4 million over two years, a number of partners were recruited to realise the vision. It is notable that the speed of development did not allow Tourism Victoria to develop the expertise in-house, hence its reliance on outside parties. Partners during the preliminary phase included AAA Travel (content) and Bookright and WorldRes (e-commerce and booking partners).

One of the objectives of the Victoria-On-Line initiatives was to assist business, and particular smaller enterprises outside Melbourne, to accelerate their e-commerce and internet-based distribution capacity. At the time of writing there was a desire by Tourism Victoria to accelerate the take-up rate amongst the small business sector. This challenge is common to destination marketing organisations worldwide, but has been encountered relatively early by Tourism Victoria because of the decision to take an active and interventionist approach to online distribution. Equivalent organisations elsewhere will be observing Tourism Victoria's pioneering activities in this area with great interest.

Tourism Victoria has embraced the opportunities provided by the internet, but Riley is convinced that digital transmission through methods such as WAP technology is the way of the future. Using this medium, tourists will be able to identify and access the smallest and most dispersed establishments such as bed and breakfasts by mobile phone when travelling around regional Victoria.

Riley describes Tourism Victoria's greatest assets as its own staff's knowledge base leading to solid partnerships and the provision of valued advice. To this end all staff position descriptions require candidates to be familiar with online delivery.

SUMMARY

Australia's various state and territory tourist commissions have an interesting marketing dynamic because they combine public sector management structures with the freedom to act more commonly associated with the private sector. Tourism Victoria has placed particular emphasis on the pursuit of partnerships with the tourism industry and this approach has informed much of its marketing activity. The focus on destination markets, rather than with the marketing of a single product creates particular challenges and opportunities. It places particular emphasis on the need for consultation and to keep all relevant parties informed about every stage of the marketing process. This means that communication is critical, particularly if misunderstandings are to be avoided. So far, it appears as if Tourism Victoria has managed to retain the strong support of its industry partners and thus deliver benefits to the government and people of Victoria. It has aggressively pursued an increase in market share in both the domestic and international market. In doing so it has given a strong emphasis to marketing research as an element of strategic planning. Research has also underpinned the emphasis on brand development (through the 'Jigsaw' campaign) and on adversity and marketing segmentation. It is this highly integrated approach to marketing which has helped Tourism Victoria establish its credentials as the leading state-based tourism commission in Australia.

Primary period covered by case study: 1998/2000

REFERENCES

Department of State Development Victoria. 1998, *1997/98 Annual Report*.

Faulkner, W. 1993, 'The Strategic Marketing Myth in Australian Tourism', pp. 27–35 in P. Hooper (ed.), Building a Research Base in Tourism, Proceedings of the National Conference on Tourism Research, Sydney, Bureau of Tourism Research.

Government of Victoria. 1992, *Tourism Victoria Act*, no. 9834, 1996 reprint (consolidated for all amendments up to and including Act no. 31 of 1994).

Tourism Victoria. 1997, *Strategic Business Plan 1997–2001. Building Partnerships*.

Tourism Victoria. 1999, *Annual Report 1998–1999*.

Tourism Victoria. 2000, Melbourne's Great Indoors (Brochure).

QUESTIONS

1   To what extent has marketing research played a role in the marketing decision-making process of Tourism Victoria?

2   Relative to businesses within the private sector, what limitations are experienced by Tourism Victoria in connection with its marketing activities/actions?

3   a) What overseas markets does Tourism Victoria believe to be most appealing in light of the geographic and product attributes of the destination?
    b) On what basis have these markets been selected?

4   Briefly describe To   ination branding.

5   What would you co

6   To what extent wc   ocused organisation?

7   To what extent is ar   control or influence over all

8   Briefly describe the   gths.

9   a) What inherent di   rts to maintain the qual
    b) How has Tourism

10 Why does Tourism Vi   mpo-nent of its business p

10. SYDNEY MONORAIL

INTRODUCTION

This case provides an exemplary example of a formalised approach to marketing planning. In doing so it highlights the significance of research in shaping marketing decisions, the strong linkage that should exist between markets and service offerings, selected approaches to quality control that are available to mid-sized tourism firms, and the relationship between promotional and distribution efforts and identified target markets. It also emphasises the importance of the link between human resource management and strategic marketing planning.

BACKGROUND

The Sydney Monorail (SM) is the only privately owned transport business of its kind in Australia, and is the only monorail system in the world to operate through the centre of a major city linking it with a nearby entertainment/ shopping precinct (see Figure 10.1). SM began operations in 1988 as Harbourlink, and was originally built and operated as a division of the multinational firm, TNT Ltd. In August 1998 Connex, a multinational transport company headquartered in France, purchased the Monorail from TNT Ltd. After operating the Monorail for several years Connex sold it to Metro Transport Sydney, an Australian company. Rather than operate the transport system itself, Metro Transport Sydney early in 2001 awarded Connex the operating contract for the Monorail, which it continues to hold.

Note: Most of the marketing practices designed to ensure quality outcomes for passengers that are outlined in this case have continued into recent years under Connex's management. This is reflected in the Connex Passenger Charter for its light rail service that it also operates in Sydney—see Appendix 1. Nonetheless, the author of this case has chosen to base it around the earlier period of 1997/99 for two reasons: First, the highly integrated nature of the marketing process evident at this time; and secondly, ownership/ operating changes that have made it problematic to explore the marketing process after this time.

Figure 10.1: Sydney Monorail route map

Darling Harbour's award-winning Monorail gives you a bird's-eye view of Sydney and easy access to all attractions of Darling Harbour, including Powerhouse and Maritime Museums, Chinese Gardens and Imax. With seven stations and a service every 3-5 mins the Monorail is the easiest way to travel around the City of Sydney.

The perfect way to see all the attractions and more is the Monorail Supervoucher. The Supervoucher, available from any of the Monorail stations, allows unlimited travel on the Monorail for one day, as well as providing discount admission to either the Powerhouse or Maritime Museums, VIP shopping offers and special savings on food and parking.

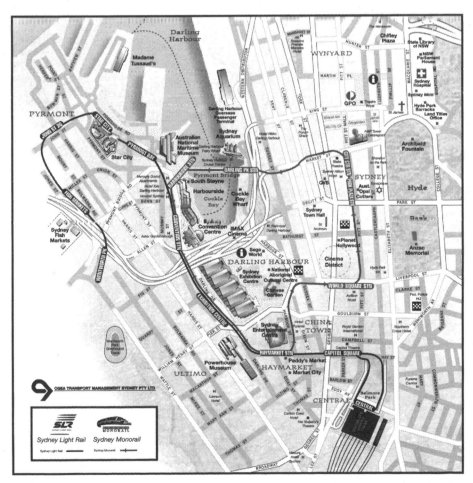

Source: Connex, 2000a.

MARKETING PLANNING PROCESS

The marketing plan for SM is based on a calendar year and is developed with the company's three-year business plan firmly in mind. The results of regular market research and an environmental audit provide the foundation for strategic marketing decisions that the plan is designed to action. The general areas covered by the marketing plan conform to a traditional marketing planning model and involve:

* environmental audit (encompassing outcomes from market research);
* target markets;
* marketing objectives;
* overall marketing strategy;
* product, pricing, promotion and distribution strategies and tactics; and
* feedback/review.

Responsibility for developing the plan lies with the marketing department under the leadership of the marketing manager. Development of the plan occurs over a period of three weeks, although data central to its compilation is collected on an ongoing basis. Once the marketing plan is in place, regular quarterly reviews monitor progress towards established marketing objectives. These objectives relate to: the level of utilisation of monorail services; the sale of added value products at monorail stations (e.g. service packages combining attraction entry with monorail transport); further development of products for specific target markets (e.g. meeting, incentive, convention and exhibition, and tourist markets); and revenue and service quality.

RESEARCH

Research plays a vital role in providing information upon which sound marketing planning decisions can be made. In recognition of this, SM has instituted a research program that is primarily directed at two main groups: monorail users and employees. Additionally, research is conducted with non-users to establish what (if any) 'barriers' may exist to their use of the transport service. The primary research tools used by SM are described below.

Annual consumer survey and focus groups

The consultancy firm Price Waterhouse conducts a detailed annual survey of Monorail users. Additionally, three times a year focus groups are conducted with staff, monorail users and non-users in order to gain deeper insights into specific issues covered in the annual survey. Matters explored by these research activities include:

- perceptions regarding value for money;
- cleanliness and comfort of the Monorail and its stations;
- friendliness and helpfulness of staff;
- facilities such as the entry system and token vending machines;
- perceptions of the quality of information provided by staff; and
- adequacy of printed material available at stations.

Results from this research are used to identify areas where further refinements can be made and to track overall performance on a continuing basis (see Table 10.1). Action plans are developed to deal with identified problems.

Table 10.1: Annual customer survey results 1995, 1996 and 1997

Classification	1995	1996	1997
Staff are polite	88%	98%	94%
Staff handle problems well	74%	94%	93%
Staff are helpful	83%	97%	97%
Stations are clean	90%	95%	92%

Source: Price Waterhouse, 1998.

Shadow shopping

A research firm is employed to conduct shadow shopping exercises throughout the year. This form of research involves employees of the contracted research firm acting as customers in order to assess the level of service currently being offered by staff. Matters examined by this means include:

- reception/approach by staff member (e.g. were they friendly? was eye contact made?);
- knowledge of SM's services and the Sydney area in general;
- general appearance of monorail stations and front line staff; and
- closing comments from staff members to customers.

The results of these interactions between staff and 'customers' are summarised and given to the deputy general manager, who then meets personally with staff members whose performance is judged as being below the standard set by the company. These meetings are used not as a form of punishment but as a means of developing a formal action plan to improve future performance. It is also note-worthy that employees who are deemed to have performed well in shadow shopping interchanges are rewarded in the form of points. Points are additionally awarded for such matters as on-time arrival at work, low levels of absenteeism and effective handling of money (e.g. daily balancing). Points are accumulated over one year and can lead to an end of year bonus.

Information gained from shadow shopping is also used to categorise employees with similar needs for training purposes. Group sessions are then conducted to improve those areas where weaknesses have been detected.

'Enjoy your ride?' cards

'Enjoy your ride?' cards (see Figure 10.2) are placed in bright orange display units in highly visible locations at monorail stations. These cards provide customers with the opportunity to describe their impressions of the service they have received as well as other matters (e.g. cleanliness of stations). These cards also seek information on the demographic characteristics of customers. Data from these cards is analysed regularly and used to identify both trends in user markets (e.g. the emergence of new market segments and changes in market mix) and problems in the service delivery process. Additionally, customer contact details (if supplied) are kept for direct marketing purposes, and to contact the individuals concerned for possible future involvement in customer focus groups.

OVERALL MARKETING STRATEGY

The Sydney Monorail once viewed itself essentially as a means of transport between the city and the Darling Harbour precinct. Over time, however, it came to realise that such a view was constraining its capacity to respond to challenges (e.g. new competitors in the form of ferries and water taxis) and opportunities (e.g. growth in inbound tourism) within the business environment in which it operated. In recognition of this, the guiding strategy pursued by Sydney Monorail moved to one of seeking to position itself as a quality tourist attraction that was integral to the Sydney experience, as well as being a modern form of transport linking the Darling Harbour precinct to Sydney's CBD. The two-part nature of this positioning strategy reflects the two core markets served by the Monorail: tourists/visitors to the area and commuters. This strategy also points to the desire of SM to move beyond being perceived simply as a means of transport, to one of being a 'must do' tourist attraction in its own right. As will be shown later in the case study, this strategy is clearly expressed in SM's marketing mix decisions.

MAJOR MARKETS

SM's choice of strategy is designed to best achieve its objectives in the context of its chosen markets. From the markets detailed below, you will note that some effort has been given to clearly identifying viable segments that had the potential to be developed through the creation of specific services. In order of market share in 1999, these were as follows.

Figure 10.2: 'Enjoy your ride?' card

TELL US WHAT **YOU** THINK·

Help us ensure you always enjoy your Monorail ride.
Our aim is to satisfy our customers but we need your help.

Please complete this card and return to us by mail (postage is free) or place it in
one of the boxes provided on the stations.

STATION(S) USED _____

TIME VISITED _____ AM / PM   DATE _____

STAFF NAME(S) _____

Please tick the box below that best describes your impressions & experience.

	Excellent	Good	Fair	Poor
Staff	☐	☐	☐	☐
Service	☐	☐	☐	☐
Cleanliness	☐	☐	☐	☐
Comfort	☐	☐	☐	☐
Value For Money	☐	☐	☐	☐
Overall Experience	☐	☐	☐	☐

Will you ride again?   Yes ☐   No ☐

Please make any comments and suggestions:

_____
_____
_____

Your Name: _____ Phone No: _____

Thank You

SASS 1110TNT

Source: Connex, 2000a.

Tourist market (51 per cent, i.e. 21 per cent international and 30 per cent domestic)

The tourist market is SM's largest market segment. Tourists are seen as a 'natural' market due to the transport linkage provided by the monorail between major tourist precincts in Sydney, specifically Chinatown, Darling Harbour, the Spanish Quarter and Sydney City. Additionally, the monorail experience can be seen as unique in that it offers scenic vistas of Sydney, and of Sydney life, as well as having a degree of novelty value, all of which provide a basis for the desired strategic position sought by SM in the context of this market.

Leisure market (21 per cent)

The leisure market is made up of a number of sub-groups including those looking for shopping and entertainment opportunities, local joyriders looking for a fun/exciting ride, casino patrons, and the local family market.

This market is essentially local in nature, with demand from most of the sub-groups noted here being dependent upon the capacity of the Darling Harbour precinct, or adjacent areas, being able to constantly create reasons for repeat visitation. Events, such as festivals, are integral to this process.

Commuter market (18 per cent)

This market is broken into two sub-markets: casual commuters (8 per cent) who use the monorail less than twice per week and regular commuters (10 per cent) who use it at least three times per week. The location of a number of parking stations on the monorail route accounts for the significance of this segment. Additionally, the growth in high density housing in the area has also added to the significance of this market.

Meetings, incentive, convention and exhibition market (9 per cent)

This market is made up of those attending meetings (7 per cent), participating in incentive programs (0.5 per cent) and charters (1.5 per cent). This market has become increasingly significant as the number of hotels/venues has grown within Darling Harbour, and along the monorail route, and reflects the need that events, such as conferences, have to transport large groups between city locations. Occasionally this involves hiring a whole train or a number of carriages. It is interesting to note that this market was not one that received specific attention until the early 1990s.

Education and seniors market (1 per cent)

The smallest of the target market groups, these segments comprise school-aged children on educational trips, as well as senior citizens involved in organised tours of the Darling Harbour area. This latter group holds some potential for future growth due to the changing demographic profile of the Australian community.

MARKETING MIX
Product

Sydney Monorail offers a range of products, from basic transportation to service packages combining monorail travel with entry into tourist attractions, car parking, and cruises of Sydney Harbour. These products have been developed with the needs of one or more of the target markets noted previously in mind. These products include:

* *Superticket*—a combined ticket that offers all Monorail transfers, entrance into Sydney Aquarium and the Chinese Gardens, a lunch or dinner cruise on Sydney Harbour on Maltilda Cruises and discounted shopping at Darling Harbour;
* *Day and family passes*—discounted day-use tickets;
* *SEE School Packages*—a package for school groups that includes a Captain Cook Cruise, entrance to Sydney Aquarium and Sydney Tower and all Monorail transfers;
* *Sydney Convention Pass*—a product designed for conference delegates that can be included in conference packages, allowing unlimited Monorail travel for one or more days;
* *Monorail and Matilda Cruises combined ticket*—a ticket that allows Monorail passengers to continue their journey from Darling Harbour to Circular Quay by boat;
* *Ride passes*—stored-value multiple-use cards that offer a discount on 'bulk' purchases of Monorail rides. The minimum number of rides that can be bought in this way is eight;
* *Sydney for Seniors*—a combined ticket that includes morning tea on a Captain Cook cruise, entrance to the Sydney Aquarium and the Powerhouse Museum, lunch at the Ken Done cafe and complimentary monorail transfers;
* *Park and Ride*—a combined ticket allowing parking at participating parking stations in Darling Harbour, and monorail travel to and from the station;
* *Monorail supervoucher*—a day pass containing a variety of discounted vouchers for attractions and other service providers in Darling Harbour (see Figure 10.3) noteworthy in that it was created after extensive research revealed that the common profile of a visitor to Darling Harbour was one of a person who visited one major attraction, used car parking, engaged in some type of shopping and spent money on food and drink.

Other products offered by SM include individual train charters (Champagne Charters), theme nights that involve the hiring of the entire monorail system, or a specific station, for use in the staging of special events. Additionally, SM has partnered with the Novotel and Ibis hotel chains, incorporating monorail services into some of their accommodation packages. It is also noteworthy that SM has the capacity to act quickly to tailor products to meet the needs of particular customers. For example, passes are developed on demand for inbound operators that combine monorail travel with entrance to Darling Harbour attractions.

Figure 10.3: Supervoucher day pass

Source: Connex, 2000b.

Another aspect of note regarding the Monorail product is that people with disabilities have been specifically catered for, with lifts or specially designed 'garavanta' chairs, that provide access to platforms.

Given the nature of the SM product, it can be observed that it is heavily reliant on the capacity of the entertainment/leisure precinct (Darling Harbour) in which it is located to stimulate visitation to the area. To this end the many events held in Darling Harbour, along with the attractions and facilities located there (e.g. IMAX Theatre, Sydney Aquarium, and extensive shopping and dining opportunities) are central to the Monorail's success. Additionally it is these facilities and attractions that provide opportunities for the creation of the service packages marketed by SM.

Product quality and human resource management

Significant effort is given by SM to staff recruitment and selection. All jobs have detailed personal specifications that clearly identify the skills, knowledge, qualifications and personal characteristics necessary to perform the various jobs within the organisation. For example, preference is given to applicants for front line positions at monorail stations if they possess a second language. This policy has resulted in some 25 per cent of staff in these positions having this desired ability. Additionally, a variety of practices have been instituted in order to ensure staff are able to perform their roles to the best of their abilities, to reward and acknowledge them for doing so, and to correct behaviour that is not conducive to the achievement of organisational objectives. These practices and procedures, detailed below, collectively act to ensure a high level of service quality.

Operations work committees

These committees, comprising volunteer front line staff, meet monthly to discuss ways in which the day-to-day operations of the organisation can be improved.

Staff publications

A staff magazine has been introduced (*In the Customers' Shoes*) that provides feedback to staff about customer comments, as well as tips from each manager, on a rotational basis, about how to improve on customer service. The staff newsletter, *The Link*, provides information on new initiatives undertaken by management, updates staff on new products offered by the attractions in Darling Harbour, and overviews any new developments in the precinct.

Staff incentive scheme

The purpose of this scheme is to assist in focusing employees on achieving objectives outlined in the company's business and marketing plans. Specifically this scheme focuses on rewarding employees who:

* achieve sales objectives on monorail stations;
* exceed customer service benchmarks; and
* maintain a sound record of punctuality and work attendance.

The best performing employees are rewarded with an invitation to attend the Sydney Monorail's Overseas Customer Service Conference, while the next 12 best performing staff members are rewarded with an invitation to attend the Sydney Monorail Customer Service Conference in Australia. It is noteworthy that SM has won two Australasian Incentive Association Awards for 'Best Application of a Trade Incentive' as well as the prestigious Society of Incentive and Travel Executives Crystal Award for 'Best Program — Asia Pacific'.

Staff training

All front line staff undertake a structured customer service training program, and **all** staff take part in a one-day customer service training course. Additionally, a 'buddy' system operates for all new employees whereby they are assigned to an experienced staff member for a period of two weeks, after which time they are assessed and, if deemed acceptable, allowed to work independently. Study leave and financial supports are provided to staff undertaking further study outside the organisation.

Complaints handling system

Written and phoned-in complaints are immediately actioned by the relevant manager, following the procedures outlined in the *Quality Manual* (an internal publication that sets out procedures and practices designed to maintain customer service standards). Customers unhappy with the level of service received are encouraged to return through the issuance of complementary passes. In the rare instances of breakdowns, or technical difficulties, proactive measures are taken to acknowledge the inconvenience to customers. In the past these have included the issuance of a written apology to customers, the provision of coffee and pastries at monorail stations, and management staff acting to greet customers at stations in order to apologise for any inconvenience caused.

Collectively, these, and other measures, resulted in a more than 10 per cent increase in customer service ratings over the period 1996 to 1997.

Quality accreditation

The Sydney Monorail is quality accredited to AS/NZS/ISO 9002 standards and operates to a series of procedures and practices (often embodied in checklists) outlined in the *Quality Manual* mentioned previously.

Pricing strategy

SM needs to maintain a high volume of sales as the profit on each ticket is small. In 1998 the difference between the fare charged and the average fare needed to break even was only 22 cents. This low per unit profit margin greatly reduces the capacity of SM to pay commissions and engage in discounting. One outcome of this situation is that SM has sought to develop a range of higher value products that involve 'packages' of services combining monorail services with, for example, entry to attractions, accommodation and harbour cruises. Other products, involving extended use of monorail transport e.g. day, family and convention passes, also reflect this need to increase the profit generated from each individual sale.

In establishing ticket prices SM is aware of the different levels of price sensitivity that exist between market segments. For example, the family sub-market was identified as being particularly sensitive to price, and so a product (the family pass) was created that offered significantly more value for money than existing products.

There is also evidence of SM using price as a market development tool. In New Zealand, for example, discount vouchers (10 per cent) on day passes were distributed to tour wholesalers as a means by which they could add value to their own offering. The result of this, and other activities directed at this market, was a 3 per cent increase in monorail usage by New Zealanders over the period 1996/97.

Promotional strategy

A significant part of SM's marketing plan deals with its promotional strategy. This strategy employs a number of cooperative and stand-alone promotional activities directed at specific trade and consumer markets. These activities, as would be expected, vary by market segment, as the following discussion makes clear.

Tourist market

The primary promotional tools used to communicate with tourism industry intermediaries packaging services for, or selling/providing information directly to, tourists are attendance at domestic and overseas trade shows such as the Australian Tourism Exchange, overseas sales missions, and involvement in product workshops for hotel concierges.

In addition to using trade intermediaries to access this market, the Sydney Monorail undertakes stand-alone advertising in publications such as *Sydney Tourist Guide*, *What's on in Sydney?*, *FAC Airport Guide*, *This Week in Sydney* and *Sydney Transport Map*. Cooperative advertising, largely with suppliers involved in monorail packages, also takes place in various publications including *Harbour Connection*, *Travel Australia* and the general brochure produced for Darling Harbour.

In order to assist in tracking the effectiveness of publications targeting tourist markets, SM participates in the *Tourism Publications Study*, which is conducted by NV Marketing Pty Ltd.

Leisure market

Advertising is the primary means by which communication with this market is achieved. Specifically, press advertisements are placed in regional newspapers and the *Sydney Morning Herald*. Additionally, cooperative advertisements are run with both the Darling Harbour Authority (now Sydney Harbour Foreshore Authority) and attractions within Darling Harbour.

Commuter market

'On-site' promotional material (i.e. posters and promotional leaflets) placed within particular parking stations and monorail stations are the major means used to promote monorail services to this market. This material was developed cooperatively with Wilson's and Secure parking stations in Darling Harbour, and was designed largely to stimulate demand for a combined 'Park and Ride' ticket.

Meetings, incentives, convention and exhibition market

A range of promotional tools is used to access this market. Advertising is conducted in MICE industry publications including *CIM*, *Rostrum* and *Who's Who in the Meetings Industry*. Additionally, a number of trade shows specific to the MICE industry are attended, such as Sydney on Sale and Asia Pacific Meetings Expo. SM is also involved in almost every site inspection conducted by the Sydney Convention and Visitors Bureau for major international and domestic conferences for which Sydney is bidding. Familiarisations are also provided for meetings and incentive industry staff.

Education and seniors market

A range of service packages has been developed for these markets. Product suppliers, such as Captain Cook Cruises, who are involved in these packages, work with Sydney Monorail to create advertisements for placement in the publications *Sydney Seniors* and *Education News*. Occasionally promotions are run targeting this market. One such effort involved providing a substantial discount on Sydney Aquarium entrance to day pass holders during a school holiday period.

Other promotional activities employed by SM include:

*   production of a brochure (over 450 000 are distributed annually locally, interstate and overseas);
*   production of a free Sydney Monorail 'rip-off' map that can be used by staff at monorail stations to provide customers with directions to attractions and shopping precincts on the monorail route;
*   occasional radio advertising in the Sydney market;
*   encouragement of other attractions and operators in Darling Harbour to use the Monorail for their promotions free of charge;
*   provision of advertising support for cooperative partners in the Darling Harbour area (e.g. the Novotel and the Powerhouse Museum) in the form of space at monorail stations for advertising and brochure display; and
*   making available the outside surface of a train for advertising purposes to the Sydney Harbour Foreshore Authority at no cost so that they may promote their various festivals and special events.

It is significant to note that SM endeavours to link promotional activities directly back to product sales. For example, sales stemming from attendance at trade shows are closely monitored, as are the results of sales promotional activities in periods such as school holidays.

Distribution strategy

SM sells its services to end consumers directly, and via a range of intermediaries. In the case of tourist and MICE market segments, a significant amount of business is transacted through intermediaries, most notably tour wholesalers, inbound tour operators, hotel tour desks, incentive houses and professional conference organisers.

In order to maintain and further develop its relationship with its distribution channel members, SM:

*   attends trade shows such as the Australian Tourism Exchange, the Travel Australia Business Show, and the Incentive Travel and Meetings Executive Show;

* attends annual industry conferences, specifically those conducted by the Australian Tourism Export Council, the Tourist Attraction Association, the Australasian Incentive Association, and the Meetings Industry Association of Australia;

* undertakes sales missions to tour wholesalers in New Zealand; and

* maintains memberships of a number of industry bodies, specifically the Australian Tourism Export Council, the Sydney Convention and Visitors Bureau, Australian Incentive Marketing Association and the Tourist Attractions Association.

In terms of electronic distribution channels, information on the Monorail is available directly from SM's own web site, as well as other web sites including the Australian Tourist Commission (to become part of Tourism Australia at the end of 2004) and the Darling Harbour Authority (now the Sydney Harbour Foreshore Authority). These web sites are designed for end-consumers. There is little likelihood that the internet will be used to sell SM services, due to the small unit cost involved.

CONTROL AND FEEDBACK SYSTEMS

The major control systems employed by SM have already been noted. These include: regular scheduled meetings to examine progress towards marketing objectives and to identify modifications that need to be made to elements of the plan; formal assessments of front line staff performance; the collection of customer feedback on service delivery; and the creation and use of a *Quality Control Manual* that acts to set out company-wide practices and procedures for ensuring product quality.

Information germane to marketing planning is collected throughout the 12-month period of the plan. This information is made use of throughout the year in order to bring aspects of the plan's application in line with changing internal or external circumstances. At the end of the period covered by the plan, this information is again used as the foundation for the next planning cycle.

SUMMARY

Various approaches to the marketing planning process can be found in operation within the tourism industry. Few firms, however, are as formal and systematic in their approach as the operators of the Sydney Monorail. The outcomes of such an approach are clear from the overview provided here. First, the discipline inherent in SM's approach to marketing planning generates strong linkages between overall marketing strategy, product development and design, pricing, promotion and distribution. Secondly, the value of market research in identifying target markets, monitoring service delivery standards and in identifying changes within markets, or the emergence of new markets, is clearly evident here. Thirdly, the link between human resource management practices and product quality has been acknowledged by SM, resulting in the adoption of various practices and procedures. Last, the need to build into marketing planning control processes, and to 'pour' information gleaned from one planning cycle into the 'top' of the next is something that SM understands as being central to successful marketing practice.

Primary period covered by case study: 1997/99

REFERENCES

Connex 2000a, Sydney Monorail Route Map.

Connex 2000b, Supervoucher Day Pass.

Price Waterhouse. 1998, *Monorail User Study* (internal document).

Sydney Monorail Quality Control Manual (undated).

QUESTIONS

1   If given the task of marketing planning for SM, what elements of the current approach would you wish to keep and what modifications/additions would you consider making?

2   Discuss the relationship between the products SM has developed and its target markets. Try to link specific products to specific markets. (Consider using a table for this purpose.)

3   What cooperative marketing activities are noted in this case study? Why does SM engage in such activities?

4   What incentives exist for customer service staff to perform at a high level within SM? Can you suggest any other means of motivating SM staff than those they are using?

5   a) Describe, and then discuss, the link between SM's human resource management practices and its concern to maintain high levels of service quality.
     b) While the Passenger Charter provided in Appendix 1 relates to Connex's light rail system in Sydney, it can fairly be assumed they deal with their monorail customers in a similar way. Based on this Charter, how is Connex acting to measure and maintain service quality/standards ?

6   What marketing challenges and opportunities does SM's location within an entertainment/leisure/shopping precinct create?

7   What systems does SM have in place to monitor its performance regarding its stated marketing objectives? Would you suggest any changes in this area?

8   What has SM's response been to the low per unit profit that it is able to generate?

9 What role does the internet play in SM's marketing activities? Is SM right in concluding that the internet offers limited scope as a vehicle for selling its products?

10 Select one of SM's target markets and suggest additional means to those presently used to communicate with this segment.

APPENDIX 1
CONNEX PASSENGER CHARTER

1. TIME

Your transport network should provide you with a punctual journey, minimising your waiting, connection & transport time:

* Connex is committed to punctuality by ensuring that a minimum of 95% of departures are within −1 and +3 minutes of that set out in the published timetables except in circumstances beyond our control.

* Connex is committed to reliability by ensuring a minimum of 98% service delivery is achieved except in circumstances beyond our control.

2. SAFETY

Your transport network should provide you with the best possible levels of safety and security:

* Connex is committed to providing a safe and secure environment for our passengers. We provide 24 hour CCTV monitoring of all stops and two way voice communication from stops to our Operations Control Centre.

3. EASE OF ACCESS

Your transport network should be practical and easy for you to use. Connex is committed to ensuring an open access network, by providing:

* 100% disability access through low floor vehicles and open access stops.
* Customer Service Staff to assist you with your ticket purchase and local information.
* Continuous improvement of directional signage within local and statutory boundaries.

4. INFORMATION

Your transport network should keep you well informed at all times:

* Connex is committed to ensuring information is up to date and easy to read.
* And available at stops, on-board and remotely, prior to travel, via the internet.

5. LISTENING

Your transport network should have a respectful relationship with you:

* Connex is committed to listening to you with consideration, to respond to all correspondence within two working days.
* Connex is also committed to ensuring a resolution within five working days.
* Connex registers all complaint & feedback information in accordance with the Privacy Act, and makes this information available to you.
* Connex insures all customer service staff are assessed via a Mystery Shopper program four times annually.
* Connex is committed to monitoring customer satisfaction by asking you how you feel about our service at least once annually.

6. COMFORT

Your transport network should make your journey as comfortable and as pleasant as possible:

* Connex is committed to developing a friendly atmosphere with guaranteed daily cleaning of interior and a regular general cleaning of both interior and exterior of its trams.

7. TRAINING OF PERSONNEL

Your transport network should ensure that it develops its staff to give you the best possible service:

* We will ensure that each Connex employee is assessed monthly on all aspects of their role including customer service, appearance standards, following procedures and professional conduct.
* We will ensure that each employee participates in training programs at least annually to ensure that we provide a friendly and professional service at all times.

8. VALUE FOR MONEY

Your transport network should provide you with the best possible value for money:

* Connex is committed to ensuring that clear information explaining how to choose the best ticket for you is widely communicated.

9. CONTRIBUTION TO THE LOCAL ECONOMY

Your transport network should contribute to the regional economy:

* Connex is committed to supporting the local economy through our recruitment policies. In addition, Connex actively supports local business through partnerships and sponsorships.

10. RESPECT FOR THE ENVIRONMENT

Your transport network should be environmentally conscious:

* Connex is committed to the protection of the local environment through waste recycling initiatives and use of emission free vehicles.
* Connex is committed to preservation of the local environment through landscaping initiatives that are consistent with the native flora and fauna.
* Connex is committed to responding to all noise complaints with appropriate action in a timely manner.

Source: <www.metromonorail.com.au>.

11. INTREPID TRAVEL

INTRODUCTION

This case study demonstrates the means by which Intrepid Travel has identified and targeted a market segment whose members align with the responsible travel ethos of the organisation. Intrepid Travel offers innovative and high quality travel products that promote social and cultural awareness of the Asian region. These products are often tailored to individual needs. The company works actively with the tourism industry to reduce the adverse impacts of travel on small local communities, by undertaking research to understand these effects, and developing a code of practice for tour operators. It has also developed strategic relationships with community and charitable organisations whose constituents align with the values espoused by Intrepid Travel. A percentage of the revenue from bookings made by members of these organisations is passed back to the relevant organisation.

BACKGROUND

An enthusiasm for travel to the remote regions of South-East Asia prompted the foundation of Intrepid Travel Pty Ltd in 1989. The personal travel philosophies of founders, Geoff Manchester and Darrell Wade, set the foundation for the types and styles of travel product for which Intrepid Travel has become known. Today, Intrepid Travel is a highly successful adventure tour operator.

From its beginnings as a micro-business with Manchester and Wade leading all the tours, the organisation has grown to a multi-million dollar business. Its gross sales now exceed $35 million per annum and it employs approximately 200 staff—50 staff in its Melbourne head office, four in its London branch office, two in Los Angeles and more than 140 group tour leaders throughout Asia. Management of Intrepid considers the company to be a leader in the field of adventure travel, and claims, with considerable authority, to be 'the' specialist small group adventure tour company to Asia, with more than 2000 departures a year, and over 100 different itineraries.

Intrepid aims to become 'the internationally recognised benchmark in socially aware adventure travel, by supplying innovative and high quality travel products which promote social and cultural awareness of the Asian region'

(Warrell Consulting 1999). Intrepid's commitment to ethical travel earned it a High Commendation in the 2002 British Airlines Tourism for Tomorrow Awards. These awards recognise the leading sustainable tourism products and projects in the world.

MARKETING PLANNING PROCESS

Intrepid's first marketing plan was prepared in 1999. Prior to this, marketing planning was limited to bringing together the company's product managers, operations staff, and sales staff once a year to develop a distinctly-positioned, competitively-priced product for the following year. These yearly meetings were used to establish sales targets in the various source markets. They were known as the 'Product Weekend' and also performed the function of a staff retreat. Decisions made at this event were subsequently acted upon, and incorporated into new brochures for distribution throughout Intrepid's travel agency network both in Australia and overseas. This decision-making approach was in large part based upon an intuitive understanding of the market, as opposed to a detailed analysis of market trends. This sense of the market developed largely through the very close links that Intrepid's owners and staff maintained with their customers and distribution channel members. Due to its small size, Intrepid is also able to respond quickly to changes in any of its markets, allowing it to exploit opportunities for growth as they arose.

As Intrepid grew in terms of overall sales and tour departures (Table 11.1), the effectiveness of its informal approach to marketing planning became more questionable. The company's significant growth had resulted in large fixed overheads, which had to be covered, and more formal procedures were required so that it could ensure coverage of these costs. In 1999 Intrepid's management decided to adopt a more structured approach to marketing and employed the services of a marketing consultant to write a comprehensive five-year marketing plan with a specific 12-month action plan. The key objective of the plan was to maintain an annual revenue growth rate of 30 per cent. Although the marketing planning process did not involve any direct interaction with consumers, it did involve detailed discussions and debates amongst Intrepid's staff. One major consequence of such discussions was the sense of ownership they engendered in the final marketing strategy and associated plan.

The marketing plan listed a number of critical success factors for Intrepid's continued success. They included:

* maintenance and further development of strong and supportive relationships with large travel agency groups and international general sales agents (GSAs);

Table 11.1: Sales and departures—1989/2002

Year	Net Sales (AUD Million)	Growth %	No. Itineraries	No. Departures	No. Countries	Countries added to portfolio	Countries dropped from portfolio
89/90	0.15	–	2	–	1	Thailand	
90/91	0.46	211	4	–	2	Malaysia	
91/92	0.81	77	8	–	3	Indonesia	
92/93	1.1	36	9	–	3	–	
93/94	2.1	92	20	–	5	Vietnam & Laos	
94/95	3.9	83	26	357	5	–	
95/96	4.8	23	33	500	6	Burma	
96/97	7.4	57	38	608	8	China & Cambodia	
97/98	9.2	24	58	832	9	The Philippines	
98/99	12.2	32	76	1063	10	Japan	
99/00	16.8	38	97	1220	11	Tibet & India	Burma
00/01	27.0	61	119	2052	11	Nepal	
01/02	28.1	4	159	2260	15	Sri Lanka, Mongolia & Central Asia	
02/03			117	2230	16	Egypt, East Timor,	Philippines

Source: Intrepid Travel, 2002.

* a differentiated product range high in quality;

* a staff with extensive product knowledge;

* high levels of customer service; and

* further development of the Intrepid brand name so that it became synonymous in the market place with quality, reliability and exceptional value for money.

The plan also identified the key selling points of Intrepid's products as being: 'no frill service'; providing access to 'off the beaten track' locations; its western tour leaders; the high number of trip types and departures to Asia which are more than any of its competitors; its guaranteed departure policy; the overall value for money offered by its tours; and its responsible travel ethos.

Intrepid's more formal approach to marketing planning also required it to be more proactive in identifying and exploiting market opportunities, and in protecting itself against potential threats to its business. Additionally, the plan called for the introduction of key performance indicators (KPIs), which were subsequently introduced, focusing on areas such as sales, yield and customer service levels. Monitoring of KPIs is now a major function of Intrepid's marketing staff. The success of this more formalised marketing planning process was confirmed at its first major 12-month review when it was determined that established sales and revenue objectives set out in the plan had been met, and in many cases, exceeded.

EXTERNAL FACTORS IMPACTING UPON MARKETING DECISIONS

Intrepid operates tours to a range of developing countries, many of which are quite remote. It also draws a growing percentage of its business from countries other than Australia. Thus, there is a wide range of external factors with the potential to impact upon Intrepid's marketing decisions.

Many of Intrepid's destinations experience some form of political instability. This can impact upon tourist demand for some products, making it difficult for Intrepid to plan long-term. In order to deal with this environmental issue, Intrepid continually diversifies its product portfolio to reduce the risk of problems within particular countries.

Intrepid's experience of running tours in Burma is a good example of how political issues can impact upon its business. When Intrepid became concerned about the suitability of travelling in Burma, it engaged informed commentators to make presentations about the situation to the company. Following these presentations, the owners and staff decided that operating tours in Burma may be misinterpreted by others as indicating support for the Burmese government's violation of human rights. As a result of these discussions, the company decided to discontinue tours to that country.

Rapidly changing consumer preferences make it increasingly difficult to ensure that Intrepid's product range remains in line with consumer desires and associated market place trends. To date, however, Intrepid has benefited from many of these trends, including: an increasing propensity to travel overseas; a growing desire for an adventure dimension to be incorporated within the holiday experience; an enhanced concern and awareness regarding the environment; and a growing tendency for consumers to seek out well-recognised brand names to reduce the risks associated with travel to 'exotic' locations. One noteworthy recent example of how Intrepid has had to respond to changing market place preferences resulted from the September 11 terrorist attacks. Intrepid found itself after this time needing to quickly expand the number of tours to its core tour destinations of Indochina, China and Thailand, and decrease its tour frequencies to India and Indonesia.

Other environmental matters of concern to Intrepid are changes in technology, particularly in the area of distribution, increasing competition (see later discussion), and fluctuating exchange rates. The latter is a particularly significant issue given that many of the contracts Intrepid has with its suppliers are written in American dollars.

COMPETITORS

The major competition to Intrepid's business is independent backpacking. This type of travel is usually facilitated by guidebooks, such as the *Lonely Planet* series. Such companies offer a complementary product to Intrepid in one sense, but may also be regarded as competitors since their travel publications encourage and facilitate travel by individuals to destinations that are packaged by Intrepid, rather than them purchasing one of the company's tours. As westerners become more familiar with destinations in Asia, it is likely that tourists travelling alone and using travel information from guidebooks to inform their travels will increase in comparison with those travelling on organised tours.

Intrepid's major direct competitor in Australia is Peregrine Adventures through their 'Geckoes' range. Peregrine also runs tours to a number of other regions of the world, but its turnover is similar to that of Intrepid. Currently, Peregrine carries less than 30 per cent of the number of tourists to Asia than are carried by Intrepid, but it is known as an aggressive marketer that is actively seeking to increase its market share.

Intrepid's main competitor internationally is the UK-based Explore Worldwide. Explore takes approximately 6000 people to South-East Asia each year, about four times as many as Intrepid carries from the United Kingdom. Compared with Intrepid, Explore tends to be more conservative, operating with larger group sizes and offering more highly structured tours. Intrepid's two other large international competitors are Travel Bag Adventures and Imaginative Traveller. As well as these direct competitors, Intrepid also has a range of indirect competitors. They include Qantas Holidays, Creative Holidays, Asia Explorer and Venture Holidays, all of which provide package holidays to destinations that are included in Intrepid's products.

MAJOR MARKETS

In 2001, the geographic origin of Intrepid's customers was fairly evenly split between Australia and the rest of the world (refer to Table 11.2 below). Approximately 46 per cent of Intrepid's clients originated from Australia, including a good mix of clients from every state in Australia, with the exception of Western Australia, which is under-represented. The remaining 54 per cent of travellers originated from a number of overseas destinations. Key international source markets in descending order of passengers were the United Kingdom, New Zealand, the United States, Canada and Japan. The 'other' category comprised largely Scandinavian and Western European countries.

Table 11.2: Country of origin of travellers (by percentage)—1993/2001

Year	Australia	UK	NZ	USA	Canada	Japan	Other
93/94	44	26	12	4	4	–	10
94/95	45	23	13	4	7	–	8
95/96	46	22	11	4	5	–	12
96/97	46	25	9	4	4	–	12
97/98	50	21	7	5	3	–	14
98/99	50	18	7	6	4	–	15
99/00	52	20	5	7	4	4	9
00/01	46	22	6	10	4	3	9
01/02	48	22	5	8	5	2	9

Source: Intrepid Travel, 2002.

Since 1998, the Japanese and United States markets have generated very substantial growth for Intrepid. Passenger numbers from the United States have doubled and passenger numbers out of Japan have started to make a significant positive impact on Intrepid's business. Although Intrepid has two agents based in Japan, it is finding that its growth is largely a result of word-of-mouth recommendations from existing clients. The Japanese are well-known for their love of travel photography, and showing these photos to their friends and family when they return home provides an incentive for others to take Intrepid trips. In effect, this acts as a personalised version of the regular promotional slide nights hosted by Intrepid (see later discussion).

Future growth for Intrepid is expected to come largely from the international market, and it is anticipated that the key source countries identified previously will continue to be its largest markets.

A demographic analysis of Intrepid's customers reveals a number of key segments. The majority of Intrepid's customers enjoy reasonably high salaries, are aged 25-45 years, and are mostly singles or couples without children. The older segment of the market is, however, important to Intrepid given that there is an ageing population in most of its source markets. Evidence suggests that, increasingly, older people are choosing to incorporate an adventure element into their overseas holidays. Older travellers also have a higher per capita spend as well as a strong interest in meeting local people, and are thus well-suited to Intrepid's product. It is noteworthy that it was the needs of this market that, in part, resulted in Intrepid introducing its Intrepid Premium product, which offers a higher level of comfort, as well as higher quality tour ingredients.

About 60 per cent of Intrepid's clients are female. Women are more likely to choose to travel in a group for added security, and tend to be more comfortable in meeting local people than are men. In addition, they are more inclined than men to go on tours that have an educational element, and are thus ideal prospects for Intrepid's tours.

Although Intrepid has focused on the package tourist to date, it has also acknowledged the significance of the FIT (fully independent traveller) market, with its Intrepid Independent product. This product allows customers to travel as individuals/couples rather than in groups.

MARKET RESEARCH

Overall, relatively little marketing research has been conducted by Intrepid to date. Though Intrepid has a substantial database containing demographic details of those who have requested brochures and those who have purchased tour products from it, limited analysis of this database has been conducted. An exploratory study using this database in 1997 found that it comprised largely young people without children, who were earning medium to high average incomes. One of the problems with this database is that there is limited opportunity to assess the level of conversion from enquiry to booking. This problem arises because the majority of Intrepid's clients book their trips through an intermediary rather than directly through it.

In 1999, a small-scale study was conducted to provide information about the travel behaviour of those listed on the database, and to assess the prospects for future purchase of adventure travel packages from Intrepid. It also sought to understand how consumers sourced their travel information. Nearly 1500 questionnaires were sent to a randomly selected sample from the database of which some 34 per cent were returned. This study found that the main reasons for choosing an adventure holiday experience were:

* cultural experiences;
* a combination of relaxation and risk-free activities;
* educational experiences;
* challenging/adventurous experiences; and
* travel with like-minded people.

In terms of what in particular would cause those surveyed to choose an Intrepid holiday, the study found the following to be central in such a decision:

* trip itinerary;
* value for money;
* responsible practices; and
* company reputation.

The survey also revealed that over 95 per cent of respondents who had been on an Intrepid tour rated their satisfaction level as high or very high. The key reasons for not taking a tour with Intrepid were found to be the preference for independent travel, lack of time and lack of finances.

Another means by which Intrepid gathers information on its services is via web-based client feedback that participants are asked to complete at the end of each tour. This research tool is designed to assess the level of satisfaction with the tour and the tour leader. Feedback sheets are also given to agents after each booking is made to assess their perspective on their dealings with Intrepid (see Appendix 3, page 156). General sales agent (GSA) satisfaction with Intrepid's service is also monitored. This is done primarily at the World Travelmart event and involves a questionnaire.

MARKETING MIX

Product

Intrepid has a diverse small group adventure product range with over 100 itineraries covering 16 different countries. It classifies its tour range under six headings:

1　Intrepid Original
2　Roam Basic

3   Intrepid Premium
4   Exploratory Adventures
5   Oxfam Journeys
6   Intrepid Independent.

Tours within these six categories vary considerably in terms of the quality of inclusions, itinerary flexibility, and travel styles and activities, thus allowing Intrepid to meet the needs of a wide variety of travellers, including independent travellers. As regards this category of traveller, it was noted earlier that Intrepid has the capacity to tailor individual itineraries around special interests (e.g. food or history) or specific types of holidays, like beach breaks. Another noteworthy aspect of the tours offered by Intrepid is the link with the secular charity Oxfam CAA. Through this linkage, a series of tours has been developed that allow participants to experience first hand the work of this organisation, and other non-government organisations (NGOs) in Asia. A percentage of the price paid by each tour participant on these tours goes to assist Oxfam's charitable activities.

Intrepid also aims to include at least one feature in each of its trips that cannot be readily accomplished by individual travellers. For example, in the case of Sabah, Borneo, Intrepid clients are housed in a Dusun village, and are invited to a private home for dinner and a night of friendship, culture and ancestral legends. This experience is made possible by the relationship that Intrepid has developed with the village community. In Langmusi, Western China, Intrepid's local guide takes groups to the Tibetan village in which he grew up. Once there, he takes them to visit the school he established for the local village children, and tour members have the opportunity to join in the class and sing and play games with the children.

Other features of note as regards Intrepid's product include its policy of guaranteed departures, itinerary flexibility (to varying degrees depending on the tour type), and respect for local communities, their culture and environment (see later discussion and Appendix 1, page 154).

Service quality

Service quality has been identified as a key factor for the ongoing development of Intrepid. The human resources manager is responsible for ensuring that new staff have a strong customer service focus. In the recent past, staff selection was relatively ad hoc, although there was always an emphasis on recruiting employees who would fit in with the ethical approach adopted by the company. Structured training programs have now been introduced to further enhance the customer orientation of staff, as well as developing their customer service skills.

As indicated previously, Intrepid's clients are encouraged to provide feedback. The resulting data provide an overall assessment of customer satisfaction, though much of the data relates to the specific performance of the relevant tour leader. Such an emphasis is understandable given the importance of these individuals to overall customer perceptions as regards service quality. Intrepid, in acknowledgement of this, conducts tour leader training in Melbourne prior to sending these staff members to their destinations, as well as providing additional training once they have arrived. An example of the latter is its in-country training courses that are conducted at the beginning of each tour season in China and India. These courses ensure that all tour leaders undertake a 'refresher' program incorporating aspects of running successful trips.

Branding

Brand awareness of Intrepid within the travel industry is adequate, however Intrepid acknowledges that its level of consumer awareness is not high. Wade believes that this is a significant issue, especially with the increasing propensity for customers to bypass intermediaries and go directly to the operator. In overseas markets, in an effort to strengthen its market branding efforts, Intrepid is now insisting that its name and logo be used more consistently. In the Australian context, Intrepid is using, amongst other things, lift-out supplements in leading Australian newspapers, such as the *Age* and the *Sydney Morning Herald*, to build its brand image.

Customer loyalty

Customer loyalty programs are considered to be important tools for increasing brand loyalty, and have been widely adopted within the tourism industry (see, for example, Imrie and Fyall 2000; McCarville 2000). Such programs work best in organisations characterised by regular repeat purchases. This has led to their ready adoption by airlines and hotels. Intrepid has assessed the costs and benefits of applying this type of model to increase brand loyalty but believes that, since its products tend to be purchased infrequently, the costs associated with implementing such a program could not be justified. Nonetheless, Intrepid acknowledges the significance of repeat purchases, with a recent analysis of its existing client base showing that some 19 per cent of its customers had made more than one trip with the company. In order to try to stimulate repeat business, Intrepid has developed an electronic newsletter that is released in five editions weekly, targeting the markets of Australia, the United Kingdom, North America, New Zealand and Rest of the World. This successful publication covers a range of topics including anecdotes, recipes, and background information on destinations, and can be subscribed to via Intrepid's web site <www.intrepidtravel.com.au>. It currently has more than 45 000 subscribers.

Pricing

Intrepid's pricing strategy is designed to reinforce its desired market position as the best value product of its type. Prices are determined using a margin over cost approach, coupled with prevailing market conditions. In recent years, Intrepid has introduced a yield management plan designed to optimise its returns from its various tour categories. Its policy of guaranteeing most of its departures at the time bookings are made, however, puts considerable strain on its efforts in this area. As a result of this, a significant aspect of Intrepid's yield management strategy involves identifying non-performing tours and increasing promotional efforts associated with them in an effort to increase yield. In some cases, tour modification or cancellation (on tours where departures are not guaranteed below an established minimum) are options.

Intrepid has found that the Asian adventure travel market is not highly sensitive to minor price rises, and this has provided it with some degree of flexibility in its dealings with suppliers.

Promotion

Until recently, Intrepid's promotional efforts centred on the production and distribution of its annual brochure. While still an important component of its marketing communication efforts, a survey undertaken by Intrepid in July 2001 caused it to rethink where its promotional focus should lie. This survey found that 53 per cent of its customers chose to travel with Intrepid after receiving advice from a travel agent, 25 per cent were influenced by friends and relatives, and 11 per cent by advertising. In response to these findings, Intrepid has placed greater emphasis on developing strategic relationships with retail travel agents, providing them with brochures, supporting materials and web-based information to support their selling efforts. Intrepid also holds slide show nights (10 to 15 nights per month) in Australian regional and metropolitan areas, as well as in New Zealand. Commonly, but not always, these events are conducted in association with retail travel agents. Familiarisations are also provided for key retailers. Given the key role played by travel retailers, it is not surprising that Intrepid seeks feedback from them on a regular basis (see Appendix 3, page 156).

Intrepid has shifted most of its advertising spend away from single advertisements to lift-out supplements in the *Age* and the *Sydney Morning Herald*. These supplements have strong 'calls to action' that require readers to contact Intrepid, and the response has been sufficiently encouraging to prompt Intrepid to continue with them. Intrepid also makes considerable use of its database, as noted previously, emailing a weekly online newsletter.

Intrepid has found that its web site is quickly emerging as its most important promotional tool. The number of 'hits' is growing rapidly and four full-time staff now work on upgrading it, ensuring Intrepid's web presence is of a high standard and that its site is effectively linked to other appropriate sites. The web site provides background information on Intrepid's travel philosophy, details its tours along with their availability, permits brochures to be downloaded or ordered, and provides online versions of traditional slide shows as well as allowing bookings to be made for upcoming slide shows in a potential customer's home area. The site also allows visitors to register for the weekly electronic newsletter, and for past clients and potential clients to engage in dialogue and to ask questions of Intrepid staff. As a way of both driving visitors to its site, and increasing direct bookings, Intrepid has created tours that can only be accessed and booked online. Always conscious of the value of market research, Intrepid has included an online client feedback questionnaire (see Appendix 4, page 157) on its web site, with discounts on future Intrepid trips being the incentive for potential clients to complete the questionnaire.

Intrepid has made significant use of public relations in its efforts to establish its market position. In this regard, Intrepid has developed strategic alliances with international organisations such as the World Wide Fund for Nature (WWF-TRAFFIC), Amnesty International Australia, Medecins Sans Frontieres (MSF), CHILDWISE—End Child Prostitution in Asia (ECPAT) in Australia, the Fred Hollows Foundation, and Oxfam Community Aid Abroad. Intrepid has also developed a partnership with Australian Volunteers International and some tours visit their volunteer placement partners in Asia. Additionally, Intrepid is a business supporter of many other NGOs including TreeProject (in Victoria), KEEP—Kathmandu Environmental Education Project, Saigon Children's Charity, KOTO (Hanoi) and may other NGOs based in Asia. These partnerships were further supported in 2002 through the establishment of the Intrepid Foundation—a charitable trust established in conjunction with CAF (Charities Aid Foundation) Australia (see Appendix 2, page 155).

Albeit based on rather limited research, Intrepid's decision to link with/ support such NGOs and charitable organisations lies with its belief that its customer base aligns with the segments of society who support such bodies. The forms these linkages take vary, and include direct contributions, inclusion of information and links on the Intrepid web site and in brochures, inclusion of activities of selected organisations within tours, and logo use in brochures/ web site.

Distribution channels

Product distribution is a critical factor for the survival of tour companies. Intrepid, by analysing its sales data, determined that a small number of retail agents/agency groups accounted for the majority of its sales. This being the case, rather than waste resources on agents that do not or cannot generate substantial business, it decided to concentrate on 'performing' agents, introducing a 'preferred' agents scheme. Such agents are rewarded by being paid a higher level of commission, providing they meet specified sales targets. Not only were individual agents classified in this way, but so were selected agency chains, specifically STA and Flight Centres.

Intrepid has also moved in recent times to make its web site more 'agent friendly', providing information on a range of product-related matters, as well as more general information on destinations, visas, and booking conditions. In developing such additional web site features, Intrepid drew on research it had conducted concerning the computer competency of agents.

Intrepid has its own sales team to service the needs of the travel trade. The team works very closely with agents, running regular training sessions, providing familiarisations, operating co-branded tours (with agency chains), and entering into special promotional deals. Recently, rather than having state-based sales representatives, account managers have been appointed to look after the larger agency chains that span a number of states. Offshore, Intrepid is represented by some 50 general sales agents (GSAs), as well as a branch office in London that services the European and United Kingdom travel industry more effectively, and an office in Los Angeles that services North America.

In 1997, Intrepid established its own retail arm known as Intrepid Direct, which sells its product in competition with retail agents. In the face of a backlash from travel agents, Intrepid has not promoted this part of its business as aggressively as would otherwise have been the case. Nonetheless, Intrepid believes that progressively this arm will account for an increasing proportion of sales as more customers use the internet to go directly to suppliers. Reflective of this is the increase in Intrepid Direct staff from one to five over the past two years, although it must be noted that the cost of maintaining a direct booking facility, is, according to Intrepid, relatively high at present compared with other booking methods.

RESPONSIBLE TRAVEL

Intrepid's responsible travel ethos, which espouses a commitment to a style of travel that is environmentally, culturally and socially responsible, is a fundamental part of its business philosophy (see Appendix 1, page 154), and has served it well in its efforts to differentiate itself from its competitors. Intrepid aims to offer tours that conserve the areas it visits and bring positive benefits to local communities. Intrepid's tour leaders play a key role in communicating such values to both its customers and the local communities in which it operates. Known as a 'grass roots travel' approach, an example of this style of travel is Intrepid's use of all forms of local public transport with a view to increasing local employment and decreasing demand for vehicles and fuel. This approach also mimimises pollution. Intrepid is also committed to 'putting back' into communities by supporting aid, development and conservation projects in the areas its tours visit. Formal activities to implement responsible travel policies at Intrepid were initiated six years ago, when its directors convened a group of staff with the purpose of ensuring that the company's activities were ethical and resulted in minimal degradation to the relevant destination communities. This group, known as the low impact group, has now been replaced by a full-time responsible travel coordinator who is supported by part-time responsible travel coordinators (RTCs) in each region in which Intrepid operates in Asia. These RTCs, who are employed primarily as travel guides, spend a week each month examining responsible tourism issues in their specific countries.

Intrepid has also become actively involved in working with the tourism industry to reduce the impacts that tour operators have on small communities in developing countries. In partnership with Victoria University, Intrepid has undertaken research to understand such impacts. The results of this work will help to reduce any adverse outcomes to communities flowing from the conducting of tours by Intrepid, and will assist in the creation of a code of practice for tour operators that will serve to influence other adventure travel operators conducting tours in village communities.

Intrepid's responsible travel activities are thought to be unique within the tourism industry, and Intrepid is now promoting them in its brochures and via its web site. This is being done to encourage other companies to adopt a similar approach, and as a means of attracting the increasing number of travellers who regard such activities as important influences on their travel decisions. However, Intrepid is mindful of the need to find the right balance in this area so that the responsible travel activities are not simply seen as gimmicks to stimulate sales of its tours.

SUMMARY

Manchester and Wade have developed a successful business, in terms of financial achievement, business growth and international reputation. This has been created by basing the company on their passion for, and ethical approach to, travel within Asia. Sound financial management has underpinned this passion. Intrepid's management style has been consumer-focused and flexible. By getting close to, and understanding the needs of its customers, it has identified and targeted a market niche that has demonstrated considerable and consistent levels of growth.

As Intrepid continues to grow, employing more people and accumulating higher fixed costs, it will need to place greater emphasis on formalised planning and market research. Such systems will help Intrepid to identify market opportunities and threats in a more proactive and systematic manner. This will become increasingly important as the company finds itself having less flexibility as it grows and subsequently a reduced capacity to respond quickly to changes in market conditions.

The increasing familiarisation of western consumers with Asia as a travel destination has been influenced by the activities of companies such as Intrepid.

The insights, understanding and confidence that travellers gain with Intrepid tours are likely to result in the adoption of a FIT approach to travel in Asia in the future. The challenge for Intrepid is to continue to develop its product range to cater for the emerging needs of these types of travellers, as well as to focus on new market opportunities.

Primary period covered by case study: 2001/02

REFERENCES

Imrie, R. & Fyall, A. 2000, 'Customer retention and loyalty in the independent mid-market hotel sector: a United Kingdom perspective', *Journal of Hospitality & Leisure Marketing*, (7) no. 3, 39–54.

Intrepid Travel 2002, Internal Management Report.

McCarville, R. 2000, 'Satisfaction—the basis of client loyalty', *Parks & Recreation*, (35) no. 11, 24–23.

Warrell Consulting. 1999, *Intrepid Travel—Strategic Marketing Plan*. <www.intrepidtravel. com.au>

QUESTIONS

1   In moving to a more formal marketing planning process, there is the risk that Intrepid Travel will become less able to respond to short-term opportunities in the market. Discuss the advantages and disadvantages of this change and identify strategies that Intrepid Travel can adopt to ensure that it maximises its ability to respond quickly to market opportunities.

2   Responsible travel appeals to a growing segment of the market and offers great potential for Intrepid Travel. How can the company promote its leadership in offering responsible travel packages without making it seem like a sales gimmick?

3   Intrepid Travel is seen as a specialist in low-impact tours to Asia whilst some of its major competitors offer tours to other regions as well as Asia. Given that Asia has been affected greatly in recent years by events such as SARS, discuss the merits of Intrepid Travel including a broader range of destinations in its product mix to offset such problems.

4   Arguably, travel guidebooks present significant competition for a tour operator such as Intrepid. Discuss how Intrepid might seek to differentiate itself from the 'do it yourself' option represented by such publications.

5   The majority of Intrepid Travel products are sold through its agent network, although a growing percentage is now being sold directly to the consumer. With the increasing propensity for consumers to by-pass various stages in the traditional distribution chain, what strategies should Intrepid Travel implement in order to capitalise on this trend without alienating its existing agents?

6   It is clear that Intrepid Travel has not made substantial use of marketing research in the past. Discuss the actions that the company can take to ensure that it effectively monitors trends in its source markets in general, and in connection with its own customers in particular.

7   How does Intrepid Travel attempt to ensure the quality of its service offerings? Can you suggest any other means by which Intrepid Travel might go about maintaining/enhancing its service quality?

8   Identify key promotional activities undertaken by Intrepid Travel. Discuss the appropriateness of these activities to both its industrial and consumer markets.

9   What business value (if any) does Intrepid Travel's links with various NGOs and charitable organisations have?

10   Identify the key aspects of Intrepid Travel's product on which it seeks to differentiate itself from its main competitors (tour companies). Would you describe such aspects of Intrepid Travel's product as offering a strong basis for differentiation and market positioning?

APPENDIX 1:
INTREPID TRAVEL OPERATING PHILOSOPHY

Intrepid Travel's web site <www.intrepidtravel.com> provides the following information on its philosophy.

Responsible travel

Intrepid is committed to a style of travel that is environmentally, culturally and socially responsible—we call this 'Responsible Travel'. With your participation we aim to travel in a way that conserves the areas we visit and bring positive benefits to local communities.

Our travel style

- Grass roots travel using local public transport where possible—minimises demand for special tourist vehicles and fuel.
- We choose small-scale locally owned accommodation and homestays where available and local restaurants and markets for dining, retaining revenue in local communities.
- Our leaders facilitate communication of our values to travellers and local communities, educating them in sustainable tourism practices.
- We employ local guides to aid travellers' understanding of local culture and etiquette.
- Small groups allow travellers to experience cultures at first hand, offering greater opportunity for cross-cultural understanding.
- We are committed to putting back into the communities and regions we visit by supporting many aid, development and conservation projects in these areas.

APPENDIX 2:
INTREPID FOUNDATION

Intrepid Travel's web site <www.intrepidtravel.com> provides the following details on the Intrepid Foundation.

The Intrepid Foundation for Conservation and Communities

Travel can be such an enriching experience. Many people return from a holiday with all their photos and wonderful memories and think, 'If only there was some easy way I could contribute something back to the people and communities I've visited.'

To enable travellers to donate money to projects in Asia, we have created The Intrepid Foundation. The Foundation has been developed in conjunction with CAF Australia, a registered charity that aims to increase the flow of resources to charities and non-profit organisations. The purpose of the Foundation is for Intrepid and our travellers to readily contribute to worthy projects in Asia. The Intrepid Foundation Committee, made up of Intrepid Travel staff and travellers, decides grant recipients and contributions to this fund are disbursed annually. Administration costs will be entirely funded by Intrepid Travel and 100% of your donation will reach your nominated program or project.

You may contribute to any of the following programs:

TIF Endowment Fund

Donations are held in perpetuity and the interest earned will fund projects for many years to come, making your donation go further than its original value. Intrepid Travel will be donating substantially into this 'corpus' in the first few years.

Intrepid Partners Program

Donations to this program contribute to the work of non-government organisations working in Asia. The activities of these organisations collectively include: health care, education, human rights, child welfare, sustainable development, environmental and wildlife protection. Organisations we have supported in the past include: Amnesty International, Medecins Sans Frontieres, World Wide Fund for Nature—TRAFFIC, Plan, Child Wise (ECPAT) and The Fred Hollows Foundation.

Community Project Fund

For the grass-roots work of non-government organisations based in Asia, identified by Intrepid Travel as making a valuable contribution to the local community. These include many small organisations or projects that you may visit during your Intrepid trip e.g. KOTO in Hanoi, Project for the Blind in Tibet and the English teaching project in Kiau community, Borneo.

APPENDIX 3:
INTREPID TRAVEL AGENT FEEDBACK FORM

| -Asia & Middle East- | ▲▼ | | -Latin America & Antarotica- | ▲▼ | | | -Europe- | ▲▼ |

| ▸ trip information | ▸ trip styles | ▸ about us | ▸ industry | ▸ intrepid foundation |

welcome to intrepidtravel.com

express newsletter
subscribe here ▼
email address

subscribe

trip finder◯

[   ] GO

what is trip finder?

photo album

the trip for you!

specials

booking tuk tuk

what's a tuk tuk?

agent feedback form

Thank you for taking the time to complete the following feedback form.

details:

country in which you are based*:	Select ▲▼
your name*:	
agency*:	
passenger surname*:	
file number*:	
date booked:	
name of trip:	
trip style:	Select ▲▼
how would you rate the standard of service from Intrepid Travel?:	Exceptional ◯ 5 ◯ 4 ◯ 3 ◯ 2 ◯ 1 Poor
how would you rate the quality of information provided in response to any queries you had?:	Exceptional ◯ 5 ◯ 4 ◯ 3 ◯ 2 ◯ 1 Poor
did you feel that your queries were handled in a friendly, helpful and professional manner?:	Exceptional ◯ 5 ◯ 4 ◯ 3 ◯ 2 ◯ 1 Poor
did you advise your client to book an Intrepid Travel trip?:	◯ Yes ◯ No
if you recommended Intrepid Travel, can you tell us why:	please write details here
would you recommend your clients book with us again?:	◯ Yes ◯ No
if no, can you please tell us why:	please write details here
did you download your dossier and pre-trip information from our web site?:	◯ Yes ◯ No
how would you rate the standard of documentation and pre-trip information provided?:	Exceptional ◯ 5 ◯ 4 ◯ 3 ◯ 2 ◯ 1 Poor
can you make any suggestions as to how we can improve our documentation and pre-trip information?:	please write details here
are you aware of Intrepid Travel's responsible travel philosophy?:	◯ Yes ◯ No
is this philosophy important in your decision to recommend Intrepid Travel?:	Important ◯ 5 ◯ 4 ◯ 3 ◯ 2 ◯ 1 Unimportant
email address:	
check this box to subscribe to express	☐
	Intrepid Express is our online newsletter which offers you a chance to WIN a trip every week and keeps you up to date with news from the road, recipes, new trips and special offers. Intrepid do not sell, rent or pass on your name or details to third parties. Subscription to the express newsletter is permission based - you can unsubscribe at any time. Full details can be accessed at privacy.

Please note fields marked * are required

submit form   clear form

APPENDIX 4:
INTREPID TRAVEL TRAVELLER
FEEDBACK FORM

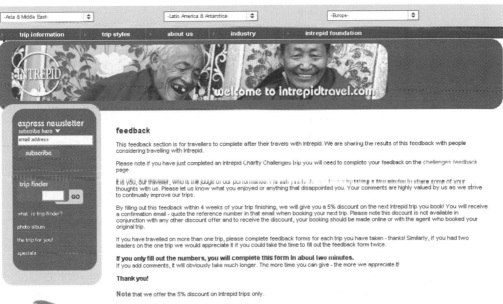

booking tuk tuk

what's a tuk tuk?

feedback

This feedback section is for travellers to complete after their travels with Intrepid. We are sharing the results of this feedback with people considering travelling with Intrepid.

Please note if you have just completed an Intrepid Charity Challenges trip you will need to complete your feedback on the challenges feedback page.

It is you, our traveller, who is the judge of our performance. We ask you to do this from by taking a few minutes to share some of your thoughts with us. Please let us know what you enjoyed or anything that disappointed you. Your comments are highly valued by us as we strive to continually improve our trips.

By filling out this feedback within 4 weeks of your trip finishing, we will give you a 5% discount on the next Intrepid trip you book! You will receive a confirmation email - quote the reference number in that email when booking your next trip. Please note this discount is not available in conjunction with any other discount offer and to receive the discount, your booking should be made online or with the agent who booked your original trip.

If you have travelled on more than one trip, please complete feedback forms for each trip you have taken - thanks! Similarly, if you had two leaders on the one trip we would appreciate it if you could take the time to fill out the feedback form twice.

If you only fill out the numbers, you will complete this form in about two minutes.
If you add comments, it will obviously take much longer. The more time you can give - the more we appreciate it!

Thank you!

Note that we offer the 5% discount on Intrepid trips only.

* these fields are required.	
Where did you travel?	Please select ⬍
	If other:
Your first name *	
Your surname *	
Your country *	Select country where you live... ⬍
Your leaders name *	
Your trip name eg: Angkor Adventure *	
Your trip code eg: KSV128	
Country you started your trip*	
Your trip departure date *	Day ⬍ Month ⬍ 2004 ⬍
Who was the agent you booked with? *	
Your email address *	
Check this box to subscribe to express	☐
Intrepid Express is our online newsletter which offers you a chance to WIN a trip every week and keeps you up to date with news from the road, recipes, new trips and special offers.	Intrepid do not sell, rent or pass on your name or details to third parties. Subscription to the express newsletter is permission based - you can unsubscribe at any time. Full details can be accessed at privacy.
Our travellers feedback is available to others thinking of travelling with Intrepid (we figure your advice is less biased - and therefore more appreciated than our own). Please write a comment here for posting to the web if you wish... (50 words or less).	
Rating of your overall experience	Please choose ⬍
Comments on your overall experience	
Rating of your itinerary	Please choose ⬍
Comments on the itinerary	
Rating of your leaders enthusiasm	Please choose ⬍
Rating of your leaders knowledge	Please choose ⬍

continued

Rating of your leaders organisation	Please choose ⇕
Rating of your leaders communication	Please choose ⇕
Rating of your leaders approachability	Please choose ⇕
Rating of your leader overall	Please choose ⇕
Comments about your leader	[text box]
Highlights of your trip	[text box]
Low points of your trip	[text box]
Rating of your accommodation	Please choose ⇕
Comments on your accommodation	[text box]
Rating of the included meals	Please choose ⇕
Comments on meals included	[text box]
Transport	Please choose ⇕
Comments on the transport	[text box]
Included Activities	Please choose ⇕
Comments on included activities	[text box]
Local Guides	Please choose ⇕
Comments on local guides	[text box]
How successful were we at providing you with opportunities to interact with locals and experience their way of life?	Please choose ⇕
Comments on providing you with opportunities to interact with locals and experience their way of life?	[text box]
How successfully are our philosophies on Responsible Travel implemented on this trip? (ie sensitivity/respect for local cultures and the environment)	Please choose ⇕
Comments on responsible travel	[text box]
How successful was your leader in explaining and demonstrating 'Responsible Travel' practices?	Please choose ⇕
Comments on leader responsible travel	[text box]

We are particularly concerned about the impacts of our trips to small remote villages, such as the hilltribe communities in Thailand and Vietnam. If as part of your trip you visited such a community could you please complete the following questions.

How would you rank your experience of staying in the village community?	Please choose ⇕
How would you describe the level of interaction you were able to have with local people?	Please choose ⇕
How would you rate your Intrepid leader's performance in providing you with information on the village, including what to expect and appropriate behavior and dress standards.	Please choose ⇕
Please add any comments you would like to make, including any changes you would suggest to improve the village stay.	[text box]
Agents knowledge of Intrepid	Please choose ⇕
Rating of agents level of service	Please choose ⇕
Did your trip match your expectations	Please choose ⇕
Did you get value for money?	Please choose ⇕
Comments on value for money	[text box]

Suggested improvements	

Why did you choose Intrepid?
- [ ] Small group size
- [ ] Itinerary
- [ ] Trip length
- [ ] Style
- [ ] Departure date
- [ ] Price
- [ ] Responsible Travel
- [ ] Guaranteed departures
- [ ] Local Leader
- [ ] Private Itinerary

Where did you hear about Intrepid?
- ○ Travel Agent
- ○ Friend/Relative
- ○ Advertising
- ○ Internet
- ○ Article

Would you travel with Intrepid again? [Please choose ⇕]

Would you recommend Intrepid? [Please choose ⇕]

What is your next destination? [_____]

What other style/type of trip would you like us to offer? [_____]

What is your country of origin? [_____]

What is your age? [_____]

What is your profession? [_____]

What is your income bracket (USD)? [Please choose ⇕]

How many trips have you done? [Please choose ⇕]

Did you receive a trip dossier? No ○ Yes ○

Rating of dossier [Please choose ⇕]

Did you receive the pre-departure information? No ○ Yes ○

Do you have any comments on your Travel Agent and/or pre-trip information?

[submit feedback] [clear form]

Intrepid Travel collects the information requested in this feedback form for the purposes of monitoring the quality of our trips, assessing our level of customer satisfaction and for the marketing of future trips. The information you provide is not used or distributed for any other purpose. If you choose not to complete parts or all of the form we are unable to complete the tasks listed above with the same accuracy.
You can access the information you have provided at any time by contacting the **Group Operations Manager** in our Melbourne Office.

12. MELBOURNE AQUARIUM

INTRODUCTION

The Melbourne Aquarium is a relatively new nature-based high technology attraction that opened in early 2000. Shortly after its opening, it experienced an outbreak of legionnaire's disease that affected over 100 people and caused two deaths. By necessity, management of the Aquarium spent much of the first year of the Aquarium's operation trying to counter the adverse publicity associated with this outbreak. Nonetheless, the Aquarium overcame this initial setback to go on to become one of Melbourne's major tourist attractions, winning the state's major tourism award for attractions.

This case study begins by providing a brief background to the Aquarium and its owners Oceanis Australia, before going on to discuss the feasibility study conducted prior to its establishment. The Aquarium's marketing system is then examined, including its use of marketing research, strategic marketing efforts, market segmentation approaches and marketing mix. Additionally, given the impact of the outbreak of legionnaire's disease on the Aquarium's initial marketing efforts, some time is devoted to exploring how it responded to this significant marketing challenge, and the lessons that flow from its response.

BACKGROUND

The Melbourne Aquarium was opened in January 2000 as a state-of-the-art, total entertainment facility showcasing the creatures of the Southern Ocean. Owned and operated by the Melbourne Underwater World Trust, the Aquarium belongs to Oceanis Australia, a privately-owned company that specialises in building, operating, designing and managing aquariums in the Asia-Pacific region.

Oceanis Australia's first venture into aquariums was the purchase of Underwater World, on Queensland's Sunshine Coast, in 1993. Following the success of this operation, Oceanis Australia opened the Chang Feng Ocean World in Shanghai, China in 1999. This was closely followed by the opening of the $33 million Melbourne Aquarium in early 2000. In late 2001 the company launched the Busan Aquarium in South Korea.

Oceanis Australia's operations are developed and managed in line with the following guidelines:

* *Aquariums as 'edutainment' complexes*—this is a modern concept for the operation of aquariums, and one that focuses on delivering conservation messages through high quality entertainment and education.

* *Employment of state-of-the-art technology and design*—the company has consciously moved away from offering fish museums to providing all-encompassing entertainment venues. The focus of these venues is on family, fun, fish and food.

* *Engagement of specialists*—the group employs a team of highly skilled staff in all areas of its operations to ensure the delivery of high quality visitor experiences.

The vision that its owners have for the Melbourne Aquarium is of an attraction that is:

> dedicated to the entertainment and education of its visitors in a manner which increases conservation awareness, and encourages actions which positively contribute to the improvement of the world's aquatic environment.

Following on from this vision, the Aquarium's mission is to be the number one tourist attraction in Melbourne, to leverage this position in order to educate and communicate a conservation message, and to obtain world's best practice standards in customer service and exhibition design. Such outcomes are sought by ensuring the organisation provides interactive, exciting, educational and entertaining visitor experiences that promote relevant subjects and issues in a financially sustainable way.

Oceanis Australia considered a number of sites in and around Melbourne prior to the final selection of the Aquarium site. The final choice is centrally located on the southern edge of Melbourne's central business district, and bordered by the Yarra River, Flinders Street and King Street. Close to many of Melbourne's premier tourist attractions, and within a half-kilometre of more than 2000 hotel rooms, the Aquarium is also easily accessed by public transport. Both Melbourne's major railway stations are situated within 500 metres of the Aquarium, and the free City Circle tram stops nearby.

Oceanis Australia has a 25-year lease on the site, which is owned by the Victorian Government, and is responsible to the Melbourne City Council for its management. Due to its riverside location, and proximity to existing infrastructure, development of an aquarium on the site posed a number of serious design, construction and operational challenges for the company. The final design is a unique and contemporary building consisting of four levels above and below water. Its shape and style are evocative of a sleek ocean liner moored to a riverbank, and representative of 'next generation', high technology.

Immediately upon opening, Melbourne Aquarium was an instant success with the public. In its first four days of operation it received 98 000 visitors, and after trading for just three months visitor numbers had exceeded the 360 000 mark. However, despite having followed government guidelines, and hiring reputable businesses to design, install and maintain its water-based airconditioning system, the Aquarium suffered a severe outbreak of legionnaire's disease on 26 April 2000 with 113 people being infected. Two people later died as a direct result of contracting the disease.

FEASIBILITY STUDY

To determine the likelihood of success of a state-of-the-art aquarium in Melbourne, Oceanis Australia initially undertook an extensive feasibility study. This process involved preparing a SWOT analysis. Through this means the major strengths of the proposed development were identified as:

* architectural uniqueness;
* all-weather nature of the attraction;
* likely mass appeal due to its multifaceted nature—embracing the environment, research, education and conservation;
* depth of management experience; and
* overall uniqueness of the experience that would be provided.

A number of potential weaknesses were also identified, including the:

* general image of aquariums within the broader community as offering fairly bland, standardised experiences;
* extent to which entry prices would be perceived as value for money;
* concerns held by some in the community regarding holding animals in captivity;
* perception that 'every city has one'; and
* the site's exposure to traffic and noise.

To further explore some of these strengths and weaknesses, and to assess the market's response to a range of key factors, focus group interviews were conducted involving potential target markets in Melbourne and Victoria's regional areas. Factors explored included admission price, propensity to visit, estimated time at the facility, and likelihood to revisit. The results, which were incorporated into a detailed marketing plan, forecast that visitor numbers would peak in year one, drop over the following two years, and then stabilise from the fourth year. The majority of visitors in the early years were anticipated to be mainly local residents. The capture rate of international visitors was forecast to increase over time as the attraction gained exposure and recognition in the international market place and was included in wholesale and inbound programs and tour group packages.

The SWOT analysis also revealed the key external factors that would impact on the business's success and marketing decisions. Key opportunities were seen to be:

* positioning the Aquarium as an icon (and therefore a must see) attraction for Melbourne and Victoria;
* the development of sponsorship as an additional revenue source;
* the possibility of forming strong marketing partnerships with other new attractions in the same area, such as Docklands and Federation Square;
* the potential to leverage the Commonwealth Games (and other major events) to increase local and overseas demand; and
* the use of the Aquarium as a venue for corporate and other functions.

Major threats were identified as:

* (arguably) the oversupply of aquarium experiences in Australia;
* the competition that the development would likely face from the various new attractions opening in Melbourne (e.g. the Museum of the Moving Image, Federation Square);
* water quality (for the exhibits);
* plant failure and disease; and
* fluctuations in demand (particularly from overseas markets) due to economic and other factors.

Examples of this last point in recent years have included the closure of Ansett Airlines, and the September 11 terrorist strike and subsequent turmoil within the international aviation industry.

COMPETITIVE ENVIRONMENT

The Aquarium believes in the need to build a critical mass of quality tourist attractions in Melbourne, and therefore views all new major tourist attractions as future strategic partners rather than as threats to its business. When a new attraction is launched, the Aquarium evaluates the short-term impact on its business, taking into account that most new attractions have a 'honeymoon period' in which visitation is particularly high. This may result in a short-term loss of business for the other attractions drawing on the same market. However, once an attraction's initial novelty has worn off, its presence is a long-term benefit for other attractions in the area as it increases the appeal of the destination.

At the time of writing there was no other attraction in Melbourne that was in direct competition with the Aquarium, although there are a number of major tourist attractions in Melbourne and its surrounds that target the same market segments. These include the Melbourne Museum, Luna Park, Royal Melbourne Zoo, Rialto Observation Deck, Sovereign Hill, Phillip Island Penguin Parade, and Healesville Sanctuary. In a narrow sense, the Sydney Aquarium is seen as the key competitor with the Aquarium, with UnderwaterWorld on the Sunshine Coast competing to a lesser degree.

MARKET RESEARCH

Market research plays a vital role in the successful marketing of the Aquarium. The Aquarium engages an independent market research firm to undertake a number of research tasks (such as tracking service quality), and staff at the Aquarium undertake others. The Aquarium runs a visitor satisfaction survey on a continual basis, as well as a quarterly survey to determine who visits and why. All promotions conducted by the Aquarium, or any in which it partici-pates, are carefully tracked for assessment purposes. Postcodes are collected from all visitors to keep track of their origin. This information is then used by the marketing team to identify those areas of the state in which to focus its marketing efforts.

Since the legionnaire's disease outbreak at the Aquarium, market research is also used to keep track of the public's perception of the safety of the attrac-tion. The marketing team still receives regular phone calls to see whether the Aquarium is free of the disease and safe to visit, and they welcome these calls, saying they provide an opportunity to develop a better understanding of the market and to allay the fears of prospective visitors.

STRATEGIC MARKETING PLANNING AND PERFORMANCE ASSESSMENT

Melbourne Aquarium's initial marketing plan was based on the feasibility study referred to earlier. The key goals of this plan were to:

- establish and maintain a brand image for Melbourne Aquarium;
- create the motivations and desire to ensure maximum visitation and yield to ensure profitability (from local, intrastate, interstate and international markets);
- establish the Aquarium as a centre of excellence and established provider of educational services;
- establish the Aquarium as a unique, high profile centre of excellence for function events, such as product launches;
- establish the Aquarium as an icon tourist attraction and benchmark for the highest industry standards of professionalism;
- develop a targeted sponsorship realisation strategy; and

* raise the profile and awareness of the Aquarium through free and positive publicity.

The marketing strategy for 2003/05 essentially seeks to further progress these goals, and is based on an extensive in-depth review of marketing strategies and practices conducted in late 2002.

Maintaining the integrity of the Aquarium's brand is considered a key aspect of its marketing strategy, and, as such, it is the marketing team's job to ensure that every form of communication issued, no matter which department it is issued by, conforms to the Aquarium's strict brand guidelines. One important change that was introduced to the Aquarium's brand since opening has been a revised tagline. Initially the Aquarium's tagline was 'Journey into Subspace'. However, research showed that this added no value to the brand and lacked any meaning. Instead it was replaced with 'Journey into the Southern Ocean' which makes reference to the Aquarium's point of difference of featuring creatures of the Southern Ocean.

The Melbourne Aquarium also seeks to position itself in the broader community as a good corporate citizen, sponsoring various charities and festivals around Melbourne, including the Smith Family Foundation, the River Festival, and various wine and food festivals.

The Aquarium's marketing team meets on the first Friday of every month to report on the previous month, share information and ideas for future marketing activities, and identify any 'fine tuning' that might be required to current practices. The Aquarium also conducts a quarterly review of its marketing plan, the results of which are presented to its board. Based on this review, marketing practices may be altered to better reflect the current business environment. A comprehensive marketing review is conducted every 18 months. A two-day marketing retreat for the entire marketing team is held each year to finalise the yearly marketing implementation strategies and budgets for the following year.

The Aquarium regularly monitors its marketing performance against key performance indicators. These indicators cover: visitation figures; average ticket price; amount of free publicity; level of sponsorship revenue; visitor satisfaction levels; number of student education group visitors; function income; average retail spend per head; and average food and beverage spend per head. Weekly reports are prepared comparing these indicators against established targets and the previous year's performance.

The Aquarium's success in the broader business environment has been recognised in the form of major tourism and Property Council awards. The most important award received to date was the Victorian Tourism Industry's award for the Major Tourism Attraction in 2001. The award is widely-recognised amongst wholesalers and inbound operators, and further supports the Aquarium's marketing position as Victoria's number one tourist attraction. The Aquarium incorporates the award logo on all its collateral materials, considering it to be an important element in its promotional strategy. The award is leveraged in all marketing communications, and is even used as the tagline in all emails leaving the Aquarium.

MAJOR MARKETS

The Aquarium's target markets vary according to the particular activity and focus. Having said that, the Aquarium's key markets are drawn from various geographic and psychographic mixes. Geographic segments targeted are: Victoria (Melbourne and surrounds and regional Victoria); interstate (New South Wales, Queensland, South Australia, Tasmania and other); and international (Japan, Asia, North America, United Kingdom/Europe, New Zealand, Middle East, and emerging markets). Respectively, these markets comprise 80 per cent, 10 per cent and 10 per cent of the Aquarium's total market. Over the next few years, it is expected that this market mix will change with the international market growing significantly. Such growth, however, is expected to be offset by a similar fall in the local market.

In terms of family life cycle stage, it is young families that are the predominant market for the Aquarium, with retirees and the school market also being major sources of visitors. Although there is a very low yield from the school market, indeed, it barely runs at break-even, it is important in the sense that by servicing it the Aquarium is seen as a 'good corporate citizen', acting to educate the young about the importance of environmental preservation. This market is also regarded as important as children will tend to bring their families back to the Aquarium if they enjoy a school visit.

The functions market, while presently small, has substantial potential for growth. There are three levels within the complex on which functions can be held, and a variety of 'unique' inclusions assist the aquarium in its efforts to attract this market. Such inclusions, for example, extend to the ability of speakers to address an audience from inside a shark tank. As with the school market, there is an increased likelihood that business people who have attended a function at the Aquarium, and have had their appetites whetted, will subsequently return with their families.

Since opening in January 2000, to the end of 2002, the Aquarium has welcomed 2 200 301 visitors through its doors. These figures were lower than those forecast (see Table 12.1) but surprisingly high considering the circumstances under which the Aquarium was operating.

The Aquarium also markets itself to business organisations in an effort to obtain sponsorship revenue from its exhibits. Exhibit sponsors benefit from this relationship by: having guaranteed product exclusivity at the Aquarium; having their association with the Aquarium communicated to the Aquarium's target markets; and enhancing their community standing by being linked with an environmentally responsible organisation. The Aquarium regards

Table 12.1: Visitation figures 2000/2002

	2000	2001	2002
January	100 878	128 267	93 827
February	87 176	45 346	37 559
March	93 483	54 035	59 619
April	119 434	76 894	59 000
May	23 384	41 700	37 533
June	50 988	53 667	44 678
July	75 643	77 574	65 968
August	50 375	51 233	47 153
September	76 274	47 190	42 691
October	55 671	51 993	48 323
November	55 690	42 889	38 055
December	66 514	48 303	51 272
TOTAL			
Actual visitation	855 510	719 091	625 678
TOTAL			
Forecast visitation	969 200 (–13%)	881 100 (–22%)	721 300 (–15%)

Source: Melbourne Aquarium, 2002.

looking after sponsors as a priority, and holds an annual sponsors' night in their honour.

Recently updated forecasts for the year 2003 put annual visitation at approximately 617 500. These figures have been revised down significantly from the 1999 forecasts for those years, and reflect such factors as the impact of the legionnaire's disease outbreak, a downturn in inbound arrivals to Australia and difficulties in the aviation industry that have existed since the events of 11 September 2001.

MARKETING MIX

Product

Open every day of the year, the Melbourne Aquarium is classified as a 'marine-based tourism attraction' which specialises in showcasing marine life in the Southern Ocean.

Positioning itself quite differently from other aquariums in Australia, the Melbourne Aquarium focuses on creatures of the Southern Ocean, and incorporates a unique portfolio of interactive rides and exhibits. These include simulator rides, a 270-degree acrylic tube viewing tunnel, a 360-degree fish bowl viewing and function area, and temporary exhibition space, all of which combine to deliver high quality education and entertainment in a highly interactive facility.

Making the experience educational as well as entertaining is the key challenge for the Aquarium, and this objective is achieved through the delivery of truly interactive and multi-sensory products. Visitors commence their journey into the Aquarium's ocean depths by entering a wall of light. An animated host fish, 'Hook', guides visitors through their underwater world journey, which takes them through:

* the coral atoll (a 10-metre diameter tank exhibiting living coral and the colourful inhabitants of the coral reef environment);
* the exhibition gallery;
* the mangrove exhibit where patrons can feed stingrays;
* the billabong exhibit featuring giant Murray cod;
* a submersible research station;
* exploration exhibit;
* the fishbowl, the world's first 100 square metre fish bowl viewing area and function facility;
* the suspended walk through clear tube underwater tunnels;
* the ocean theatre; and
* a state-of-the-art simulator ride which changes theme every six months. At the time of writing, this ride simulated the experience of swimming with sharks.

The Aquarium augments its core product with an extensive range of activities and events. These include unique function facilities, licensed cafe and snack bar, children's birthday parties, themed aquarium souvenir shop, formal and informal education programs, hand-held audio tour guides, interpretive tours, back-of-house tours, and an opportunity to 'Dive with the Sharks'.

Based on focus group research, the current re-visit cycle by the Melbourne market is estimated to be approximately 15 months, and changing exhibits and programs at least every six months is seen as the key to developing strong repeat visitation. To achieve this goal, Oceanis Australia has instituted a masterplan group, which is responsible for the development of new product concepts for all of its four aquariums. Comprising one representative from each of the education, curatorial and marketing departments, the group reports back to the senior management team every six months. Their ideas are then incorporated into a rolling three-year plan. To determine the success of the new products, and the popularity of older exhibits, visitor feedback is monitored via a visitor survey.

From the outset, the Aquarium recognised that in years four or five of its operations, a major overhaul of the facility would be required in order to promote repeat visitation. As part of this overhaul, a second stage development is planned which will be located on the other side of King Street and will be connected by walkways to the existing facility. It will also link with the planned Plenary Hall that will add to Melbourne's convention hosting capacity.

Service quality

Delivering world's best practice in customer service is one of the key objectives of Oceanis Australia. To achieve this end, an annual staff training calendar is in place, and all staff have an annual performance review which takes into account the staff member's career aspirations and the company's goals. To monitor the success of this program, and the overall level of customer service, an independent company is commissioned to regularly track service quality. The company does this by remaining anonymous and visiting, calling or emailing queries, and then seeing how such requests are handled. At the end of every month the senior management team receives a detailed report from the consultants and feedback is shared with staff.

Pricing

As the Aquarium is privately owned and funded, unlike many of its nearest competitors, its prices must provide sufficient income to ensure the financial sustainability of the business.

Prior to the facility opening, different pricing scenarios were tested with focus groups in both Melbourne and regional areas around the state. The results varied somewhat between capital city and the regions, with the family price seen as a stronger issue in the regions than in metropolitan areas. As a result, the concession and family prices were varied. At the time of writing the prices of entry to the Aquarium were listed as $22 for an adult, $12 for a child, $14 for a concession admission, and $55 for a family ticket (two adults and up to three children). Groups of 10 or more receive a 20 per cent discount off the entry price and a range of meal options have been packaged for groups. Yearly memberships to the Aquarium are also offered, these being $45 for an adult and $105 for a family.

The prices of other attractions were central concerns in setting final admission prices, with consideration being given to the relative durations of stay at the various attractions and the type of experience on offer. A similar analysis was performed for the average visitor expenditure on souvenirs and food and beverages. Prices at other attractions are tracked on a regular basis.

Research undertaken with focus groups also indicated that the Aquarium needed to be careful not to outprice itself in the market. As such, Aquarium management acknowledges that it needs to be innovative in the pricing area and to be seen as providing more than the other attractions in return for visitors paying a higher price. One innovative solution implemented by the Aquarium in recent times is the inclusion of a free *Aquarium Guide* with each ticket purchased. This is something that visitors would need to purchase separately from their entrance ticket at many other attractions. To encourage visitors to spend on other items whilst they are at the Aquarium, and as the amount visitors spend on gifts and souvenirs depends largely on the range and quality of merchandise available at attractions, the Aquarium provides a large, well-stocked shop.

Promotion

The Aquarium manages its own advertising and promotional activities, including an extensive 12-month calendar of events and sponsorships, which are tailored to cover a range of different interest groups. These include a conservation stream that comprises a World Environment Day event, and a general community stream, which includes events for Secretaries Day and Christmas in July. The Aquarium also sponsors teams and events that fit its image, and result in its enhancement in the eyes of the general public. Examples include the sponsorship of races on the Yarra River, and the sponsorship of the Channel 7 football team, the Hammerheads. The Aquarium also has partnership arrangements with the *Herald Sun* newspaper, Channel 7 and Prime TV.

The media plays a key role in building awareness and communicating the Aquarium's marketing and general communications messages to the public. As a result of the Aquarium's policy of being open and accessible to the media during the legionnaire's disease disaster, it has developed very close working relationships with the media.

Oceanis Australia is an advocate of the benefits of cooperative marketing. The group believes that to increase visitation to its own facilities it must be actively involved in increasing the destination's attractiveness to prospective visitors. Management at the Aquarium believes that this is best done by working with other major tourism bodies, the government and major tourism attractions. As Melbourne's premier tourist attractions have not had a tradition of working and marketing collaboratively, Oceanis Australia has found itself playing a leading role in bringing such organisations together in united marketing efforts. For example, the Aquarium has developed and introduced an Attraction Pass that combines Melbourne's 11 premier attractions and entitles the pass holder to visit six of the 11 attractions on offer. The pass was introduced initially into the international market, and has now been offered in the domestic market via the nationwide network of motoring organisations.

The Aquarium is also actively involved in packaging with other local and statewide organisations and attractions. For example, the Aquarium is involved with the Entertainment Card (which is offered in the form of a coupon book offering discounts to movies, theatres and sporting events). Through its association with this card, the Aquarium offers a two for one entry discount coupon that has proven to be a significant demand generator. Other packages in which the Aquarium is involved include—a nature-based day package that incorporates a visit to one of Melbourne's Zoos, an 'early bird' tour designed for people arriving into Melbourne early in the day, and a tour linking the Aquarium with regional attractions.

Customer loyalty programs

As repeat visitation is seen to be a key issue for the success of the Aquarium, customer loyalty programs have recently been introduced. One of these is a membership program designed to encourage people to revisit the Aquarium more than once a year. Although members do not have to pay for their additional visits, the packages are structured in a manner that encourages them to bring guests by entitling them to discounts. Repeat visitation on these packages can also involve expenditure on other items including food and beverages. Initially planned for launch in year one, the program was put on hold following the outbreak of legionnaire's disease. Since the commencement of the program in November 2001, the Aquarium has welcomed 3000 members, and its popularity is growing. Whilst time-consuming to administer, this program is considered very important by management.

Another program that has recently been developed is geared towards corporations. Developed in response to September 11 and the resultant downturn in business, the Aquarium has introduced Family Days, where businesses invite staff and their families to the Aquarium for the day.

Distribution

The Aquarium distributes its product through a variety of channels. These include the retail sector, the nation's motoring organisations, inbound operators, wholesalers, various specialist groups (for example, social and football clubs, hotel concierges, coach companies and travel agents), and has plans to soon be selling its product via the world wide web.

The international market is seen to offer the major growth potential for the Aquarium, and Tom Smith believes that developing personal relationships with inbound and wholesale operators is vital to the success of the business. As a result, the Aquarium's marketing team makes its own sales calls in Asia, and works closely with Tourism Victoria and key wholesalers in the United Kingdom, European, North American and New Zealand markets.

The Aquarium has a focus on attracting visitors from regional areas of the state as well as Melbourne, and has developed a series of structured incentive programs for hotel concierges, coach companies and travel agents. It also produces monthly updates that are sent to each of these key groups, and Aquarium staff make regular face-to-face visits. Social and football clubs are also seen as offering access to large numbers of individuals, and, as such, direct mail and other special campaigns are run in conjunction with them.

It is noteworthy that the Aquarium management places significant importance on sending 'thank yous' to channel members for delivering business to the Aquarium.

At the time of writing, the Aquarium's web site <www.melbourneaquarium. com.au> was in stage two of its development. This stage will focus on delivering e-commerce solutions to the travel trade whilst continuing to provide quality information to the general public and media. The new site will be more interactive, include games, and offer more downloadable materials.

DEALING WITH DISASTERS—LEGIONNAIRE'S DISEASE AND THE MELBOURNE AQUARIUM

Some three months after its opening, news broke on 26 April 2000 of an outbreak of legionnaire's disease at the Melbourne Aquarium. The problem made front-page news around Australia and, indeed, received substantial coverage overseas. One hundred and thirteen people were affected by legionnaire's disease, of whom two subsequently died.

The Aquarium did its best to limit the damage from this event and to terminate the crisis quickly. As soon as the outbreak was discovered, the Aquarium's air conditioner cooling towers were doused with purification chemicals, thereby eradicating the problem. Although management at the Aquarium offered to immediately close the facility in order for tests to be conducted, the Department of Human Services said that this was unnecessary once the towers had been doused. Despite having been given the 'all clear' by the relevant authorities, the Aquarium decided to completely replace the air-conditioning units to allay any community fears.

The Aquarium implemented a policy that all information would be released to staff prior to it being released to the media. This was done as a means of trying to reduce stress on staff, particularly as some had been subjected to criticism in the community due to their association with the facility. Additionally, during the weeks immediately after the legionnaire's disease outbreak, senior management of the Aquarium would each walk around the facility at least three times per day in order to maintain contact with staff and boost morale. This had a very positive effect on staff.

Daily visitation to the Aquarium dropped by over 90 per cent as soon as the problem occurred, and visitation remained low for the next two months. Although the facility did not close, the 120 staff had relatively little to do for over two months. Given that the staff had worked in the facility during the infected period, many were worried about whether they had picked up the disease, and extensive medical tests were conducted on all staff. None, as it turned out, had contracted the disease. Doctors were brought in to give lectures to staff on the background to the disease, and provided information on how to help manage the crisis.

There is some evidence that the downturn in business at the Aquarium, which resulted from the legionnaire's disease outbreak, extended beyond the Melbourne Aquarium. Visitation to the aquarium in Sydney also fell sharply during this period, as many people associated the problem with aquariums as a whole, and visitation at other attractions around Melbourne also dropped around this time. Such decreases in demand indicate the flow-on effect these disasters can have on other businesses.

There is an argument that 'any publicity is good publicity'. If this is the case, then the Melbourne Aquarium should have benefited greatly as there was enormous publicity associated with this problem, both within Australia and overseas. The fact that a Liberal Party function had been held in the facility during the contamination period made for an even better media story. There is no doubt that the publicity increased awareness of the facility but the challenge was to then convince the public that it was safe to revisit.

Like most large organisations, Melbourne Aquarium had a disaster management plan, but like most others, the plan was 'generic in the extreme' and did not cover the day-to-day consequences of a disaster such as this. It took a few days to sort out the manner in which the organisation would communicate with the public, which was thirsting for information on the issue. Tom Smith, the then Marketing Manager of the Aquarium, became the organisation's central contact with the media. The organisation's approach was to be completely open with the media, providing interviews and access to the facility at all times, with the only restriction being that all company comment would come via Tom Smith.

In the weeks after the tragedy, Tom Smith visited the victims of the disease and their families in order to explain what had happened and what was being done to resolve the problem and ensure that it did not happen again. Generally, this was well received by the victims, although understandably some were quite angry about what had transpired.

The Aquarium's management, while deeply involved in dealing with the disaster that had befallen the business, recognised that there was a need to position the organisation for the time when the crisis was over. To this end, a 're-launch' budget was established with a view to restoring the organisation's credibility and bringing visitors back to the facility. This budget was used to implement a comprehensive four-month, four-step, communications plan. As senior staff at Oceanis Australia felt that it would be inappropriate to promote the facility whilst there was any risk of previous visitors developing symptoms of legionnaire's disease, or whilst any of the victims were still in hospital, it was not until July, some three months after the problem occurred, that the re-launch of the facility finally took place.

Step one of the plan was a nationwide advertising campaign apologising for what had happened. The advertisements gave Oceanis Australia an opportunity to acknowledge the support it had received from staff, the public and the government. Advertisements talked about the changes that had occurred at the Aquarium, and included photographs of the air-conditioning towers being replaced. In order to personalise some of the communication messages, there were stories about the staff at the facility themselves.

The second step was to generate positive media attention for the Aquarium by promoting it in association with high profile personalities. A number of celebrities were photographed at the Aquarium during this stage, and an example of one outstanding media opportunity was when the Aquarium secured an important press conference for popular footballer Paul Salmon, otherwise known as 'Fish', to announce his retirement. This cost the Aquarium the sponsorship of a football game, but the resultant positive media coverage of the Aquarium was considered well worthwhile.

The next step was another nationwide advertising campaign. This time the campaign included a tagline that noted that there had been a problem at the facility but that it had been addressed and no longer existed.

The final step was another nationwide advertising campaign which was run without the tagline, and which included a series of discounts for certain target groups, such as seniors and residents of selected suburbs that had generated significant demand in the past. Throughout the disaster, the Aquarium did not alter its pricing policy. Rather, it introduced special promotions instead, realising that such short-term discounts and the like would not significantly impact upon its long-term financial sustainability.

For the remainder of 2000, Tom Smith gave guest lectures at a large number of meetings throughout Victoria to promote what had been done to rectify the problem and to share the knowledge that had been gained as a result of this crisis. The intention was so that others could learn from the experience of the Melbourne Aquarium.

As sponsors are a key to the ongoing success of the Aquarium, it is understandable that Oceanis Australia was concerned about the future of these relationships following the outbreak. Having planned the annual sponsors' dinner prior to 26 April, the Aquarium decided to proceed with the event, which it saw as providing a good opportunity to explain what had happened. A representative of every sponsor attended the function, and all expressed their genuine commitment to continuing their relationship with the Aquarium.

Even now, three years down the track, the legionnaire's disease disaster still impacts on the business. As a result, the Aquarium continually monitors and evaluates the public's perception of the facility's safety.

SUMMARY

In spite of its initial setbacks, the Melbourne Aquarium has become a successful major tourist attraction in Melbourne. Its strategic approach to marketing is evident in its efforts to position itself as one of Melbourne's premier tourist attractions, and in the way it has supported such positioning efforts through an appropriately crafted marketing mix. Market research, a detailed understanding of its target markets, and its commitment to monitoring its marketing performance have also been integral to its success. Additionally, the Aquarium's structured and considered approach to the significant problem which befell it soon after it opened, provides clear insights into the crisis management process which should be of interest to marketers in the full range of tourism enterprises.

Primary period covered by case study: 1999/2002

REFERENCE

Melbourne Aquarium, 2002, Internal Management Report

QUESTIONS

1 Evaluate the approach to disaster management that was adopted by Melbourne Aquarium and suggest ways that this could have been improved in order to enhance further the short- to medium-term results achieved by the facility.

2 After a major setback, such as the outbreak of legionnaire's disease and the more recent SARS, there is often the temptation to use price reductions to encourage visitation. Discuss the pros and cons of using price in such a way and whether there are differences depending on whether the setback is localised (legionnaire's) or general (SARS).

3 Compare the marketing segmentation approaches evident in both this case study and that of the Sydney Aquarium discussed elsewhere in this book. What (if any) differences are there, and to what extent do you see these differences as significant?

4 Discuss the costs and benefits of customer loyalty programs for facilities such as the Melbourne Aquarium, and indicate whether you believe that the benefits of such programs exceed the total costs of operating them.

5 Discuss the rationale for Melbourne Aquarium's decision to form relationships with other competing attractions. In your answer ensure you make some observations about the nature of the tourist experience in destinations.

6 Reliable and timely market research data are vital to underpin marketing plans. What forms of market research are evident in this case study? Can you suggest any additional approaches to obtaining market-related information given that the Aquarium's marketing manager has a relatively modest budget for undertaking this activity?

7   Attractions usually experience a honeymoon period in their first year of operation during which visitation is very high. As a result of the legionnaire's outbreak, the honeymoon period at the Melbourne Aquarium lasted only three months. Discuss the action that management of the Aquarium could have taken after the legionnaire's problem to continue or reinstate the honeymoon period.

8   Setting an entry price that provides an acceptable profit level for the attraction owner without being seen as excessive by the market is not an easy task. This is even more difficult in the case of the Melbourne Aquarium where a number of its main competitors, such as the Museum, are government-owned and thus not driven to the same degree by a profit incentive. Critically examine the approach that Melbourne Aquarium has used in establishing its entry prices.

9   Repeat visitation is a vital aspect for tourist attractions. Identify and discuss the appraches that management at the Melbourne Aquarium are currently using to enhance the level of repeat visitation, especially amongst local residents. Can you suggest other approaches that could be used for this purpose?

10   What insights does the approach used by Melbourne Aquarium in dealing with the outbreak of legionnaire's disease provide to tourism marketers in general?

13. MELBOURNE AIRPORT

INTRODUCTION

Melbourne Airport was purchased by Australia Pacific Airports Corporation when the Airport was privatised in 1997. Although the Airport is located in Australia's second largest city, its single terminal facility and absence of any form of curfew provide it with some important competitive advantages.

Since privatisation, Melbourne Airport has focused heavily on building strong partnerships with its many key stakeholders and has placed a strong emphasis on the delivery of exceptionally high service quality. These foci have been important in Melbourne Airport's success in recent years as reflected in the number of prestigious industry awards it has won.

Melbourne Airport makes good use of marketing research to underpin its business plan and it employs various ongoing monitoring tools to ensure that its performance is in line with customer expectations. As the Airport has no direct control over either the patronage at Melbourne Airport or the many thousands of people employed in the many businesses at the airport, there are substantial challenges for management of the airport in building the business.

BACKGROUND

Melbourne Airport is one of Australia's major passenger and freight gateways. From the time of its establishment at Tullamarine on Melbourne's north-western outskirts in 1970 until 1987, Melbourne Airport was operated by the Federal Department of Transport. From 1988 until 1997 this responsibility fell to the newly created publicly owned Federal Airports Corporation. However, in July 1997, in the first round of airport privatisations in Australia, the Airport came up for lease. For the sum of $1.3 billion, the Australia Pacific Airports Corporation Ltd (APAC) secured the management rights to operate Melbourne Airport for 50 years with an option to extend the lease by another 49 years. This agreement maintained the existing sub-leases at the Airport, which included those for the two domestic terminals leased and operated by Ansett and Qantas.

APAC is an 85 per cent Australian-owned, non-listed company. Established in 1995, the company has four shareholders:

- AMP Asset Management Australia Ltd, Australia's largest pension and insurance company (50 per cent holding);
- Deutsche Asset Management (Australia), as the manager of the SAS Trustees Corporation's Interest (25 per cent holding);
- BAA plc, the world's largest private airport operator (15 per cent holding); and
- Hastings Fund Management, as manager of the Australian Infrastructure Fund and Utilities Trust of Australia (10 per cent holding).

APAC currently operates two airports in Australia, having also taken over the management of the Launceston Airport in May 1998 in partnership with the Launceston City Council. APAC intends to substantially increase its holdings of airports in the Australia Pacific region over time.

APAC's mission is to 'be one of the world's leading airport companies, and to fully realise Melbourne Airport's potential as an international gateway and hub for passengers and freight'.

It works towards achieving this goal by applying seven underlying principles to its business planning and management, which are:

1   to provide a safe, secure and efficient range of services;
2   to be a world top ten airport;
3   to ensure quality customer service and satisfaction;
4   to maximise opportunities for growth and development;
5   to develop skilled employees, with recognition and incentive to excel;
6   to be a responsible corporate citizen and neighbour; and
7   to realise a return on shareholder investment.

APAC's number one priority is to ensure that airports under its control are operated safely and securely. To this end, it has put in place an extensive program of safety testing and checking, as well as providing regular training and awareness programs for staff. It also employs outside experts to conduct regular checks in addition to the periodic reviews by regulators to ensure that the airports comply with all navigation and security regulations.

Whilst airports are not attractions in their own right, poor operating performance at an airport can be a major disincentive to passengers and airlines. As a result, Melbourne Airport aims to be ranked in the top tier of international airports. To meet this goal, it has focused upon the delivery of outstanding customer service by efficiently managing the diverse requirements of its many stakeholders including passengers, airlines, staff, retailers, immigration, customs, government and regulatory authorities. Melbourne Airport states that this approach to customer service is one of its major strengths, and the key reason behind its success.

A major objective for APAC is to increase the number of flights into and out of Melbourne Airport. This is because airports make at least part of their profit from charging airlines for terminal use on a per passenger basis. Thus, in its effort to increase flight numbers, Melbourne Airport operates without a curfew and is the only major airport in Australia to do so. This initiative has led to higher growth in international flights and passenger numbers than any of Australia's other airports in the period since privatisation.

Since taking control of Melbourne Airport, APAC has been proactive in positioning itself as a strong supporter of initiatives being developed and operationalised by, key tourism organisations, federal, state and local governments, as well as the broader business community. This strategy for Melbourne Airport has been successful, resulting in passenger numbers rising from 14.5 million passengers in 1995 to over 17 million in 2001 (although the number had declined marginally in 2002 to 16.5 million passengers), a thriving global freight service, and a number of prestigious international and national awards in recognition of its performance.

MARKETING PLANNING PROCESS

Success in marketing has been one of the major strengths of Melbourne Airport. The airport's marketing plan is a fundamental guide for the day-to-day operations of the airport and is developed in consultation with the airlines. The plan, which takes into account the directions set out in the Airport's 20-year master plan, includes a range of key performance indicators which are reviewed regularly. The plan is used to set the direction of the organisation and to ensure that appropriate attention is given to the key issues impacting upon the airport.

Once per quarter, the marketing plan is updated. This is done by bringing together the Airport's key staff in a half-day workshop to review the Airport's key markets, and to identify new opportunities and threats to its business. This process ensures that the Airport's internal and external environments are continually monitored, and strategies are set in place as required.

Melbourne Airport also monitors and carefully analyses the trends and opportunities identified in the projections prepared by the Australian Tourist Commission and the Tourism Forecasting Council. (Both of these organisations will become part of Tourism Australia at the end of 2004.) In this way, the Airport can ensure that it has the facilities and services in place to meet the needs of its international airline partners.

EXTERNAL FACTORS IMPACTING UPON MARKETING DECISIONS

A number of external factors present serious challenges to the management and operations of Melbourne Airport.

A major challenge for any airport's management is that demand for its services is controlled almost entirely by other parties. Whilst it facilitates travel, it does not in itself generate demand, and must rely on the local business sector, the travel behaviour of the local community, and the attractiveness of the destination to draw tourists, and create demand for its services. Airports, therefore, are heavily influenced by external factors and, although airport operators can seek to influence these, they have limited direct control over the business that they receive. Recognising this fact, Melbourne Airport works closely with influential organisations to develop strategies which will enhance travel to and from Melbourne and, therefore, increase its business prospects.

At the time of writing, worldwide confidence in the aviation industry was low. Following the September 11 terrorist attack in 2001, the world's major airlines lost more than US$17 billion, nearly wiping out their cumulative profits for the preceding four years, and tripling their previous worst-ever annual loss a decade earlier. Consumer confidence in international travel has been further diminished as a result of the Bali bombings in 2002, the war against terror in Iraq and the more recent severe acute respiratory syndrome (SARS), which drastically reduced airline travel to and from Asia in particular. In Australia, the collapse of Ansett Airlines further emphasised the problems the industry faced. By April 2003, analysts were revising airline losses down further, with Merrill Lynch predicting that American airline losses in 2003 could be US$7.4 billion, higher than the original estimate of $6.4 billion. This lower figure was also partially due to a general slow down in the world economy. In combination, these factors are expected to result in a drop in the number of airlines worldwide from 300 to 200 in the medium- to longer-term.

Despite this turmoil, Melbourne Airport has generally performed well throughout these difficult times. For two weeks following the September 11 attack, flights around the world were overbooked, and Melbourne airport was extremely busy as people sought to return to their home bases. Immediately after this time, however, passenger numbers dropped substantially. Fortunately, the Christmas vacation prompted passengers to return to the skies, and this resulted in a substantial increase in passenger numbers with the airport recording the second highest number of passengers for this time of year in its history. This success continued throughout February and March of 2002, again setting records for these months.

Overall passenger numbers at Melbourne Airport for the third quarter of 2002/03 were consistent with the same period the year before. This was due to an increase in domestic travel that more than offset the decline in international travel. The domestic capacity that was lost as a result of the collapse of Ansett has been largely replaced by Qantas and Virgin Blue, although it is still below the total seat capacity available in January 2001 when Qantas, Ansett, Virgin and Impulse were all operating. Melbourne Airport expects international passenger numbers to rebound from the impacts of the Iraq war and SARS as they did following September 11 in 2001.

The demise of Ansett also had a significant effect on Melbourne Airport's business. Overnight around 40 per cent of the Airport's domestic flights ceased as a result of the collapse, and this also affected the movement of Ansett's Star Alliance partners who had used Ansett to transport its international passengers throughout Australia. In addition, Ansett was a Melbourne-based airline, and the airport's largest customer after Qantas. This meant that its most significant impact was on Melbourne. The demise of Ansett resulted in job losses at the airport and this impacted on businesses in the nearby areas, which supplied the airline and its staff. These included caterers, and businesses in the areas of freight, operations and maintenance. An economic impact study by Sinclair Knight Merz in March 2003 estimated that 2400 jobs at the airport were lost due to the closure of Ansett.

According to Melbourne Airport's Airline Business Coordinator, Stephen Palombo, the morale of the remaining staff at the airport was very low during this time, as the generally busy environment of the Airport had been replaced with a 'ghost town' like feeling in the former Ansett terminal. Given the Airport's policy of employing local people, the demise of Ansett had a significant impact on the local community as well. However, no research has been conducted in this area to date.

A number of other issues affect the demand for air travel, and thus affect the success of the Airport. These include: the depreciation of world currencies; rising third party insurance costs; the increased emphasis on security; air service agreements between Australia and other destinations resulting in passenger capacity constraints; the plight of economies from which airline services emanate; and the decisions of major companies as to where to locate their corporate headquarters, which also impacts upon the number of airline services that are required for the city.

COMPETITION

Sydney Airport is Melbourne Airport's most significant competitor. Whilst Sydney is Australia's major gateway, its airport has had some problems due largely to the fact that the domestic and international terminals are separated, air traffic is congested, there is a curfew, and airport neighbours, who live immediately adjacent to the airport, are not fully supportive of the airport. Until more recently, relatively little attention has been paid to customer service at Sydney Airport, although substantial investment was made at the airport in the lead up to the Sydney Olympics and some of the longstanding problems at the airport were addressed. Subsequently, effort has been made to improve the 'total journey experience' at Sydney Airport and a campaign has been launched to reposition it as a 'place where people truly connect'.

In the post-Olympic period, Sydney as a city has become more competitive in the tourism market, so as to utilise the new facilities that were built for the Games. This will likely further increase the travel business that goes via Sydney at the expense of Melbourne and its airport.

Qantas's recent launch of Australian Airlines, a low-cost international airline, is likely to have some impact on the operations at Melbourne Airport. The very unstable airline operating environment in recent times, however, makes it difficult to gauge the full impact of this launch.

Australian Airlines has been launched in two stages. During stage one, flights are scheduled from its base in Cairns to a number of Asian destinations. These flights are unlikely to have any significant impact on the operations of Melbourne Airport as few Melbourne-based travellers to Asia will in all probability fly via Cairns when it is possible to fly to the same destinations from Melbourne on other airlines. The second stage of the new airline's launch has the potential, however, to have a significant impact on Melbourne Airport. This stage will see flights scheduled from a second base in southern Australia to a number of ports in South-East Asia. At this stage, the location of the second base has not been decided, but either Melbourne or Adelaide is the most likely option.

Melbourne Airport is hopeful that the new airline's second base will be in Melbourne. The destinations scheduled for flights from this base include Phuket, Bangkok and Bali, all of which are very popular destinations with Melburnians which, until the Bali bombings and SARS, had experienced substantial growth in recent times. Despite the popularity of these destinations with Melburnians, Qantas has recently withdrawn its daily flight service from Melbourne to Bangkok. There is some speculation that this reduction was made to accommodate the entry of Australian Airlines into the market.

The commencement of Bali's first international airline, which had been postponed after the Bali bombings, will also provide a boost for tourism and to Melbourne Airport as travel between Melbourne and Bali begins to increase again. Air Paradise International began flying between Melbourne and Bali in February 2003 and provides the only non-stop service between Melbourne and Bali operated by any airline. Air Paradise will operate three direct weekly services between Melbourne and Denpasar.

MARKET RESEARCH

Although Melbourne Airport does not conduct significant levels of market research in relation to travel trends, it makes extensive use of forecasts and other studies conducted by groups such as Tourism Victoria, the Australian Tourist Commission, the Bureau of Tourism Research and the Tourism Forecasting Council. By these means it stays abreast of key changes in the market. The services of a media monitor are also employed to ensure that management is well informed on events likely to impact upon its operations.

Melbourne Airport is, however, actively involved in monitoring passenger satisfaction with the facilities and services at the Airport. A team of five interviewers conduct intercept interviews with 1000 passengers each month, asking about a variety of issues, ranging from the price of food at the airport to the quality of signage provided. The results of these surveys are used to underpin business plans and to improve facilities in order to enhance the overall performance of the Airport in the eyes of the travelling public.

OVERALL MARKETING STRATEGY

Melbourne Airport's key business objectives are to be seen as a leading international airport and to increase revenue through increased volume rather than via increased charges. To achieve these objectives, Melbourne Airport has adopted a very 'customer-focused' approach to complement the substantial investment that has been made in the Airport's 'state-of-the-art' infrastructure.

In seeking to make Melbourne Airport Australia's southern gateway, the Airport's management has listened to its customers so that it is able to offer the range and level of services that best meet its customers' needs. It treats airlines and other key stakeholders as partners, rather than simply tenants, and is active in seeking to build strong relationships in these areas.

Recognising that the level of business at the Airport is largely controlled by the actions of others, Melbourne Airport is very active in forming partnerships with key bodies able to influence the amount of business that comes to Melbourne. For example, Melbourne Airport is a very active member of various committees in the tourism sector that seek to promote Melbourne as a destination. By belonging to such groups, Melbourne Airport is better able to influence the decisions of these committees and use its promotional budget more effectively by linking it to initiatives driven by others. Melbourne Airport's key staff regularly visit the head offices of international airlines in order to promote the benefits of Victoria in general, and Melbourne in particular. The attractiveness of Melbourne as a tourist destination, and its success in the meetings, incentives, conferences and exhibitions (MICE) market, substantially influences the number of passengers seeking to fly to Melbourne, which in turn influences the number of services that major airlines schedule for Melbourne.

Actual and forecast visitor numbers

With more than 300 000 passengers passing through Melbourne Airport in December 2001, it was the second busiest December for the airport on record, and second only to the previous Olympic year. This increase was largely due to the addition of extra seats and services into Melbourne in the last quarter of 2001.

Despite the difficulties experienced when Ansett collapsed, capacity on trunk route operations has been sustained through the introduction of new services by both Qantas and Virgin Blue. Qantas has introduced its new Citiflyer program between most Australian capital cities. In this program, flights operate between Sydney and Melbourne every half hour, and between Brisbane and Melbourne every hour during peak times. Furthermore, with the use of larger aircraft on these sectors, overall domestic capacity has been maintained.

Since 1995, international air services into Melbourne have increased by an average annual growth rate of 6.3 per cent, resulting in a net growth of 44 per cent. International seating capacity has shown an average annual growth rate of 4.6 per cent and a total growth of 31 per cent over this period. International air services have grown faster than seat capacity due to the continuing trend towards increased services and frequencies using smaller capacity aircraft.

Table 13.1 below provides an analysis of Melbourne Airport's passengers in the period 2000/01 and 2001/02. In 2000/01, the largest increase in business would appear to be in transit passengers—this was from a very low base. In contrast, the real growth can be seen to come from the domestic market, at close to 10 per cent of a much larger passenger base (13.51 million). Again the sharpest change in 2002 was in the number of transit passengers, which fell quite sharply but from a low base.

Table 13.1: Change in Melbourne Airport's overall passenger numbers—2000/01 and 2001/02

Passenger Type	Number of passengers 2001 2000 & 2001	Growth in passenger numbers B/N	Number of passengers 2002 2001 & 2002	Change in passenger numbers B/N
Domestic	13.51 million	+9.5%	12.81 million	−5.2%
International	3.36 million	+12.25%	3.41 million	+1.5%
Transit	0.32 million	+33.9%	0.26 million	−18.8%
Total	17.19 million	+10.4%	16.48 million	−4.1%

Source: Melbourne Airport, 2002.

Recognising that the number of leisure travellers using the Airport is closely linked to the operation of the state government's peak tourism body, Melbourne Airport and Tourism Victoria work very closely to develop strategies to maximise visitation to Victoria.

In its new strategic plan (2002–2006), Tourism Victoria dedicates a section to the role of the aviation industry in Victoria. The objectives of this section include:

* achieving an average growth in international services of between four and five per cent a year over the next five years;

* maximising the benefits of Melbourne Airport being a 24-hour operation;

* increasing the number of domestic late night services; and

* closing the link between Victoria's tourism performance and the capacity and ease of air access to and within Victoria.

The plan notes that immediate priorities for the industry are aimed at speeding Victoria's recovery from the impacts of the September 11 terrorist attack and the collapse of Ansett airlines.

Tourism Victoria's aviation plan states that visitor growth into Melbourne is likely to result from new air links which have previously been disregarded, and notes that whilst international airlines are fully utilising the 24-hour operations of Melbourne Airport, domestic airlines have so far failed to realise the value of operating late night services (11 pm to 6 am). Currently, there are over 90 per cent of domestic aircraft lying idle at Australian airports between these hours, and this business is likely to be popular for medium- to long-haul domestic sectors, such as flights from Melbourne to the Northern Territory and some ports in Queensland, which currently have few direct services.

The report also identifies a lack of direct services from North Asia (Taiwan, Korea and North China) as a deterrent to building visitation from these markets. However, the recent introduction of Qantas's single class international leisure carrier, Australian Airlines, should help overcome this limitation by establishing direct services to these markets. It should be recognised, however, that visitors from North Asia are less interested in Melbourne as a holiday destination compared with some other regions in Australia. This is attributable to the fact that Melbourne's climate is closer to countries in North Asia than is the weather in cities such as Sydney, Brisbane and Cairns, and Melbourne is not a great group tour city.

Finally, the plan states that Melbourne Airport will continue to develop as Melbourne's gateway, by adding more major accommodation and retail outlets, and introducing substantial entertainment activity to secure its position as one of the world's best airports.

MAJOR MARKETS

Melbourne Airport has four distinct key markets that it considers in all of its marketing endeavours. These are airlines, passengers, business/tourism community, and airport neighbours, each of whom has quite different needs. Consequently, Melbourne Airport has developed a range of strategies to address the needs of each group.

Airlines

Melbourne Airport actively encourages airline growth to stimulate passenger demand. In 2001, domestic airlines added 191 new services weekly, an increase of up to 27 flights daily. However, the Ansett collapse in 2001 saw Australia's domestic flight capacity effectively halved overnight. It is now gradually returning to normal through increased scheduling of flights by Qantas and Virgin Blue.

International airlines decide which airports they will use for flights to and from Australia and the frequency of such services. There are now 22 international carriers that use Melbourne Airport mainly because the airport has 24-hour-per-day access and the best minimum connection times in Australia. The number of European airlines flying to Melbourne has decreased in recent years, but this has been more than offset by the increase in the number of carriers from the Asian region.

Melbourne Airport attempts to 'pick winners' by building close working relationships with international airlines that have the largest share of passenger traffic to Australia and those that have the greatest growth potential. Melbourne Airport's aim is to become a hub airport for as many airlines as possible. As such, it must be able to identify new carriers that have the potential to become major participants in the market, and not simply rely upon traditional carriers.

Melbourne Airport has targeted Qantas, Singapore Airlines, Malaysia Airlines and Thai Airways. The success of its approach can be seen in the increases in international airline services to Melbourne Airport over the past three years:

* Singapore Airlines now has 17 scheduled flights per week (although at the time of writing three of these had been suspended due to SARS);

* Thai Airways has introduced 11 flights into Melbourne. These replace 12 flights which were previously scheduled as direct flights into Brisbane and Sydney, and which then flew to Melbourne. As a result of the change in scheduling, more passengers disembark in Melbourne now and more freight can be moved in and out of Victoria, which has significant advantages for the Victorian economy and the airline's retail and catering areas; and

* Malaysia Airlines has increased from seven to 14 services per week. However, it should be noted that Malaysia has recently changed its aircraft type from a Boeing 747 to a Boeing 777, effectively reducing capacity but maintaining flight numbers.

Qantas is currently undergoing a period of significant international flight expansion out of Melbourne as follows:

* from June 2002, Qantas introduced five new services per week to New Zealand. This was due in part to the Ansett collapse and the

consolidation of Air New Zealand's flights, resulting in reduced capacity between the two countries; and

* from July 2002, Qantas introduced direct daily flights from Japan to Melbourne as well as four direct flights per week from Melbourne to Japan. The previous daily service was via Sydney, and these new services will provide considerable business and tourism opportunities for Victorians with Japan.

Good relationships with the domestic airlines are also of vital importance in strengthening international airline business. The more frequent and better timed are the domestic services, the better are the connections with international flights. This makes the Airport more attractive to international carriers.

APAC recently purchased the former Ansett terminal, which the airport's Chief Executive Officer, Chris Barlow, says will allow the Airport to provide airlines with more terminal options and thus increase the Airport's competitiveness.

Passengers

Airport success is dependent upon both airlines and passengers, as without airline services passengers are not able to access direct services, but without sufficient passenger demand airlines will not continue to offer their services. The success achieved by Melbourne Airport in recent years in attracting increased international airline services to Melbourne has meant that the previous criticism of 'few direct services to Melbourne' is no longer valid. The airport's active promotion to potential passengers of the benefits it offers to passengers is much appreciated by the airlines. These key benefits include 24-hour-per-day access, single terminal convenience, frequent interstate connections, and high quality service.

On the international stage, Sydney is widely recognised as the gateway to Australia. Sydney's major icons, namely the Opera House and the Sydney Harbour Bridge, have strong international recognition, enticing a major percentage of international tourists to enter and leave Australia via Sydney. The very successful 2000 Olympic Games enhanced further the image and reputation of Sydney, which made it harder for Melbourne to compete. This in turn had an impact upon the demand for flights to Melbourne.

To justify additional inbound international services to Melbourne, it is vital to maximise the number of passengers using Melbourne Airport as their departure point from Australia. Melbourne Airport has sought to expand the catchment of the airport by seeking to make Melbourne the terminal of choice for residents of Tasmania, Adelaide and Canberra. By doing this, the population of the potential outbound market increases from 4.5 million people to over 6 million. The importance of 24-hour access is supported by the fact that the peak time-slot for international departures from Melbourne Airport is now between midnight and 1 am, and, since 1997, 35 per cent of all new services have scheduled departure and arrival times between 11 pm and 6 am when other Australian airports are closed.

Table 13.2 below illustrates the overall growth of Melbourne Airport compared with other airports in Australia between 1996 and 2002. It demonstrates that international passenger growth through Melbourne Airport has been the highest in Australia in recent years with a 6.8 per cent growth in 1998/99, 9.6 per cent growth in 1999/2000, 12.5 per cent in 2000/01 and 1.3 per cent in 2001/02. While the growth was only marginal in 2001/02, it compared very favourably with the almost 8 per cent decline that Sydney experienced.

Table 13.2: International passenger arrivals into Australian airports: percentage growth on previous year 1997/2002

Year	Melbourne	Sydney	Brisbane	Perth
1996/97	8.4	7.5	10.3	8.6
1997/98*	5.9	0.9	(0.1)	6.5
1998/99*	6.8	4.3	3.3	1.9
1999/00	9.6	8.6	2.9	3.6
2000/01**	12.5	8.4	2.7	3.8
2001/02***	1.3	(7.9)	(4.0)	(0.6)

* Asian currency crisis
** Olympic Games in Sydney
*** September 11 terrorist attack

Source: Melbourne Airport, 2002.

The origin of the airport's international passengers, and how these numbers compare with Australia's other airports, are illustrated in Table 13.3. This table suggests that whilst Melbourne Airport is above average in attracting flights from Europe, South-East Asia and New Zealand, it is significantly weaker than other Australian airports in attracting passengers from North-East Asia. This supports Tourism Victoria's recently announced strategy aimed at increasing flights from this region (Tourism Victoria 2002).

Business/tourism community

The broader business community within which an airport is located plays a vital role in influencing passengers to come to that city. In particular, this includes organisations running major special events, conferences and conventions.

Table 13.3: Origin of Melbourne Airport's international passengers—2002

Country	Australian airport average (%)	Melbourne airport average (%)	% Difference
Americas	10	11	1
Europe	22	25	3
NE Asia	20	12	(8)
Other	3	4	1
SE Asia	22	26	4
NZ/Pacific	21	23	2

Source: Melbourne Airport, 2002.

To foster partnerships in these areas, Melbourne Airport builds strong relationships with groups such as the Melbourne Convention and Visitors Bureau, Tourism Victoria, Victoria Major Events, Committee for Melbourne and the Victorian Employers' Chamber of Commerce and Industry. Being actively involved with their committees means that Melbourne Airport can respond to opportunities and help influence the direction that such organisations take.

The meetings, incentive, convention and exhibition (MICE) industry in particular is very important in this endeavour, and Melbourne Airport has introduced services at the Airport to deal specifically with MICE and major event passengers. This includes working with Customs to more efficiently manage large group arrivals and a groups and tours desk. Comprehensive theming in the terminal buildings is available to promote major events, including up to 90 pillars that can be used to hang banners promoting major events that are being held in Victoria.

Melbourne Airport works with local businesses to enhance the level of freight that enters and leaves via Melbourne Airport, and around 80 per cent of airline freight in and out of Melbourne is carried on passenger aircraft. There is a symbiotic relationship between tourism and freight. An increase in passenger services leads to an increased capacity and frequency of freight services, which leads to lower unit costs to exporters. Increased freight services helps subsidise the cost of passenger services.

Airport neighbours

APAC has an underlying philosophy of being a proactive and responsible member of the local community, so the neighbours of Melbourne Airport form another important target market for it. Although airport neighbours could be considered part of the external environment, Melbourne Airport considers them to be one of its client groups, especially since many airport staff live locally.

If the interests of the airport neighbours are not given a high priority, there is a significant chance of a community backlash against the Airport. One only has to consider the situation in relation to Sydney Airport to understand the problems that can occur when an airport loses the support of its neighbours. The fact that Melbourne Airport runs a 24-hour-per-day operation makes this issue that much more important as both aircraft and truck movements can be quite noisy and have the potential to disrupt a neighbourhood. The curfew-free status of Melbourne Airport has led to a substantial increase in the number of flights arriving and departing in the early hours of the morning, and while this provides great benefits for the airport, it also increases noise, which puts at risk Melbourne Airport's relationship with the local community. To minimise this potential problem, Melbourne Airport has very tight air corridors in place, especially after dark, and these are strictly enforced. The success of Airport management in dealing with the noise issue to date is reflected in the number of noise complaints from people who live in the area. Such complaints have fallen in recent times, and in the last audited period averaged only 1.5 per week. This is the lowest level of complaint per aircraft movement of any major airport in Australia. It should also be noted that Melbourne Airport has environmental systems and procedures in place to deal with the range of environmental impacts of its operations, and those of businesses within its precinct, on the local community and the broader environment. These systems are outlined in an Airport-wide Environment Strategy and Environmental Management System, and the Airport's environmental performance is evaluated under the Commonwealth *Airports Act 1996* and *Airports (Environment Protection) Regulations 1997*.

The Airport works with local councils to develop appropriate planning regimes around the Airport to ensure that it can continue to operate on a curfew-free basis without detracting from the amenity of the local community.

MARKETING MIX

Product

Services

Melbourne Airport has a broad business base, encompassing passenger facilities, freight facilities, a business park, an office park, and a large retail and food precinct, all of which ensure that it is not overly dependent on deriving income from any one sector.

The Airport's passenger facilities compare favourably with leading airports around the world and have been regularly updated over the years. First opened in 1970, the Airport underwent a major refurbishment in 1994/95, and since APAC took control of the facility capital works have totalled around $200 million. Although Melbourne Airport has funded much of this work alone, most of it has been done in partnership with the private sector at the Airport, again demonstrating the importance of strategic partnerships to its business.

The fact that there is a single terminal allowing passengers to very easily and quickly move between the domestic and international gates at the Airport is a major asset, especially compared with airports such as Sydney, Perth and Brisbane where passengers must use buses to move between domestic and international terminals. Having domestic and international terminals under a single roof creates efficiencies for airlines, in that they do not need to have separate domestic and international teams, and are, therefore, able to quickly move staff and equipment between terminals.

New aerobridges at Melbourne Airport have been designed to handle all types of aircraft, so that airlines are not constrained to having to schedule particular types of planes to fly to Melbourne. The Airport's automated baggage system handles 3000 bags per hour and the international terminal handles about 1800 passengers per hour. The Airport is currently upgrading to accommodate the new generation A380 plane which is so well suited to long haul destinations such as Melbourne.

Melbourne Airport's income from retail operations is derived from four streams. These include: duty free, food and beverage, currency exchange and specialty stores; long- and short-term car parking; car rental concessions; and advertising sites. In 2000/01, retail revenue grew by 12 per cent continuing the upward growth trend over the previous two years, with the main reasons for growth considered to be the improvement and expansion of the retail outlets and new car parking facilities.

APAC honoured all existing retail leases when it took control of the Airport. However, as the leases expire, new terms and conditions have been introduced to ensure that the range of products offered match the needs of the passengers who use the Airport. Before new leases are signed for retail concessions at the Airport, a comprehensive assessment of applications is made in order to ensure that the most suitable retailers are accepted. In particular, this assessment examines the retailer's reputation, recruitment practices, and training programs. This is done to ensure that the service delivered by the retailer is at a very high level, consistent with the overall objectives of Melbourne Airport.

The fact that over 50 per cent of passports presented at the Airport are Australian has led to an emphasis on products catering for Australian travellers. The product mix also reflects the fact that 23 per cent of the Airport's passengers are business travellers, 27 per cent are visiting friends and relatives, 42 per cent are leisure and 7 per cent are education. As a result, the focus of the Airport's retail precinct has been on general merchandise rather than on high-priced fashion shops. This approach has been very successful.

Much effort has been made to improve the previously held, but justified, reputation that Melbourne Airport had expensive shopping. Under the new leases with retailers at the Airport, a price guarantee has been built into agreements, such that prices at the Airport must not be dearer than shops in Melbourne. Educating consumers that prices at the Airport now compare favourably with city prices has required considerable effort, and there are indications that the message is now being accepted. However, more work is required to convince travellers that the prices charged at Melbourne Airport are generally better than those charged in many airports in Asia, and acceptance of this may take some time. As part of the Airport's Airside Masterplan, the number of retailers will be expanded over the next five-year period.

Melbourne Airport is Australia's second biggest airfreight hub, handling 27 per cent of Australia's airfreight exports and 27 per cent of its imports. In recent times, major global freight companies, such as DHL and Lufthansa, have made Melbourne Airport a key base for their air freight programs, and Lufthansa has chosen Melbourne as the base for its new 'round the world' freight service. This is largely because of the Airport's curfew-free status and its ability to offer companies the infrastructure and flexibility they require.

Melbourne Airport manages a large piece of land, and is home to over 150 businesses employing more than 12 000 people. Recent property developments in terminal, freight and business park infrastructure have cost $310 million, and these projects have been a major force behind the Airport's growth. The Airport has another 350 hectares of land, which is zoned commercial and is considered suitable for future development. One part of this development will take place in an area dedicated for a state-of-the-art Office Park. Stage one of this development has commenced, and the completed park will have an office area of 17 000 square metres. Another 250 hectares of vacant land at the Airport has been set aside as the home of the future Melbourne Airport Business Park, and APAC has recently appointed Australand Holdings and Santilli Group of companies as the preferred developers of this site.

Since the early days of the Airport, there has been a hotel located within a few hundred metres of the terminal. The original facility was not large enough for a major international airport, and a new four star hotel with 280 rooms was opened late in 2000. This facility, which is operated by the Hilton group, is only 75 metres from the airline check-in counter and can be accessed completely under cover. In addition, and in direct contrast, the recent opening of Accor group's Formula 1 motel is geared towards the budget traveller and provides yet another style of product within the Airport's diverse product portfolio. This hotel is located only a few minutes walk from the airport terminal. Thus the Airport now has 1200 hotel beds located within 400 metres of the terminal spread across three grades of accommodation and price.

Service quality

Melbourne Airport's 'obsession' with the delivery of high service quality is the distinguishing feature that separates the Airport from so many other such facilities. The focus of the Airport's attention is very clearly on the passengers, as to a large extent airlines will be satisfied providing that their passengers are satisfied. Great efforts are made to ensure that passengers' waiting times are minimised, the ambience of the setting is as pleasant as possible, the retail precinct is relaxed and offers a wide range of value for money quality products, and there is adequate visitor information.

In forming opinions about the level of service quality at the airport, passengers would normally be judging the performance of non-Melbourne Airport operations, such as retail services and baggage trolley availability, and this makes the task for Melbourne Airport that much more difficult. As Melbourne Airport itself employs less than 1.5 per cent of the airport's workforce, it is a challenge to ensure that the overall quality standards at the Airport are maintained.

Substantial effort is made to ensure that new tenants at the Airport have a history of offering high quality service, and performance criteria are written into the leases. Recently, for example, it took over six months of evaluation of various applications for a new coffee shop operation at the Airport before the final decision was made. The airlines seem most appreciative of this attention to detail, as it enhances the passenger experience, and ultimately reflects well on the airlines themselves.

Melbourne Airport's vision is to provide retailing in the international terminal that offers variety, value for money and quality customer service for all. This is supported by its ongoing market research to identify customer needs and trends. The Airport shares the results of this research and works with retail partners to assist them in achieving improved sales and greater customer satisfaction.

Quality of service monitor (QSM) is a fundamental plank in the Melbourne Airport operation. As mentioned earlier, 1000 passengers are questioned each month about their perceptions of their experience at the Airport, and even the interviewers used are accredited with standards required by 'Interviewer Quality Control Australia', reflecting further Melbourne Airport's commitment to providing excellent practice across all areas of its operation. The questionnaire that is used for this purpose is part of a package produced by BAA, which allows the results of this monthly survey to be benchmarked against a number of other international airports, such as Heathrow and Gatwick. Melbourne Airport, however, is the only Australian airport to employ this international airport monitor and the results are used to ensure that high quality customer service is maintained and increased. Areas surveyed include quality of baggage trolleys, check-in, baggage reclaim, food and beverage outlets, parking, passport control, security, and airport cleanliness. The results of these surveys have led to improvements in both the facilities and services on offer. For example, feedback from passengers led to the introduction of a range of Asian cuisine at the airport, and complaints about airport trolleys led to the development and introduction of an improved trolley design. The results of these monthly surveys are given to the various service providers at the Airport in order to encourage them to monitor and improve their own service standards. Melbourne Airport receives an average rating of 4.3 on a 5-point scale, and this rating outperforms the other airports using the measure. QSM results are also provided to Customs, Immigration and Quarantine to help improve customer service at the Airport.

Melbourne Airport continually monitors and analyses key performance indicators to assess its level of service quality. QSM and Customer Comment Cards (CCCs) are part of this process, and action is taken where necessary to improve service quality, such as ongoing staff development, and working with business partners to assist them to raise their performance. CCCs are distributed in the international terminal, and these cards collect feedback on all aspects of the 'airport experience'. Melbourne Airport acts immediately upon such feedback, responding directly to customers where necessary.

Melbourne Airport's international check-in counters are owned by the Airport and leased to the various airlines in 15-minute blocks so that airlines can best match the expected passenger demand for their various flights. Airlines do not need to bear the cost of permanent facilities nor pay rental based upon full load estimates as happens at many other airports, as that approach results in airlines taking fewer counters than needed in order to reduce costs. Conversely, Melbourne Airport's approach assists the airlines to improve customer service.

Signage and visitor information are vital components in delivering a high quality experience for passengers. Much effort has been expended over the past three years in the provision of suitable signage, and, in 1997, Melbourne Airport was ranked first in the world in this area. With respect to visitor information, Melbourne Airport now operates the visitor information service in the international arrivals hall 21 hours per day every day, from the first to the last flight, to ensure that the needs of passengers are adequately met. There is no other facility in Australia that offers such an extensive visitor information service. The provision of quality visitor information assists in promoting Melbourne and Victoria as popular tourist destinations.

As part of its focus on providing quality information to customers, Melbourne Airport now operates a real-time flight information service on its web site. Flight information is updated every two minutes and this saves the airlines having to handle the very high volume of arrival and departure time enquiries themselves. The web site is very popular with the travelling public, featuring links to many other organisations, both within the tourism industry and outside, and promoting and linking to upcoming event web sites in Melbourne.

Pricing

Airports generally use two main mechanisms for raising revenue from aircraft movements, namely, airport charges per aircraft, and aeronautical charges per passenger. In total, these charges usually make up less than 4 per cent of an airline's overall operating cost. Melbourne Airport's pricing is particularly competitive, with aircraft costs half those of Sydney Airport at the time of writing (refer to Table 13.4 below).

Aircraft Type	Melbourne	Sydney	Saving per annum
	Table 13.4: Comparison of Sydney and Melbourne Airport charges as at June 2002		
Daily 747	$4400	$8050	$1.332 million
Daily 777	$3610	$6600	$1.091 million

Source: Melbourne Airport, 2002.

Currently, the Airport lists its proposed airport charges prior to the end of each financial year, which enables airlines to factor into their budgets any variation in charges. Until June 2002, the Australian Consumer Competition Commission (ACCC) regulatory authority had to approve any increase in charges. However, since then, airports have not been required to meet any regulation regarding pricing, and instead are governed by a new monitoring system. Following on from this change, Melbourne Airport has decided to base its pricing structure on a per passenger basis rather than per aircraft as was previously the case. The per passenger rate shares the risk with airlines during downturns.

PROMOTIONAL STRATEGY

Branding

Very soon after taking management control of the Airport, APAC commissioned a major brand value and positioning study of the Airport. This study involved an assessment of the core values of the Airport from a customer perspective, and found that the key descriptors were 'sophisticated, stylish and effective'.

Since these features align very closely with the core values of Melbourne itself, as determined in other studies, it was decided that the word 'Melbourne' should be emphasised in the name of the Airport. Previously the Airport had been unofficially known as Tullamarine Airport, a name that had no substantial brand recognition. The name of the airport officially became Melbourne Airport, and the word 'Melbourne' became the emphasis in all of the Airport's promotional materials.

General promotional activities

Partnerships are an important part of the Airport's promotional strategy. Just as Melbourne Airport has developed partnerships with key stakeholders such as the airlines, it has formed partnerships with other key institutions that can be used to underpin its promotional activities. Brand value drives these partnerships, and an example of such a relationship is the Airport's decision to partially sponsor a Chair (the Melbourne Airport Chair of Marketing) at Victoria

University. Given that Victoria University is located in close proximity to the airport and draws students from the Airport's immediate surrounds, this relationship directly benefits the local community, assists the Airport in its research efforts, and reinforces the Airport's position as a good corporate citizen. Melbourne Airport also demonstrates its bona fides in this area by actively supporting a wide range of good causes such as the *Safe sex* campaign for the AIDS Council, a women's refuge in Broadmeadows, the Red Cross, the Salvation Army, and the *Swim between the flags* campaign.

Geoffrey Conaghan, Melbourne Airport's Manager of Corporate Affairs, has a talk spot on ABC radio 774. This radio spot is aimed at the 26-years-of-age and above 'white collar' audience in Melbourne and the intention of this 8-10 minute slot is to position Melbourne Airport as the barometer of what happens in the city. It covers what's happening at the Airport, visitor trends, major conferences and events and who's in town, and endeavours to create a relationship between the Airport and the city it serves.

The Airport uses its growing list of industry awards as part of its promotional strategy to demonstrate its contribution to the airport, transport and tourism industries, and, as part of these awards, the City of Melbourne gains recognition on local, national and global stages. These awards include:

* Melbourne Award from the Committee for Melbourne in recognition of the Airport's contribution to the Victorian economy and the quality of Melbourne's civic life;
* in 1999, Melbourne Airport was named Australian Major Airport of the Year in recognition of its commitment to quality and outstanding contribution to transport and aviation;
* International Air Transport Association 'Top 5 World Airports' award;
* *Business Traveller Magazine*'s 'World's Top 10 Airports' in 2002 (for the seventh consecutive year);
* multiple Australian Tourism Awards;
* Victorian Tourism Award and Hall of Fame;
* Best Airport in Asia Pacific;
* Most Valued Employer of Graduates; and
* IATA Eagle Award 2003 for outstanding world business practice by an international airport.

Melbourne Airport ranked in the Top 10 of *Business Traveller Magazine*'s World's Best Airports and was the only Australian airport that ranked each year since 1993 in its report of the world's Top 10 airports. Fourth only to Singapore, Hong Kong and Amsterdam—Schipol Airport, the *Business Traveller* passenger survey ranked Melbourne Airport as a leading airport achieving Top 10 rankings in the individual categories of Best Airport Shopping, Ease of Access and Efficiency.

Working hard to ensure a high reputation as a corporate partner and citizen means that Melbourne Airport does not need to focus on reactive media or public relations consultants to enhance its image with its various stakeholder groups.

As indicated earlier, the Melbourne Airport web site has become an integral component of APAC's promotional strategy and is referred to in all of Melbourne Airport's printed material.

SUMMARY

Since privatisation, Melbourne Airport has performed extremely well on all measures of success despite the very turbulent external environment that has existed in the last couple of years. Given that Melbourne is Australia's second largest city and not the major international gateway to Australia, Melbourne Airport has to be very strategic in the manner in which it builds its business. Melbourne Airport has two major competitive advantages, namely, a single terminal under one roof and being curfew-free, aspects that the Airport features in all its promotional efforts.

Much of Melbourne Airport's success, however, has come from its absolute commitment to high levels of service quality and to its focus on developing solid partnerships with its many key stakeholders and working with the Victorian Government. This success was demonstrated in the Olympics year when Melbourne Airport had 12.5 per cent international passenger growth compared with Sydney's 8.4 per cent growth—the host city's airport. Substantial effort is expended in the development and maintenance of systems in both of these areas, and it is clear that benefits are flowing.

Examples of indicators of the Airport's success are its many awards, its strong and consistent international and domestic passenger growth, and sound financial performance. Nonetheless, Melbourne Airport must continue to be highly competitive and customer-focused to ensure that the demand for its facilities continues to grow, particularly in the light of the dynamic nature of the environment in which it operates and the recent privatisation of its main competitor, Sydney Airport.

Postscript

In December 2003 Qantas announced it would begin operations of a new domestic cut price airline (Jetstar) in May 2004. This airline will be based at Melbourne Airport.

Primary period covered by case study: 2000/02

REFERENCES

Melbourne Airport, 2002. Internal Management Report.

Tourism Victoria, 2002. Strategic Plan 2002–2006—Aviation.

QUESTIONS

1   Since the events of 11 September 2001 there have been greatly increased security measures at all airports, which have added to passenger inconvenience. Does this undermine Melbourne Airport's marketing plan, which has the provision of high quality customer services and attempts to reduce passenger waiting times as fundamental elements?

2   Although Melbourne Airport has substantial unused capacity in the hours between 11 pm and 6 am, this time period is not very convenient for passengers. Discuss the strategies that Melbourne Airport can adopt to encourage further utilisation of this time period by airlines.

3   From the perspective of an airline passenger, what is Melbourne Airport's core, tangible and augmented product?

4   Melbourne Airport is not an attraction in its own right and is not able to control its different markets. It must rely on relationships with other parties to help entice business to Melbourne. Identify the market segments that Melbourne Airport is best able to influence, and the strategies that it can employ to enhance the number of patrons through the Airport.

5   How important is it for organisations such as Melbourne Airport to be seen as 'good corporate citizens'? Identify and evaluate the approaches that Melbourne Airport has adopted to enhance its profile in this area.

6   From a marketing perspective, discuss the rationale behind, and feasibility of, Melbourne Airport's decision to try to become the airport of choice for residents of Tasmania, South Australia and Canberra for their international travel.

7   What value is there in Melbourne Airport's efforts to link its branding efforts to that of the City of Melbourne?

8   One of the key competitive advantages of Melbourne Airport appears to be its 'curfew-free' status. If Sydney Airport was relocated and it too became curfew-free, what marketing strategies could Melbourne Airport adopt in order to remain a strong competitor?

9   Critique the overall marketing strategy being adopted by management at Melbourne Airport and indicate whether you believe that this approach is sustainable.

10   Given the heavy reliance of Melbourne Airport on flights to and from Asia, what opportunities does Airport management have to protect this business at a time when international events have greatly reduced the number of flights from Asia?

14. SMARTRAVEL SOLUTIONS

INTRODUCTION

Smartravel Solutions is involved in business-to-business marketing (B2B) rather than consumer-based marketing. In servicing the needs of the travel industry generally and travel agents in particular, it is dealing with a relatively small number of clients. It is focused on the provision of technologically-based solutions to the challenge that travel agents confront in attempting to provide competitively priced products to consumers. The complexity of the behind the scenes transactions relating to commissions, rebates and discounts cannot be transmitted to consumers. The latter expect efficiency and simplicity. This case study is an interesting example of an organisation which is attempting to communicate complex solutions in a simple, concise and user friendly manner.

BACKGROUND

The advent of electronic commerce (e-commerce) is in the process of transforming the way in which travel-related products are distributed. A key feature of the case studies presented in this book is the recognition by established organisations of the need to embrace new technology. The case study featured in this chapter is an interesting example of a company that has enthusiastically embraced e-commerce in the form of business-to-business marketing using the internet.

The application of e-commerce to tourism is particularly potent because the tourism phenomenon involves customers travelling from places throughout the world to reach a given destination. When the consumer commits to a major travel purchase, he or she relies on the convenient availability of up-to-the-minute and accurate information. Since travel agents are located close to where consumers live or work they are likely to play an ongoing role. They will, however, need to offer information to their customers and supplement this with appropriate service and advice. Historically, training and recruitment in the travel sector has placed a strong emphasis on the employment of staff proficient in technical functions such as fare calculation and ticket issuance. Over the past two decades, technological applications have reduced the need for paper tickets and have facilitated calculations that previously relied on considerable manual effort. In view of these changes which have affected the travel sector, the authors considered the inclusion of a case study focused specifically on e-commerce applications to be essential.

Smartravel Solutions is a component of Concorde International Travel, which was founded in Melbourne in 1949. The principal activities of the Concorde International group are the development, marketing and wholesale distribution of airline product, internet travel resources and technology, tour packages, travel products and airline representation (Concorde International Travel 2002).

In the late 1970s, the activities of Concorde expanded to encompass air ticket wholesaling (consolidation), airline representation and (subsequently) internet technology services as a support to its traditional and electronic travel businesses. In 1987 the scale of the group was transformed following the acquisition of a 50 per cent shareholding by British Airways. At the time of writing, British Airways retains its half share with four individual Concorde partners having the remaining shareholding. Subsequent to the involvement of British Airways, the group's annual turnover has increased to $1.7 billion, with a return on investment of 24 per cent. According to the company's profile, all purchases and acquisitions have been funded from company revenue. A major leap in revenues occurred in 1996 when Concorde Inc. purchased Qantas Vacations, the largest wholesaler from North America to the South Pacific region (Additional information about the organisation is available at <www.concorde.com.au> and <www.smart ravel.com.au>).

The company consists of four main business units:

* Air Tickets (consolidator)
* Concorde Holidays (tour wholesaler)
* World Aviation Systems (general sales agent)
* Smartravel Solutions (technology and distribution).

The present case study focuses on the activities of Smartravel Solutions. This division was established in 1997 in recognition of the growing importance of the internet and its related technologies, and is currently Concorde's fastest growing division. One of its roles is the provision of technological support for the core infrastructure of Concorde International Travel as well as for other travel industry organisations. It specialises in providing internet travel resources to organisations in the following sectors: ticket wholesaling, traditional travel agencies and electronic travel agencies. A key component of Smartravel Solutions is the 'SmartFares' database. According to Richard Noon, General Manager of Smartravel Solutions, the database is at the forefront of fares databases worldwide, winning the Best Agency Support Services

Award in the 2003 Australian Federation of Travel Agents National Travel Industry Awards.

One of the core businesses of Smartravel Solutions is the provision of 'SmartFares' for retail and wholesale applications using airfares database technology. SmartFares provides 130 000 fares daily and is claimed to be the largest distributor of airfare content in Australia. All of Australia's major retail travel groups, as well as many individual travel agents, use SmartFares to maintain their internal private fares databases and their retail internet services.

Although online bookings currently account for less than 3 per cent of revenue, consumers are increasingly turning to the internet to undertake travel-related research. Consumers are comfortable with the use of the internet for locating fares and for comparing prices. Having completed what they regard as sufficient online research, the consumer then heads for a travel agent to carry out the booking process. As consumer confidence grows, it is likely that online bookings will increase.

This increase is already evident in the case of airlines in Australia. New entrants Impulse Airlines and Virgin Blue Airlines have attracted a significant and increasing share of their bookings via the internet. This shift has promoted the established carriers Qantas and Virgin to adopt a more proactive stance towards online bookings. The anticipated increase in online bookings is likely to lead to the emergence of new distribution channels. In anticipating this change, management at Smartravel Solutions has developed products such as SmartWeb and SmartFares which can assist travel agencies to stay competitive online. This reinforces the relationship between Concorde and retail travel agents by demonstrating a commitment to working in partnership and assisting the retail sector to face up to the mounting challenges which confront it. As a component of its proactive approach to product development, Smartravel Solutions has a direct relationship with all computer reservation systems (CRSs) and the latter play a fundamental role in the development of product offerings by the division.

MARKETING PHILOSOPHY AND PLANNING PROCESS

The marketing philosophy of Smartravel Solutions is to provide innovative technology to help travel agents enhance their existing business operations and adapt to the current travel environment. Within Concorde, the Smartravel Solutions division is positioned as providing advanced innovative technological support for travel agents.

As previously mentioned, Concorde is a highly diversified group with a substantial turnover. Both Concorde and Smartravel Solutions have business plans that provide broad group-wide strategic parameters. According to Noon, new business initiatives within the Concorde group need to be underpinned by a thorough assessment of risk and potential return. The strategic plan is viewed as the essential underpinning for sound commercial decision-making and defines the overall mission and objectives of the group. A marketing plan has subsequently been developed to reinforce the broad strategic parameters. This process involves identifying the current marketing situation, threats and opportunities, objectives and issues, marketing strategies, action programs, and budgets and controls. All marketing plans typically cover a period of one year.

BRANDING STRATEGY

Smartravel Solutions has adopted a multi-brand strategy (see Figure 14.1) with a number of different brands included within the overall product range.

Figure 14.1: The Smartravel Solutions multi-brand strategy

Source: Concorde International, 2000.

MARKETING RESEARCH

There are two main approaches to marketing research at Smartravel Solutions—exploratory and descriptive. In view of the technology focus of Smartravel Solutions and the rapidity of change, marketing research plays a major role. Such research provides the division with confidence about the validity of its decision-making, and underpins the anticipation of future market developments and how the company should respond to them. The main market research tool used is online surveys.

Online surveys have proved to be extremely successful. For example, Smartravel Solutions launched a 'new look SmartFares' home page linked to a user survey. According to Noon, 'within two days we had a 15 per cent response rate enabling us to determine that the "new look SmartFares" was a success. Within five days a 25 per cent response rate had been secured. At this stage the results were correlated and the findings prompted the group to make changes consistent with customer preferences.' Noon believes that there has never been such a fast and efficient means of obtaining such valuable information.

MAJOR MARKETS

Since Smartravel Solutions is an Australian-based wholesale travel agent and business-to-business marketer, its major clients are retail travel agencies in Australia. Outside Australia its role is slightly different. In addition to servicing the needs of travel agents, Smartravel Solutions provides a service to consolidators and air ticket wholesalers who wish to apply strategies and products based on the Smartravel model in their home markets.

As is the case with any company which has moved from a domestic focus to an international environment, there are ongoing differences between the conduct of its international and domestic operations. Concorde has adopted a range of approaches to its various overseas partnerships and alliances. Overseas organisations wishing to emulate the Concorde approach to business will generally do so on a franchise basis.

KEY COMPETITIVE STRENGTHS

Smartravel Solutions aims to provide a technological edge over its competitors. According to Noon, it is the group's continuous and proactive commitment to research and development (R&D) which has led to the introduction of new products not offered by competitors. The 'new look' SmartFares home page is a useful example. The company identified that the lack of tools needed by travel agents to make full use of the product offering was a deficiency. In response to this recognition, the company gathered information about the tools that agents would like. In-house surveys were carried out using a sample of 150 employees. The healthy response rate of over 35 per cent provided a clear understanding of the most valued tools and those that need to be developed. The product offering was subsequently updated, accompanied by in-house test marketing. Following the analysis of results and feedback, amendments were made and the home page was finally launched. The external survey results were collated a week after the launch of the home page. The 20 per cent of recipients who responded confirmed that the launch and product itself were consistent with initial expectations.

SERVICE QUALITY AND MARKETING

Noon states that the critical importance of service quality should not be underestimated. Nevertheless, the online focus of the business has reduced much of the direct customer contact that would be encountered in other customer-focused businesses. Despite the high level technological application as opposed to face-to-face contact, staff training and selection are regarded as vital to the success of the organisation. Staff are grouped into areas, each area reporting to a team leader who is in turn answerable to a department manager. New staff are trained by one of the existing team leaders and are provided with additional supervision by existing staff members, once they have been fully integrated into the work environment.

There are currently 35 staff members, all located at a single site. A departmental structure is employed, with each department being headed by a manager and operated by team leaders.

It is also worth noting that the information technology department of the Concorde group reports directly to Smartravel Solutions in its role as a commercial department. Although this approach is becoming more widespread in industry, it is still somewhat unusual.

CUSTOMER LOYALTY PROGRAMS

Depending on the circumstances, incentives are given to agencies to encourage better performance defined in terms of increased turnover and brand loyalty. Within the travel industry, the payment of 'overrides' is common practice. Such incentive payments are used as a way of inducing product loyalty and of boosting sales volumes. Overrides involve the payment of an additional margin over and above the established commission rate. According to Noon, customer loyalty is an important issue, and Smartravel Solutions has identified that customers regard the need for product customisation as a priority. Maintaining long-term positive relationships with key customers is viewed as a critical success factor. One example of the cultivation of such relationships is the private fares database (PFD) operated by Smartravel Solutions. A number of technological relationships depend upon this database, and its high level of customisation has prompted strong customer loyalty. Customers regard the fare structure made available through PFD as being specifically tailored to their needs and the needs of their clients.

PRICING

The most common method of pricing used is the cost-plus method where a pre-established mark-up is added to the cost of the product. Noon acknowledges that this method can work to reduce profitability, but observes that it reduces the need to adjust prices continually. He noted that price-setting methods vary considerably according to product type.

A buyer-based approach to pricing may be adopted as a result of feed-back obtained from surveys. In the case of the SmartWeb product, a number of pricing strategies have been formulated based on the value that customers perceive is added to their business. In contrast, the organisation has adopted the cost-plus pricing method in the case of SmartFares. Smartravel Solutions is sometimes willing to 'give away' level-one product offerings in order to gain market share provided that this approach does not distort expectations or create price barriers at the inception phase. He believes that customers have a greater willingness to take up and pay for an upgraded version, once they make the original commitment.

PROMOTIONAL STRATEGY AND MEDIA

The size and composition of a promotional budget is dependent on the nature of the product to be promoted. In most cases the 'affordable method' is used for the setting of promotional budgets. Although the method has a number of drawbacks, Noon states that implementation has been successful for a wide range of products. Once the total promotional budget has been identified, a decision is made as to how to divide the total promotional budget among the various elements of the promotional mix.

The selection of medium depends on the type of product. In the case of a customised fare search engine such as SmartWeb, the main promotional medium is online advertising and personal selling through the sales force. Because the major product offerings are internet-based, the main challenge confronting the B2B marketer is a reliance on the internet rather than on personal selling to bring about market penetration.

Since the Concorde group is a large and diversified organisation, its large sales force provides a competitive advantage and plays a critical role in the implementation of the organisation's promotional strategies. The appropriate combination of push and pull promotional strategies varies according to product market, the nature of the business and the product offerings available. An email newsletter is also made available on an optional basis to travel agent partners, and is an important means of communication. To communicate effectively with overseas customers, trade shows and conference speaking engagements have been used to good effect.

STRATEGIC PARTNERSHIPS AND USE OF EXTERNAL ORGANISATIONS

As mentioned previously, a number of the products offered by Smartravel Solutions are undertaken in partnership with a third party (for example, Smart-Money with travel industry automated systems). No external organisations, such as advertising agencies, are used for promotional purposes. In the case of joint venture initiatives, both companies collaborate in the development of promotional strategies.

According to Noon, Smartravel Solutions focuses on its key strengths, namely its sophisticated fares database. Since it is impractical to be an expert in all areas, partnerships have been developed with companies such as Penzance Technology that has developed and supplied advanced technology systems for online use. Other partners include Solarnet, major suppliers of travel content to all of the world's major computer reservations systems and travel industry automated systems (TIAS). Because of the technology focus, the products provided by Smartravel Solutions need to feature the latest and the most advanced technology systems available. Naturally, all of these requirements cannot be accomplished in-house and this has prompted the organisation to enter into a range of partnerships to provide access to the relevant technology.

ROLE OF THE INTERNET AND E-COMMERCE

The internet is the key platform for Smartravel Solutions and is currently associated with the fastest growth areas for the Concorde group. The internet plays a major role in the development and implementation of the marketing mix, as is evident from material included on the Concorde web site (<www.concorde.com.au>).

INSTALLATION AND APPLICATION OF NEW TECHNOLOGY

A number of external factors are taken into account during the process of strategic marketing planning. Key indicators include the number of retail travel outlets and the volume of business that they transact. An increase in the number of agents or in the volume of sales will enhance the market potential of Smartravel Solutions. Another important factor to consider is the growth of internet access for travel agents, including email. Approximately 75 per cent of the Smartravel Solutions products are internet-based. Consequently, any increase in the number of agents who have access to the internet will create enhanced sales potential. Currently 20 per cent of SmartFare page views are accessed via the internet. Noon foresees that this will increase to 40 per cent by 2001 and to 70 per cent by 2002. He states that the question of whether the internet is appropriate for a particular product is less critical than whether a particular product is appropriate for the internet. Products are consciously designed at Smartravel Solutions with an internet focus, and the early stages of R&D will identify whether a product is internet-compatible.

Smartravel Solutions works closely with a number of organisations outside the travel sector, such as suppliers of web site services. Typically, these organisations are confronting the same challenges of how to apply leading edge technology to small- and medium-sized enterprises which are encountering difficulties in adapting long-established practices and behaviours.

The development of new technology within Smartravel Solutions is another factor that must be considered. Since Smartravel Solutions offers cutting edge technology to its customers, any new marketplace development must be met with a speedy response. The division must be 'leading edge' in its internal processes if it is to remain credible with its business partners.

SERVICE QUALITY, STAFF SELECTION, TRAINING AND DEVELOPMENT FOR MARKETING

The greatest technological development that has helped the organisation to improve service and quality standards is the implementation of online surveys. These substantially accelerate the receipt of customer responses to new or existing products. Such surveys enable Smartravel Solutions to respond more quickly to market trends.

Smartravel Solutions places a high value on staff that are knowledgeable and proficient with the relevant technology and possess some formal training. After being recruited, such staff increase their product-specific knowledge and in due course are in a position to assist with the achievement of marketing objectives. A key attribute is the ability to simply jump in and to use or try to use new products. According to Noon, true learning only takes place when an employee is putting theory into practice. Given the nature of the organisational structure previously outlined, communication is not considered to be a problem. Staff typically work in teams in the pursuit of marketing objectives. Regular briefing sessions are also carried out to ensure that all areas are aware of the overall objectives.

SUMMARY

The key future challenge for Smartravel Solutions is to play and to be seen as playing a lead role in the application of advanced technology to the information needs of travel organisations. The risks and rewards associated with operating in this field are high, and consequently require high levels of vigilance. The experience of the dot com stock exchange 'bubble' has demonstrated the vulnerability of companies whose value is based on speculation and hype as opposed to true value. As a single division within a major and robust corporation, Smartravel enjoys the relative advantage of being able to adopt a leading role in technology with the solid backing of the wider group. This will require particular care in the selection of business partners as well as a clear understanding of where technological applications are most appropriate.

Primary period covered by case study: 1999/2000

REFERENCES

Concorde International Travel, 2000, Internal Management Document.

Concorde International Travel, 2002, *Company Profile*.

QUESTIONS

1   How would you describe the 'product' offered by Smartravel Solutions?

2   To what extent is Smartravel Solutions involved in client education? Should this be considered part of the product and/or service?

3   What are some other examples of B2B marketing undertaken within Australia's tourism sector?

4   What are some of the challenges confronting businesses that do not deal directly with final consumers?

5   To what extent is Smartravel Solutions vulnerable to changes in the external business environment generally and within the travel and tourism sector in particular?

6   What promotional tools are particularly relevant to a business like Smartravel?

7   a) How has Smartravel employed market research to shape the development of its product offerings?
    b) Which other tourism businesses could employ similar techniques to gather market information?

8   What are the key customer benefits provided by Smartravel's products? Before answering this question you may wish to try out the product demonstration incorporated within Smartravel's web site (<www.smartravel.com.au>).

9   How would you describe Smartravel's intended market position?

10 a) What challenges face Smartravel in its new product development process?
    b) How does it seek to deal with these challenges?

15. TRAVEL Ys INTERNATIONAL

INTRODUCTION

Travel Ys International is an online booking service that deals exclusively with YWCA (Young Women's Christian Association) and YMCA (Young Men's Christian Association) hotels worldwide. It is the commercial business unit of the YWCA of Australia and contributes an important source of funding for the fulfilment of YWCA's community service commitments. This case study traces the evolution of Travel Ys from a marketing initiative that started as an internal support service within a particular organisation (YWCA of Australia) to a global commercial business venture. The case study highlights many of the challenges of international marketing, as well as the strategic value of being first in the international market place offering an innovative and accessible mode of distribution. The latter has helped YWCA of Australia to secure a unique leadership position in the internationalisation of 'Y' brand travel accommodation.

BACKGROUND

The YWCA has a long history of tourism-related activities with the latter operating alongside its diverse community services. It established Travellers Aid in 1886 to provide overnight accommodation for women travellers. By the end of World War II there were 30 YWCA hostels in Australia offering full board and overnight accommodation for travellers. As tourism grew within Australia over the next 40 years, the number and range of accommodation suppliers expanded significantly. The increased competition that occurred at the budget end of the market saw demand for YWCA hostel accommodation decline, and by 1985 there were fewer than 10 YWCA-operated hostels (Dunn 1991). The best performing properties were those located in major cities that were able to take advantage of Australia's growing tourist market. Despite such opportunities, the decline in accommodation properties continued, and by 1994 only five YWCA of Australia properties remained in operation. With the exception of one property which had started to renovate, the rest were ageing, were experiencing increased competition and were ineffective in their promotional efforts. If YWCA of Australia was not to be forced out of the accommodation sector entirely, it needed to invest in its tourist accommodation services more seriously or seek alternative income sources. It eventually chose to pursue the first option. The ensuing relaunch of YWCA's tourist accommodation was a major marketing challenge, particularly in light of the apparent decline of the properties over the previous period and the need to attract capital investment with the intent of upgrading the quality of the product.

The relaunched product became a business unit of YWCA of Australia in 1995 and the name Travel Ys Australia replaced YWCA Travel Accommodation. Management identified the core activity of the new unit as the marketing of its five Australian YWCA hotels and lodges. In response to the marketing challenges it faced, Travel Ys embraced web-based technology, establishing an online central reservation service for the Australian properties, as well as for the international hotel properties operated by YWCA and its associated organisation, YMCA. By embracing both local and international properties with this service, Travel Ys sought to become a world coordinating point for the distribution of accommodation services, changing its name to Travel Ys International in the process. The potential network was enormous—the YWCA alone now operates over 220 travel accommodation properties in 44 countries.

The evolution of the YWCA of Australia is outlined in Figures 15.1 and 15.2.

Figure 15.1: History of YWCA involvement in tourism in Australia

1880s	The YWCA developed Travellers Aid and provided safe, temporary accommodation for women migrants 'protecting them from dangers of being strangers in a strange land'.
1950s	There were 30 YWCA hostels throughout Australia offering full board and overnight accommodation for women travellers.
1980s	Hostel numbers declined to 10. Accommodation was open to all travellers.
1990	Retaining travel accommodation services became a national priority but increased competition for budget accommodation, minimal marketing and the absence of financial resources contributed to property numbers declining.
1994	Only five properties remained—Sydney, Melbourne, Alice Springs, Darwin and Toowoomba.
1995	YWCA Travel Accommodation was relaunched as Travel Ys Australia and new tourism marketing strategies were implemented with the assistance of a Federal Government business development grant.

Source: Dunn, 1991, and Travel Ys International, 1999.

Figure 15.2: Travel Ys International 1995–2000

The table below summarises the development of Travel Ys International from 1995–2000 including strategies, achievement highlights, staff numbers and property representation.

Date	Priority & Highlights	Employees	No. of Properties
1995	Travel Ys Australia established	1	5
Priority:	**To consolidate the five YWCA properties and implement group marketing strategies**		
	• Full time tourism marketer employed • Group policies and procedures established • The Hotel Y, Melbourne relaunched following a multi-million dollar renovation		
1996		1	6
Priority:	**To further develop marketing activities and increase room sales**		
	• Toll-free central reservation telephone service started • First National Y Hotel Marketing Conference held • The Hotel Y won an Australian Tourism Award for Best Budget Accommodation		
1997		2	8
Priority:	**To expand Australian property representation** **To investigate internet-based technologies**		
	• Marketing services sold to independent (non-Y) hotels • Government grant received for Internet research project • Second Australian Tourism Award won by The Hotel Y		
1998		3	9
Priority:	**To establish alliances with YMCAs in Australia** **To develop an internet-based reservation system**		
	• First YMCA hotel joined • Central reservation service extended to include toll-free NZ fax service • Initial web site activated		

continued

Figure 15.2: Travel Ys International 1995–2000 (cont.)

Date	Priority & Highlights	Employees	No. of Properties
	• Y on the Park hotel, Sydney—relaunched following a $5 million renovation • Award wins continue: —Victorian Hall of Fame Award— The Hotel Y, Melbourne —NT Brolga Award—Banyan View Lodge, Darwin		
1999		3	10
Priority:	**To expand internationally and establish alliances with YWCA and YMCA hotels worldwide** • Travel Ys International launched, replacing Travel Ys Australia • E-commerce activities developed		
2000		4	60
Priority:	**To further develop the on-line booking service, increase property numbers and establish new tourism alliances** • 60 hotels represented in 28 countries • Negotiations under way with complementary travel partners such as car rental firms etc.		

Source: Travel Ys International, 1999.

MARKETING PLANNING PROCESS

Travel Ys International conducts an annual two-day strategic planning conference that incorporates small-scale workshops immediately prior to, and after, the plenary conference sessions. At this time Travel Ys three-year strategic business plan, as well as its series of one-year action plans, is reviewed (Travel Ys International 1999). As part of this review the strategic marketing plan, along with its associated three-year financial projections, yearly action plan, and monitoring program, are examined. To provide staff with a sense of ownership over this review process, the relevant documents are distributed for comment beforehand and discussed at the strategic planning conference. The monitoring function involves a monthly review of performance based on pre-set targets, with adjustments to be made where appropriate.

In taking a strategic approach, Travel Ys International has attempted to reposition itself as a provider of marketing services to its constituent properties. In the initial stages of development, the strategy involved a fairly conventional approach using printed materials such as the production of an accommodation directory. The second stage involved interaction with the various properties worldwide via a web-based reservation system.

MARKETING PHILOSOPHY AND POSITIONING

As stated in the organisation's business plan, the vision for Travel Ys International is the development of a commercially viable business by:

* providing travellers with a central booking service for YWCAs and YMCAs worldwide; and
* assisting individual YWCAs and YMCAs to maximise their income-generating potential by marketing their accommodation services on a collective basis internationally.

Travel Ys aims to be responsive to market demands and to consumer needs. Emphasis is placed on direct marketing rather than mass marketing with a preference for one-to-one communication. There is a strong emphasis on accountability with an expectation that implementation will only occur after full consideration of the available evidence.

Travel Ys and its constituent properties are positioned between the budget and mid-range accommodation markets. There is some variation between different YWCA properties in terms of facilities and services provided. In view of this diversity, the group aims to build its brand in a way that will achieve a realistic match between customer expectations and the services provided. The fact that the brand is established, well-recognised and well-respected internationally is an advantage. Many travellers do, however, make the mistake of believing that YWCA accommodation is focused exclusively on cheap, gender-specific, no frills lodging. This is a legacy of both past promotional efforts and direct experience by some sectors of its market.

Travel Ys has adopted a strategy of updating the existing brand, of re-educating potential travellers, and of clarifying the type and style of service on offer. A key component of changing consumer perceptions, and of re-positioning was the adoption of the name Travel Ys Australia, and later, Travel Ys International, in place of YWCA Travel Accommodation. The alliance with YMCA has been particularly important for altering the perception that accommodation services are gender-specific.

MARKETING RESEARCH

According to the General Manager of Travel Ys International, Carina Slavik, Travel Ys International is strongly committed to the use of marketing research. Whilst she would welcome greater use of external resources, budget constraints have so far confined marketing research to in-house activity. Marketing research is regarded as playing a critical role in the start-up and on-going stages of business development in supporting the strategic direction of the group. It also helps to instil confidence amongst business partners.

The key marketing research activities undertaken by Travel Ys International are as follows:

* surveys of customers and businesses using face-to-face and telephone communication as well as formal self-completion surveys;
* the measurement of business performance using indicators such as the number of calls received, bookings made, room nights sold, room revenue generated, sources of referrals and origin of visitors;
* the measurement of advertising effectiveness which involves the evaluation and/or quantifying of response coupons, editorial coverage and the placement of advertising; and
* web site performance, of which the relevant measures include the number of 'hits' received, the duration of the site visit, the profile of those inquiring directly and the number of bookings received.

Since the scale of the Travel Ys organisation is small, marketing research is undertaken as one of a number of the duties of the marketing manager. YWCA was, however, successful is securing two grants from the Commonwealth Government of Australia. The first project focused on the initial establishment of the business, and the second on the development of the web site. Each project allowed for the recruitment of a hospitality and tourism graduate who was able to assist with research activity, and who had, because of the nature of the position, a strategic approach to the development of the organisation.

TARGET MARKETS

The major target market of Travel Ys International is fully independent (leisure-based) travellers (FITs). The following are the key target market segments:

* students and young travellers
* budget travellers
* seniors and the over-50s
* solo travellers.

Prior to World War II, YMCA properties across the world confined their targeting to single males, though the exclusivity was discontinued at the end of the war. In the case of YWCA Australia, it was not until the late 1970s that the exclusive focus on women ended and the organisation began to target families and school groups as well as YWCA members. Neither YWCA nor YMCA are now gender-specific, though in practice their history is still influential and the current business and customer mix closely mirrors the pedigree of the organisation. YWCA for example continues to attract a disproportionate share of female customers.

COMPETITOR ANALYSIS AND KEY COMPETITIVE STRENGTHS

The type of accommodation that can be booked through Travel Ys International ranges from small budget lodgings to four star international standard hotels. As such, competitors are also varied and include backpacker hostels, hotel and motel groups, and other not-for-profit accommodation providers. That said, Travel Ys has identified other YWCA and YMCA brands as its major competitors. These include Ys Way Alliance and YMCA, USA. Also within the YMCA network are YMCA European Alliance and YMCA Asia Alliance. The Ys Way Alliance in the United States was the first computer reservation system to be established for Y properties. It was started in the mid-1980s and currently represents approximately 20 YMCAs, though only seven of these properties are located outside the United States.

The well-established nature of the YWCA and YMCA brands is a key benefit to the respective organisations. However it is an ongoing challenge to ensure that key stakeholders, including travellers, understand the relationship between the two entities and do not assume that they are synonymous.

Travel Ys International is well-positioned strategically as the only provider of a comprehensive central reservation service for the 500 YWCA and YMCA properties worldwide. Only a relatively small proportion of the networks are currently partners of Travel Ys International, but the potential for growth is considerable.

Within Australia, the YWCA properties in central Melbourne and central Sydney are critical to the positioning of the organisation as a significant (albeit small-scale) player in the budget to middle-market accommodation field. These properties are also able to accommodate corporate and association conference business. This extends the range of possible target markets and provides the scope for further diversification. Major refurbishment was a prerequisite for the diversification that has already occurred and has provided the organisation with confidence to market its competitive advantage. A shortage of capital is an ongoing challenge, though the development of alternative revenue streams by Travel Ys International has certainly diversified the risk away from the Australian properties.

SERVICE QUALITY MANAGEMENT AND CONSUMER RETENTION

The Travel Ys product is service-based and, according to Slavik, the provision of quality customer service underpins the organisational philosophy. She stresses that Travel Ys promotional messages that carry with them expectations regarding standards and quality service need to be delivered upon, and for this reason she has sought to develop a strong customer service ethos within the organisation.

During the staff induction process, recruits are briefed about the full range of YWCA businesses and are encouraged to participate in the relevant development and review activities. This approach is indicative of the importance attached to internal marketing. Individual staff are allocated clear areas of responsibility but are also encouraged to be multi-skilled and to demonstrate a good understanding of other roles within the business. Since the staff complement is small (four people), multi-skilling has been a necessity, but has also been regarded as an opportunity to create a responsive and flexible organisation. Ongoing training is provided, largely in response to staff expressions of interest. Opportunities include participation in industry seminars, conferences and in-house training programs.

A *Procedures Manual* documents the relevant Travel Ys service delivery procedures, and updating and amending the manual is a key staff responsibility. A blend of formal and informal training is used and, according to Slavik, new staff have been quick to adopt existing customer service standards. Where there are gaps, there is an expectation that more experienced colleagues will provide assistance. The performance of a staff member is reviewed twice during the first year in the job, with an annual review taking place in subsequent years. Self-assessment is encouraged throughout the year and senior staff make themselves available for one-on-one or group discussion. Peer assessment forms a component of the annual review process.

Where conflicts or problems arise, resolution amongst the concerned individuals is the preferred first step. In the absence of resolution, group discussions are used to identify the key issues. This philosophy and approach build upon the YWCA ethos as a women's organisation and the small-scale and close-knittedness of the team.

The interface between the marketing and human resource functions is regarded as critical, though the small scale of the business unit means that all staff inevitably play a significant role in the pursuit and achievement of marketing objectives. The communication problems between different divisions evident in some larger organisations are not encountered. The selection of staff with the right approach to marketing is regarded as essential for all positions.

In view of the multi-functional nature of YWCA, effective communication with the national YWCA office is regarded as critical and meetings are held monthly to provide an opportunity for regular face-to-face communication. Participating Australian properties meet six-monthly and receive printed communication on a monthly basis, supplemented by phone or personal contact as required. This approach is intended to ensure a full range of communications. Assessments of performance and budget reviews are prepared on a monthly and an annual basis. Face-to-face meetings are the preferred approach for issues that require speedy resolution.

Since YWCA is a membership-based organisation, the issue of retaining the loyalty of members is a priority. The capacity of Travel Ys as a single division of a large entity to develop a loyalty scheme is, however, limited. On the positive side, YMCA and YWCA members receive accommodation discounts as a benefit of membership. On the other hand, it is important that Travel Ys is not seen as competing with the wider organisation for the recruitment of members. Currently there is no dedicated Travel Ys membership program, though at the time of writing various alternatives were under consideration.

PRICING

Accommodation prices are set by the individual properties and not at group-wide level. Where a booking is made through Travel Ys International, the relevant property pays a commission fee of 20 per cent. The determination of an appropriate fee structure was a major challenge for the organisation as a component of its distribution strategy. Participating hotels rejected the option of paying an advertising fee in return for being offered lower rates of commission. Many of the properties have negligible promotional budgets and lack experience in dealing with third parties or intermediaries. With a view to lowering the perceived risks of participation for the properties, a structure of performance-based fees was established based on the number of rooms sold following accepted industry norms. Since the organisation and its workforce is small, Travel Ys does not currently operate a yield management program.

PROMOTIONAL STRATEGY

A key element underpinning the promotional strategy of Travel Ys is to create awareness of the new Travel Ys International name. The 'Y' name was deliberately included and needed reinforcement through image promotion. Promotion involves printed collateral as well as an attractive and consistent web site that seeks to convey an image of quality. Advertising is targeted at customers, the travel trade and Y properties worldwide. Editorial space is secured as an accompaniment to most paid advertising, reinforced by the distribution of press kits. In response to a range of direct mailouts, customers are asked to indicate how they had found out about Travel Ys, and promotional activities are adjusted accordingly. Details from inquiry and booking forms are used to profile customers and their buying behaviour.

There is a strong strategic focus on 'one-on-one' marketing, with an emphasis on maintaining a relationship with those who have submitted a request for information, thus indicating an interest in establishing contact with Travel Ys. Since a variety of communication tools are used, it is important that each of these reinforces the availability of further information. Brochures, stationery and advertisements, for example, include reference to the web site with a view to maximising cross-selling opportunities. Key strategic objectives include raising awareness about the availability of the new international accommodation booking service and converting inquiries into future sales.

PROMOTIONAL MEDIA AND BUDGETS

In determining the appropriate media for marketing activities, the internet, direct mail-outs and print advertising have been found to be the most effective. See Figure 15.3. The use of these media may be summarised as follows:

The purpose of direct mail activity is to maintain contact with consumers and with other potential sources of business. Materials used include brochures (see Figure 15.4), postcards, posters, newsletters and stickers. In the case of advertising, the objective is to raise overall awareness and to reinforce the brand. Advertising accounts for about 40 per cent of the total promotional budget outlay. The remaining 60 per cent consists of a combination of direct mail and the preparation of collateral materials including design and printing costs. The organisation makes little use of external consultants for promotional activity. A graphic designer specialising in marketing communications has, however, been retained in a consultancy capacity over a five-year period.

DISTRIBUTION CHANNELS AND INTERNET-BASED DISTRIBUTION

Travel Ys has enthusiastically embraced the opportunities provided by internet-based distribution. At the time of writing, approximately 20 per cent of accommodation bookings were received via the internet and 80 per cent via the telephone. It is intended to reverse this situation in the future. During the earlier stages of development, the Australian-based properties participating in the Travel Ys initiative had access only to toll-free phone services.

It is anticipated that the role of the internet is likely to increase as the number of participating international properties expands. The internet site may be viewed at <www.travel-ys.com>.

EXTERNAL ISSUES FOR STRATEGY DEVELOPMENT

According to Slavik, the wider YWCA organisation needs to strengthen its commitment towards the provision of tourism accommodation services by investing in refurbishment and new product development. This issue is, however, outside the direct control of Travel Ys International. Despite its limited ability to control a range of factors, Travel Ys aims to gain an understanding of wider developments by monitoring international tourism growth trends in terms of volume, information gathering by tourists and travel decision-making

Figure 15.3: Travel Ys promotional activities

Medium	Time period	Purpose
Internet		
Web site	Continuous	Exposure to international travellers 24 hours a day, seven days a week. Information constantly updated
Email	Continuous	Direct one-to-one communication with travellers
Web advertising & links	Continuous	Exposure to key markets visiting complementary sites e.g. individual Y hotels, World Y home page, International Students Forum, cheap flights etc.
Direct mail outs	*Brochures, posters, postcards and web address stickers*	
Travellers	Quarterly and as requested	Previous and potential guests
Y accommodation	Quarterly	To reach current Y accommodation users and increase awareness amongst hotel staff
Y offices without accommodation	Quarterly	To increase awareness amongst staff and Y members
Media—broadcast, travel, women's magazines	Quarterly	Editorial exposure to general public
Print advertising		
International Y publications: *Common Concern* (YWCA), *YMCA World*	Quarterly	Target Y management to encourage them to sign up their accommodation Target Y staff, members and friends for persona ltravel and referrals
Consumer travel and target market publications e.g. senior citizens publications & publications targeting overseas university students	Varied	Branding exercise Exposure to general and target market travellers

Source: Travel Ys International, 1999.

Figure 15.4: Sample Travel Ys brochure

Where in the world
are you going?

Stay @ YWCA & YMCA

Travel Y's... accommodating
travellers worldwide

Travel Y's
INTERNATIONAL

Source: Travel Ys International, 2002.

processes. Given its already significant investment in internet technology, it is critical that the organisation monitors developments such as levels of internet access and use in different parts of the world. Travel Ys also monitors the progress of hotel property networks internationally with a view to having a better understanding of the performance of equivalent organisations overseas. Another external issue that is the subject of constant scrutiny is the level of community recognition of the 'Y' brand and the level of community acceptance of the association between YWCA and YMCA accommodation.

TECHNOLOGICAL DEVELOPMENTS

The internet is the major current marketing-focused technology for Travel Ys International. The Travel Ys web site has been fully integrated with the internal computer system in order to achieve operational efficiency and ensure that staff are familiar with relevant product content. The internet interface has become a *de facto* marketing information system (MIS) for Travel Ys International. The main functions of the web site are to communicate promotional activities and to transact bookings. Other useful applications include the conduct of consumer research, the analysis and reporting on operational performance, and other back-of-house activities such as database maintenance and invoicing. These activities reinforce marketing by contributing to the continuous improvement of service standards and quality. Technology has been fully integrated into service delivery, and bookings are computerised even in cases where initial inquiries are received over the phone. This comprehensive level of computerisation facilitates the collection of standardised information, thereby improving the monitoring of business activities and transactions. Inquiries are logged by origin and by source of referral. Using a variety of criteria, reports are generated on a periodic basis for monitoring and evaluation purposes.

SUMMARY

This case study has highlighted the important role played by distribution in tourism development and marketing. To a large extent the distribution service has superseded the situation where the physical entity constituted the hotel 'product'. The potency of distribution has been enhanced by the advent of internet-based technology that has accelerated the process of internationalisation. This case study has also shown how a brand can be transformed quite rapidly. Given the 100-year plus history of YWCA, it is remarkable how Travel Ys International has transformed the community perception of YWCA accommodation from one of a rather traditional and community-service focused branding to a global and diversified brand. The bringing together of YWCA and YMCA properties has transformed the pre-existing and fragmented products of the two organisations. A strategic alliance between the participating property networks has been created where previously only loose connections existed. The large number of participating properties has enhanced the prospect of economic viability for the initiative since economies of scale are needed to maintain the momentum of providing a dedicated and comprehensive distribution service.

Unlike many of the large international organisations, Travel Ys International has had few resources at its disposal. By adopting a number of creative solutions such as collaborative research and development and the capacity of the internet, the disadvantages of smallness of scale have been substantially overcome. In identifying and pursuing a competitive advantage, Travel Ys International has devoted considerable attention to formulating the product concept. Issues such as service delivery systems, staff selection and training, and overall quality management needed particular attention. Investment and assurance of ongoing sources of revenue was also required to ensure that the product was capable of meeting the rising expectations of consumers.

Without the necessary revenue, the organisation could not have grown and the initial skepticism of participating properties anxious to see a return could not have been overcome. However, resources alone would never have been sufficient to overcome such barriers. It was essential to identify and understand key markets through research and cultivate relationships using the internet as a main medium.

Primary period covered by case study: 1999/2000

REFERENCES

Dunn, M. 1991, *The Dauntless Bunch, The Story of the YWCA in Australia*, Young Women's Christian Association of Australia, Melbourne.

Travel Ys International, 1999, *A Global Approach to Future Success. Strategic Business Plan 2000–2003*, Young Women's Christian Association of Australia, Melbourne.

Travel Ys International, 2002, Where in the World Are You Going? (Brochure).

QUESTIONS

1   The YWCA brand is well-established. However it has been noted in the case study that '[M]any travellers do, however, make the mistake of believing that [YWCA] accommodation is focused exclusively on cheap, gender-specific, no frills lodging'. How has Travel Ys management attempted to address this concern? Can you suggest any additional measures they might employ?

2   Briefly discuss the role of the internet in the development of Travel Ys. You may wish to visit the Travel Ys web site when researching this question.

3   What initial challenges were confronted by Travel Ys as it moved into the international marketplace?

4   What role has been played by the formation of business alliances in contributing to the success of Travel Ys?

5   What functions are performed by the Travel Ys internet interface? Do you believe that it constitutes a *de facto* marketing information system (MIS)?

6   After examining Figure 15.3, can you suggest any amendments that might assist Travel Ys marketing communication effort?

7   What organisations may be viewed as competitors to Travel Ys? Taking into account its current product range, how could Travel Ys further enhance its competitive position?

8   What types of market research are undertaken by Travel Ys? What use is made of the information generated by such research?

9   To what extent does Travel Ys determine the prices charged by the various properties within its accommodation directory? In establishing its own fee structure, what challenges were confronted by Travel Ys? How were these overcome?

10   The high level of community recognition of the 'Y' brand and acceptance of the association between YWCA and YMCA accommodation is significant to the long-term success of Travel Ys. Randomly select 10 to 15 people within three broad age groups (18–30, 31–50, and 50+). Attempt to ascertain the extent to which they recognise the 'Y' brand and understand the association between the YWCA and YMCA.

BIBLIOGRAPHY

SELECTED TOURISM AND HOSPITALITY MARKETING REFERENCES

Books

Baron, S. & Harris, K. 2003, *Service Marketing: Text and Cases*, 2nd edn, Palgrave, Basingstoke.

Bateson, J. (ed.) 1999, *Managing Services Marketing*, 4th edn, Dryden, Fort Worth.

Batey, I. 2002, *Asian Branding: a Great Way to Fly*, Pearson Asia.

Beirman, D. 2003, *Restoring Tourism Destinations in Crisis: A Strategic Marketing Approach*, CABI Pub, Cambridge, MA.

Bradley, F. 2003, *Strategic Marketing: in the customer driven organization*, J. Wiley, New York.

Briggs, S. 2001, *Successful Web Marketing for the Tourism and Leisure Sectors*, Kogan Page, London.

Buhalis, D. 2003, *eTourism: Information Technologies for Strategic Tourism Management*, Pearson Education, Harlow, Essex, United Kingdom.

Buhalis, D. & Laws, E. 2001, *Tourism Distribution Channels: Practices, Issues and Transformations*, Continuum International, New York.

Burke, J.F. & Resnick, B.P. 2000, *Marketing & Selling the Travel Product*, 2nd edn, Delmar, Albany, New York.

Chon, K.S., Inagaki, T. & Ohashi, T. (eds.) 2000, *Japanese Tourists: Socio-Economic, Marketing and Psychological Analysis*, Haworth, New York.

Cooper, C. (ed.) 2002, *Classic Reviews in Tourism*, Channel View Publications, Clevedon.

Cooper, C., Fletcher, J., Gilbert, D., Wanhill, S. & Shepherd, D. 1998, *Tourism: Principles and Practice*, 2nd edn, Longman, Harlow, Essex, United Kingdom.

Coyle, J.R. 2002, *Internet Resources and Services for International Marketing and Advertising: A Global Guide*, Oryx, London.

Crotts, J.C., Buhalis, D. & March, R. (eds.) 2000, *Global Alliances in Tourism and Hospitality Management*, Haworth Hospitality Press, New York.

Crouch, G., Mazanec, J., Brent Ritchie, J.R. & Woodside, A. (eds.) 2001, *Consumer Psychology of Tourism, Hospitality and Leisure*, vol. 2, CABI, Wallingford, Oxon, United Kingdom.

Dallen, T. 2003, *Safety and Security in Tourism: Relationships, Management, and Marketing*, Haworth Hospitality Press, New York.

Dickman, S. 1999, *Tourism and Hospitality Marketing*, Oxford University Press, Melbourne.

Faulkner, W. 1993, 'The Strategic Marketing Myth in Australian Tourism', pp. 27–35 in P. Hooper (ed.), Building a Research Base in Tourism, Proceedings of the National Conference on Tourism Research, Sydney, Bureau of Tourism Research.

Frechtling, D.C. 2001, *Practical Tourism Forecasting: Methods and Strategies*, Butterworth-Heinemann, Oxford, United Kingdom.

Fyall, A., Garrod, B. & Leask, A. (eds.) 2003, *Managing Visitor Attractions: New Directions*, Butterworth-Heinemann, Oxford, United Kingdom.

Goeldner, C. & Brent Ritchie, J.R. 2002, *Tourism: Principles, Practices and Philosophies*, 9th edn, Wiley, Chichester, New York.

Gronroos, C. 2000, *Services Management and Marketing*, 2nd edn, Wiley, New York.

Gummesson, E. 2002, *Total Relationship Marketing: Rethinking Marketing Management from 4Ps to 30Rs*, 2nd edn, Butterworth-Heinemann, Oxford, United Kingdom.

Hall, C.M. 1997, *Tourism in the Pacific Rim*, 2nd edn, Longman, South Melbourne, Australia.

Hall, C.M., & Page, S. (eds.) 2000, *Tourism in South and South East Asia*, Butterworth-Heinemann, Oxford, United Kingdom.

Hall, C.M. & Sharples, L. (eds.), *Food Tourism Around the World: Development, Management and Markets*, Butterworth-Heinemann, Oxford, United Kingdom.

Harris, R. & Howard, J. 1996, *Dictionary of Travel, Tourism and Hospitality*, Hospitality Press, Melbourne.

Hefner, R.W. (ed.) 1998, *Market Cultures: Society and Morality in the New Asian Capitalisms*, Westview, Boulder, Colorado.

Heskett, J., Sasser, W.E. & Schlesinger, L. 1997, *The Service Profit Chain*, Free Press, New York.

Hoffman, K.D. & Bateson, J.E.G. 2001, *Essentials of Services Marketing: Concepts, Strategies and Cases*, 2nd edn, Harcourt, Fort Worth, Texas.

Holloway, J. 1998, *The Business of Tourism*, 5th edn, Longman, Harlow, Essex, United Kingdom.

Holloway, S. 1998, *Changing Planes: A Strategic Management Perspective of an Industry in Transition*, Ashgate, Aldershot, United Kingdom.

Howie, F. 2000, *Managing the Tourist Destination: A Practical Interactive Guide*, Continuum International, New York.

Hsu, C. & Powers, T. 2002, *Marketing Hospitality*, 3rd edn, Wiley, New York.

Hudson, S. 2003, *Sport and Adventure Tourism*, Haworth Hospitality Press, New York.

Hughes, H. 2000, *Arts Entertainment and Tourism*, Butterworth-Heinemann, Oxford, United Kingdom.

Huybers, T. & Bennett, J. 2002, *Environmental Management and the Competitiveness of Nature-based Tourism Destinations*, Edward Elgar, Cheltenham.

Jennings, G. 2001, *Tourism Research*, Wiley, Milton, Australia.

Kandampully, J., Mok, C. & Sparks, B. (eds.) 2002, *Service Quality Management in Hospitality, Tourism and Leisure*, Haworth Hospitality Press, New York.

Kay, H.K. 2002, *Selling Tourism*, Delmar Learning, Clifton Park, New York.

Kelly, I. & Nankervis, T. 2001, *Visitor Destinations*, Wiley, Milton, Queensland.

Kotler, P., Bowen, J. & Makens, J. 2002, *Marketing for Hospitality and Tourism*, 3rd edn, Prentice-Hall, Upper Saddle River, New Jersey.

Law, C. 2002, *Urban Tourism*, 2nd edn, Continuum International, London.

Laws, E. 1997, *Managing Packaged Tourism*, International Thomson Business Press, London.

Laws, E. 2002, *Tourism Marketing: Quality and Service Management Perspectives*, Continuum, London.

Leiper, N. 2003, *Tourism Management*, 2nd edn, Pearson SprintPrint, Sydney.

Lennon, J.J. (ed.) 2003, *Tourism Statistics*, Continuum International, London.

Lockwood, A. & Medlik, S. (eds.) 2001, *Tourism and Hospitality in the 21st Century*, Heinemann, Oxford, United Kingdom.

Lovelock, C.H., Patterson, P.G. & Walker, R.H. 2001, *Services Marketing: An Asia-Pacific Perspective*, 2nd edn, Pearson Education Australia, Sydney.

McColl, R., Callaghan, B. & Palmer, A. 1998, *Services Marketing: A Managerial Perspective*, McGraw-Hill, Sydney.

McColl-Kennedy, J.R. 2003, *Services Marketing: A Managerial Approach*, Wiley, Milton, Queensland.

McGuire, L. 1999, *Australian Services Marketing and Management*, McMillan, South Yarra, Australia.

Marcussen, C.H. 1999, *Internet Distribution of European Travel and Tourism Services*, Bornholms Forskninscenter, Nex, Denmark.

Middleton, U. & Clarke, J. 2001, *Marketing in Travel and Tourism*, 3rd edn, Butterworth-Heinemann, Oxford, United Kingdom.

Morgan, N. & Pritchard, A. 2001, *Advertising in Tourism and Leisure*, Butterworth-Heinemann, Oxford, United Kingdom.

Morgan, N., Pritchard, A. & Pride, R. (eds.) 2001, *Destination Branding: Creating the Unique Destination Proposition*, Butterworth-Heinemann, Boston, Massachusetts.

Morrison, A. 2001, *Hospitality and Travel Marketing*, 3rd edn, Delmar Thompson Learning, Albany.

Moutinho, L. (ed.) 2000, *Strategic Management in Tourism*, CABI, Wallingford, United Kingdom.

Page, S. 1999, *Transport and Tourism*, Longman, Harlow, Essex, United Kingdom.

Page, S. & Dowling, R. 2002, *Ecotourism*, Pearson Education, Harlow, Essex, United Kingdom.

Pearce, P., Morrison, A. & Rutledge, J. 1998, *Tourism: Bridges Across Continents*, Irwin-McGraw-Hill, Sydney.

Pizam, A. & Mansfield, Y. (eds.) 2000, *Consumer Behaviour in Travel and Tourism*, Haworth Hospitality Press, New York.

Reisinger, Y. & Turner, L. 2000, *A Cultural Analysis of Japanese Tourists: Challenges for Tourism Marketers*, Monash University, Faculty of Business & Economics, Melbourne.

Reisinger, Y. & Turner, L. 2002, *Cross Cultural Behaviour in Tourism*, Butterworth-Heinemann, Oxford, United Kingdom.

Robinson, M., Evans, N., Long, P., Sharpley, R. & Swarbrooke, J. (eds.) 2000, *Reflections on International Tourism: Management, Marketing and the Political Economy of Travel and Tourism*, Centre for Travel and Tourism, Business Education, Sunderland, United Kingdom.

Ryan, C. & Page, S. (eds.) 2000, *Tourism Management: Towards the New Millennium*, Pergamon, New York.

Swarbrooke, J. 1999, *Sustainable Tourism Management*, CABI, Wallingford, Oxon, United Kingdom.

Swarbrooke, J., Beard, C., Leckie, S. & Pomfret, G. 2002, *Adventure Tourism*, Butterworth-Heinemann, Oxford, United Kingdom.

Swarbrooke, J. & Horner, S. 1999, *Consumer Behaviour in Tourism*, Heinemann, Oxford, United Kingdom.

Sweeney, S. 2002, *Internet Marketing for Your Tourism Business: Proven Techniques for Promoting Tourist-based Businesses over the Internet*, Maximum Press, Gulf Breeze, Florida.

Tribe, J. 1997, *Corporate Strategy for Tourism*, Thomson, London.

Turner, L. & Witt, S., *Pacific Asia Tourism Forecasts 2002–2004*, 2nd edn, PATA, Bangkok.

Vellas, F. & Bécherel, L. (eds.) 1999, *The International Marketing of Travel and Tourism: A Strategic Approach*, Macmillan, Basingstoke, Hampshire, United Kingdom.

Weaver, D. & Lawton, L. 2002, *Tourism Management*, Wiley, Milton, Queensland.

Weber, K. & Chon, K. (eds.) 2002, *Convention Tourism: International Research, and Industry Perspectives*, Haworth Hospitality Press, New York.

Williams, C. & Buswell, J. 2003, *Service Quality in Leisure & Tourism*, CABI Publishing, Wallingford, Oxon, United Kingdom.

Wong, K.K.F. & Song, H. (eds.) 2002, *Tourism Forecasting and Tourism Marketing*, Haworth Hospitality Press, New York.

Zeithaml, V.A. & Bitner, M.J. 2002, *Services Marketing: integrating customer focus across the firm*, 3rd edn, McGraw-Hill, Boston, Massachusetts.

Woodside, A., Crouch, G., Mazanec, J., Opperman, M. & Sakai, M. (eds.) 2000, *Consumer Psychology of Tourism, Hospitality and Leisure*, CABI publishing, Wallingford, Oxon, United Kingdom.

Tourism- and hospitality-related journals

Annals of Tourism Research
Asian Pacific Journal of Tourism Research
Australian Journal of Hospitality Management
Cornell HRA Quarterly
Journal of Hospitality and Leisure Marketing
Journal of Hospitality and Tourism Management
Journal of Sustainable Tourism
Journal of Tourism Studies
Journal of Travel and Tourism Marketing
Journal of Travel Research
Journal of Vacation Marketing
Scandinavian Journal of Hospitality & Tourism
Tourism Management
Tourist Studies

General marketing journals

International Journal of Services Industry Management
Journal of Consumer Behaviour
Journal of International Marketing
Journal of Marketing
Journal of Marketing Management
Journal of Marketing Research
Journal of Marketing Theory & Practice
Journal of Services Marketing

Selected government and industry tourism/ hospitality organisations

The following bodies produce a variety of publications/statistical reports (some regularly, others on an ad hoc basis) that may be of interest to tourism/ hospitality marketers. Consult their web sites for details.

National and state/territory tourism commissions

Australian Tourist Commission <www.atc.net.au>
(Note: This organisation will become part of Tourism Australia by the end of 2004.)
New South Wales <www.tourism.nsw.gov.au>
Northern Territory <www.nttc.com.au>
Queensland <www.tourism.qld.gov.au>
South Australia <www.southaustralia.com>
Tasmania <www.tourismtasmania.com.au>

Victoria <www.visitvictoria.com>
Western Australia <www.tourism.wa.gov.au>
Australian Capital Territory <www.canberratourism.com.au>

Tourism forecasting and statistical bodies

Bureau of Tourism Research (BTR) <www.btr.gov.au>
Tourist Forecasting Council—see <www.btr.gov.au>
(Note: These organisations will become part of Tourism Australia by the end
of 2004.)

Industry bodies

Pacific Asia Travel Association (PATA) <www.pata.org>
World Tourism Organisation <www.world-tourism.org>
World Travel and Tourism Council <www.wttc.org>